IRAN
A COUNTRY STUDY GUIDE

IRAN
A COUNTRY STUDY GUIDE

PATRICA TAYLOR

HAWK PRESS

Published by

Hawk Press
4836/24, Ansari Road, Daryaganj
New Delhi – 110 002
Phones: 91-11-23278618, 91-11-43667199
E-mail: thehawkpress@gmail.com
www.thehawkpress.com

Contents

Preface

Iran became an Islamic republic in 1979, when the monarchy was overthrown and clerics assumed political control under supreme leader Ayatollah Khomeini. The Iranian revolution put an end to the rule of the Shah, who had alienated powerful religious, political and popular forces with a programme of modernization and Westernization coupled with heavy repression of dissent.

Persia, as Iran was known before 1935, was one of the greatest empires of the ancient world, and the country has long maintained a distinct cultural identity within the Islamic world by retaining its own language and adhering to the Shia interpretation of Islam. In 2002, US President George W Bush declared Iran as part of an "axis of evil". While Mr Bush's successor, Barack Obama, adopted a less abrasive tone, Washington long continued to accuse Iran of trying to develop nuclear weapons.

Iran has been led by a highly conservative clerical elite since 1979, but appeared to be entering another era of political and social transformation with the victory of the liberals in parliamentary elections in 2000. However, the reformists, kept on the political defensive by powerful conservatives in the government and judiciary, failed to make good on their promises. The elections of June 2005 dealt a blow to the reformists when Mahmoud Ahmadinejad, Tehran's ultra-conservative mayor, became president.

Mr Ahmadinejad's controversial re-election in June 2009 and the violent suppression of subsequent opposition protests further widened the rift between conservatives and reformists within Iran's political establishment. Hopes for more fruitful engagement with the rest of the world rose with the election of self-proclaimed moderate Hassan Rouhani to the presidency in 2013. Mr Rouhani declared soon after his election that although it was "good for centrifuges to operate", it was also important that "the wheels of industry" be kept turning.

Iran, which built its first atomic power station - at Bushehr, in the south of the country - with Russian help, insisted its nuclear ambitions were peaceful. Mahmoud Ahmadinejad, who was president from 2005 to 2013, maintained that Iran had an "inalienable right" to produce nuclear fuel. Negotiations between Iran and six world powers - UN Security Council members US, UK, France, China and Russia, plus Germany - began in 2006 but did not produce an agreement until July 2015.

By 2010, the UN had imposed four rounds of sanctions on Iran in a bid to apply pressure on Tehran over the nuclear issue. The EU, US, Japan and South Korea also imposed their own sanctions on the country.

This is a reference book. All the matter is just compiled and edited in nature, taken from the various sources which are in public domain.

— Editor

1

Country Profile

At a glance

- Politics: Domestic politics have long been characterised by a seemingly unbridgeable gulf between conservatives and reformers
- Economy: Iran holds 9% of world oil reserves; a critical shortfall in jobs has hit the young, and international sanctions imposed over Iran's nuclear programme have badly affected the economy as a whole
- International: Following years of often tense negotiations, Iran and six world powers finally reached an agreement to limit the country's nuclear activities in exchange for the lifting of sanctions in July 2015

FACTS

Islamic Republic of Iran: Capital: Tehran

- Population 80 million
- Area 1.65 million sq km (636,313 sq miles)
- Major language Persian
- Major religion Islam
- Life expectancy 75 years (men), 77 years (women)
- Currency rial

LEADERS

Supreme Leader: Ayatollah Ali Khamenei

The Supreme Leader - the highest power in the land - appoints the heads of the judiciary, military and media. He also confirms the election of the president.

Ayatollah Ali Khamenei was appointed for life in June 1989, succeeding Ayatollah Khomeini, the founder of the Islamic republic. He previously served two consecutive terms as president in the 1980s.

Iran has been led by a highly conservative clerical elite since the revolution in 1979.

President: Hassan Rouhani

Hassan Rouhani won a resounding re-election victory in May 2017 as voters overwhelmingly backed his efforts to reach out to the world and rebuild the struggling economy.

Rouhani, who is regarded as a moderate, reformist figure, spearheaded a 2015 nuclear deal with world powers. He first came to power in 2013.

MEDIA

The struggle for influence and power in Iran is played out in the media.

All broadcasting from Iranian soil is controlled by the state and reflects official ideology. A wider range of opinion may be found online and in the printed press.

However, many pro-reform outlets have been closed and their writers and editors imprisoned. Iran has been described by media freedom advocates as "among the five biggest prisons in the world" for journalists.

TIMELINE

Some key dates in Iran's history:

1794 - Mohammad Khan Qajar seizes power and founds the Qajar dynasty.

1921 - Military commander Reza Khan seizes power and is later crowned Reza Shah Pahlavi.

1941 - Britain and Russia occupy Iran during Second World War.

1953 - Coup engineered by British and US intelligence services after parliament nationalises mainly British-owned oil industry. Shah, who had fled into exile, returns.

1979 - Iranian revolution unseats the shah.

1980-1988 - Iran-Iraq war.

2002 - US President George W. Bush describes Iran, Iraq and North Korea as "the axis of evil".

2004 - US says Iran's nuclear programme is a growing threat and calls for international sanctions.

2016 - International economic sanctions are lifted after the UN nuclear watchdog, the IAEA, confirms that Tehran had complied with its promises to scale back its nuclear activities.

Country Profiles - home

One of the most hard-hitting parts of the sanctions regime was the EU's ban on Iranian oil imports, which came into force in 2012. As the EU had until then received 20% of Iran's oil exports, this had a significant effect on the country's economy.

Iran has an abundance of energy resources - substantial oil reserves and natural gas reserves second only to those of Russia - and the targeting of this key sector, which had accounted for a large part of the state revenue, combined with Iran's isolation from the international banking system, caused the currency, the rial, to plummet in value. This in turn led to runaway inflation, and sent the prices of basic foodstuffs and fuel soaring.

Conservative/liberal split

With the domestic divide between moderates and hardliners continuing to represent a deep fault-line in Iranian society, Mr Rouhani's political survival came to be seen as very much dependent on the Iranian negotiating team's ability to strike a lasting deal with world powers over the nuclear issue.

Iran is historically known as Persia, the Persian Empire was one of the greatest empires of the ancient world with a series of imperial dynasties. The empire also was frequently invaded, first by Alexander the Great, then by the Parthians, later ruled by the Hellenistic Seleucid Empire.

Iran's hereditary monarch, Shah Mohammad Reza Pahlavi, fled the country in 1979 after decades of corrupt and authoritarian rule, and mounting religious and political unrest. Exiled Ayatollah Ruhollah Khomeini returned to lead an Islamic revolution and formed the world's first Islamic republic the same year. An eight-year war with Iraq followed.

In the elections of 1992 and 1996, former president Akbar Hashemi-Rafsanjani's support increased and at the presidential election of 1997 Mohammad Khatami, Rafsanjani's cultural adviser, succeeded him. Khatami promised greater freedom and tolerance and was supported mainly by women, younger voters and intellectuals.

In June 2005, Mahmoud Ahmadinejad, former mayor of the capital, Tehran, and famous for his conservative approach and for rolling back reforms put in place by modernists before him was elected president. He has not been shy of confronting the West and has pushed ahead with a national nuclear programme that has brought international condemnation.

In June 2013 Iranians elected a moderate conservative cleric Dr. Hasan Fereidun RUHANI to the presidency. He is a longtime senior member in the regime, but has made promises of reforming society and Iran's foreign policy. The UN Security Council has passed a number of resolutions calling for Iran to suspend its uranium enrichment and reprocessing activities and comply with its IAEA obligations and responsibilities, and in July 2015 Iran and the five permanent members, plus Germany (P5+1) signed the Joint Comprehensive Plan of Action (JCPOA) under which Iran agreed to restrictions on its nuclear program in exchange for sanctions relief.

In 1979, the country, known in the west as Persia, became the Islamic Republic of Iran, ruled by a theocratic government. Chief of State is the Supreme Leader, who exerts ideological and political control over the state, he controls the armed forces and makes decisions on security, defense and major foreign policy issues.

Head of Government and head of the executive branch is the President, who is elected by popular vote for four years and can serve no more than two consecutive terms. The president's power is limited by decisions of the Supreme Leader, the influence of Islamic clerics and conservatives in Iran's coercive security apparatus and judiciary.

2

History

The history of Iran, commonly also known as Persia in the Western world, is intertwined with the history of a larger region, also to an extent known asGreater Iran, comprising the area from Anatolia, the Bosphorus, and Egypt in the west to the borders of Ancient India and the Syr Darya in the east, and from the Caucasus and the Eurasian Steppe in the north to the Persian Gulfand the Gulf of Oman in the south.

Iran is home to one of the world's oldest continuous major civilizations, with historical and urban settlements dating back to 7000 BC. The southwestern and western part of the Iranian Plateau participated in the traditional Ancient Near East with Elam, from the Early Bronze Age, and later with various other peoples, such as the Kassites, Mannaeans, and Gutians. Georg Wilhelm Friedrich Hegel names the Persians as the *first Historical People*. The Medesunified Iran as a nation and empire in 625 BC. The Achaemenid Empire(550–330 BC), founded by Cyrus the Great, was the first of the Persianempires to rule from the Balkans to North Africa and also Central Asia, spanning three continents, from their seat of power in Persis (Persepolis). It was the largest empire yet seen and the first world empire. The First Persian Empire was the only civilization in all of history to connect over 40% of the global population, accounting for approximately 49.4 million of the world's 112.4 million people in around 480 BC. They were succeeded by the Seleucid, Parthian and Sasanian Empires, who successively governed Iran for almost 1000 years and made Iran once again as a leading power in the world. Persia's arch-rival was the Roman Empire and its successor, the Byzantine Empire.

The Persian Empire proper begins in the Iron Age, following the influx of Iranian peoples. Iranian people gave rise to theMedes, the Achaemenid, Parthian, and Sasanian Empires of classical antiquity.

Once a major empire, Iran has endured invasions too, by the Greeks, Arabs, Turks, and the Mongols. Iran has continually reasserted its national identity throughout the centuries and has developed as a distinct political and cultural entity.

The Muslim conquest of Persia (633–656) ended the Sasanian Empire and was a turning point in Iranian history. Islamization of Iran took place during the eighth to tenth centuries and led to the eventual decline of Zoroastrianism in Iran as well as many of its dependencies. However, the achievements of the previous Persian civilizations were not lost, but were to a great extent absorbed by the new Islamic polity and civilization.

Iran, with its long history of early cultures and empires, had suffered particularly hard during the late Middle Ages and the early modern period. Many invasions of nomadic tribes, whose leaders became rulers in this country, affected it negatively.

Iran was once again reunified as an independent state in 1501 by the Safavid dynasty, which converted Iran to Shia Islamas the official religion of their empire, marking one of the most important turning points in the history of Islam. Functioning again as a leading power, this time amongst the neighboring Ottoman Empire, their arch-rival for centuries, Iran had been a monarchy ruled by an emperor almost without interruption from 1501 until the 1979 Iranian Revolution, when Iran officially became an Islamic republic on April 1, 1979.

Over the course of the first half of the 19th century Iran lost many of its territories in the Caucasus, which were parts of Iran for centuries, comprising modern-day Eastern Georgia, Dagestan, Azerbaijan, and Armenia, to its rapidly expanding and emerged neighboring rival the Russian Empire, following the Russo-Persian Wars between 1804–13 and 1826–8.

Prehistory

Paleolithic

The earliest archaeological artifacts in Iran were found in the Kashafrud and Ganj Parsites that are thought to date back to 100,000 years ago in the Middle Paleolithic.Mousterian stone tools made by Neandertals have also been found. There are more cultural remains of Neandertals dating back to the Middle Paleolithic period, which mainly have been found in the Zagros region and fewer in central Iran at sites such as Kobeh, Kunji, Bisitun Cave, Tamtama, Warwasi, and Yafteh Cave. In 1949, a Neanderthal radius was discovered by Carleton S. Coon in Bisitun Cave. Evidence for Upper Paleolithic and Epipaleolithic periods are known mainly from the Zagros Mountains in the caves of Kermanshah and Khorramabad and a few number of sites in the Alborz and Central Iran. During this time, people began creating rock art.

Neolithic to Chalcolithic

Early agricultural communities such as Chogha Golan in 10,000 BC along with settlements such as Chogha Bonut (the earliest village in Elam) in 8000 BC,began to flourish in and around the Zagros Mountains region in western Iran. Around about the same time, the earliest-known clay vessels and modeled human and animal terracotta figurines were produced at Ganj Dareh, also in western Iran. There are also 10,000-year-old human and animal figurines from Tepe Sarab in Kermanshah Province among many other ancient artifacts.

The south-western part of Iran was part of the Fertile Crescent where most of humanity's first major crops were grown, in villages such as Susa (where a settlement was first founded possibly as early as 4395 cal BC) and settlements such as Chogha Mish, dating back to 6800 BC; there are 7,000-year-old jars of wine excavated in the Zagros Mountains (now on display at the University of Pennsylvania) and ruins of 7000-year-old settlements such as Tepe Sialk are further testament to that. The two main Neolithic Iranian settlements were the Zayandeh River Culture and Ganj Dareh.

Bronze Age

Parts of what is modern-day northwestern Iran was part of the Kura–Araxes culture(circa 3400 BC — ca. 2000 BC), that stretched up into the neighboring regions of theCaucasus and Anatolia.

Susa is one of the oldest-known settlements of Iran and the world. Based on C14 dating, the time of foundation of the city is as early as 4395 BC, a time that goes beyond the age of civilization in Mesopotamia. The general perception among archeologists is that Susa was an extension of the Sumerian city state of Uruk. In its later history, Susa became the capital of Elam, which emerged as a state found 4000 BC. There are also dozens of prehistoric sites across the Iranian plateau pointing to the existence of ancient cultures and urban settlements in the fourth millennium BC, One of the earliest civilizations in Iranian plateau was the Jiroft culture in southeastern Iran in the province of Kerman.

It is one of the most artifact-rich archaeological sites in the Middle East. Archaeological excavations in Jiroft led to the discovery of several objects belonging to the 4th millennium BC. There is a large quantity of objects decorated with highly distinctive engravings of animals, mythological figures, and architectural motifs. The objects and their iconography are unlike anything ever seen before by archeologists. Many are made from chlorite, a gray-green soft stone; others are in copper,bronze, terracotta, and even lapis lazuli. Recent excavations at the sites have produced the world's earliest inscription which pre-dates Mesopotamian inscriptions.

There are records of numerous other ancient civilizations on the Iranian Plateau before the emergence of Iranian peoplesduring the Early Iron Age. The Early Bronze Age saw the rise of urbanization into organized city states and the invention of writing (the Uruk period) in the Near East. While Bronze Age Elam made use of writing from an early time, the Proto-Elamite script remains undeciphered, and records from Sumer pertaining to Elam are scarce.

Russian historian Igor M. Diakonoff states that the modern inhabitants of the Iranian Plateau are descendants of mainly non-Persian groups: "It is the autochthones of the Iranian plateau, and not the Proto-Indo-European tribes of Europe, which are, in the main, the ancestors, in the physical sense of the word, of the present-day Iranians."

Early Iron Age

Records become more tangible with the rise of the Neo-Assyrian Empire and its records of incursions from the Iranian plateau. As early as the 20th century BC, tribes came to the Iranian Plateau from the Pontic–Caspian steppe.

The arrival of Iranians on the Iranian plateau forced the Elamites to relinquish one area of their empire after another and to take refuge in Elam, Khuzestan and the nearby area, which only then became coterminous with Elam. Bahman Firuzmandi say that the southern Iranians might be intermixed with the Elamite peoples living in the plateau. By the mid-first millennium BC,Medes, Persians, and Parthians populated the Iranian plateau. Until the rise of the Medes, they all remained under Assyriandomination, like the rest of the Near East.

In the first half of the first millennium BC, parts of what is now Iranian Azerbaijanwere incorporated into Urartu.

Classical Antiquity

Median and Achaemenid Empire (650–330 BC)

In 646 BC, The Assyrian king Ashurbanipal sacked Susa, which ended Elamite supremacy in the region. For over 150 years Assyrian kings of nearby Northern Mesopotamia were seeking to conquer Median tribes of Western Iran. Under pressure from Assyria, the small kingdoms of the western Iranian plateau coalesced into increasingly larger and more centralized states.

In the second half of the seventh century BC, the Medes gained their independence and were united by Deioces. In 612 BC,Cyaxares, Deioces' grandson, and the Babylonian king Nabopolassar invaded Assyria and laid siege to and eventually destroyed Nineveh, the Assyrian capital, which led to the fall of the Neo-Assyrian Empire. Urartu was later on conquered and dissolved as well by the Medes. The Medes are credited with the foundation of Iran as a nation and empire, and established the first Iranian empire, the largest of its day until Cyrus the Great established a unified empire of the Medes and Persians, leading to the Achaemenid Empire (c.550–330 BC).

Cyrus the Great overthrew, in turn, the Median, Lydian, and Neo-Babylonian Empires, creating an empire far larger than Assyria. He was better able, through more benign policies, to reconcile his subjects to Persian rule; and the longevity of his empire was one result. The Persian king, like the Assyrian, was also "King of Kings", *xðâyaèiya xðâyaèiyânâm* (*shâhanshâh*in modern Persian) – "great king," Megas Basileus, as known by the Greeks.

Cyrus's son, Cambyses II, conquered the last major power of the region, ancient Egypt, causing the collapse of the Twenty-sixth Dynasty of Egypt. Since he became ill and died before, or while, leaving Egypt, stories developed, as related byHerodotus, that he was struck down for impiety against the ancient Egyptian deities. The winner, Darius I, based his claim on membership in a collateral line of the Achaemenid Empire.

Darius' first capital was at Susa, and he started the building programme at Persepolis. He rebuilt a canal between the Nileand the Red Sea, a forerunner of the modern Suez Canal. He improved the extensive road system, and it is during his reign that mention is first made of the Royal Road (shown on map), a great highway stretching all the way from Susa to Sardis with posting stations at regular intervals. Major reforms took place under Darius. Coinage, in the form of the *daric* (gold coin) and the shekel (silver coin) was standardized (coinage had already been invented over a century before in Lydia c. 660 BC but not standardized), and administrative efficiency was increased.

The Old Persian language appears in royal inscriptions, written in a specially adapted version of the cuneiform script. Under Cyrus the Great and Darius I, the Persian Empire eventually became the largest empire in human history up until that point, ruling and administrating over most of the then known world, as well as spanning three continents, namely Europe, Asia, and Africa. Their greatest achievement was the empire itself. The Persian Empire represented the world's first superpower that was based on a model of tolerance and respect for other cultures and religions.

In the late sixth century BC, Darius launched his European campaign, in which he defeated the Paeonians, conquered Thrace, and subdued all coastal Greek cities, as well as defeating the European Scythians around the Danuberiver. In 512/511, Macedon became a vassal kingdom of Persia.

In 499 BC, Athens lent support to a revolt in Miletus which resulted in the sacking of Sardis. This led to an Achaemenid campaign against mainland Greece known as the Greco-Persian Wars which lasted the first half of the 5th century BC, and is known as one of the most important wars in European history. In the First Persian invasion of Greece, the Persian generalMardonius resubjugated Thrace and made Macedon a full part of Persia.The war eventually turned out in defeat however. Darius' successor Xerxes Ilaunched the Second Persian invasion of Greece. At a crucial moment in the war, about half of mainland Greece was overrun by the Persians, including all territories to the north of the Isthmus of Corinth, however, this was also turned out in a Greek victory, following the battles of Plataea and Salamis, by which Persia lost its footholds in Europe, and eventually withdrew from it. During the Greco-Persian wars Persia gained major territorial advantages capture and razed Athens in 480 BC. However, after a string of Greek victories the Persians were forced to withdraw thus losing control of Macedonia, Thrace and Ionia. Fighting continued for several decades after the successful Greek repelling of the Second Invasion with numerous Greek city states under the latters' newly formed Delian League, which eventually ended with the peace of

Callias in 449 BC, ending the Greco-Persian Wars. In 404 BC following the death of Darius II, Egypt rebelled under Amyrtaeus. Later pharaohssuccessfully resisted Persian attempts to reconquer Egypt until 343 BC, when Egypt was reconquered by Artaxerxes III.

Hellenic conquest and Seleucid Empire (312 BC–248 BC)

In 334 BC-331 BC Alexander the Great, also known in the Zoroastrian as *Arda Wiraz Nâmag* ("the accursed Alexander"), defeated Darius III in the battles ofGranicus, Issus and Gaugamela, swiftly conquering the Persian Empire by 331 BC. Alexander's empire broke up shortly after his death, and Alexander's general, Seleucus I Nicator, tried to take control of Iran, Mesopotamia, and laterSyria and Anatolia. His empire was the Seleucid Empire. He was killed in 281 BC by Ptolemy Keraunos.

Greek language, philosophy, and art came with the colonists. During the Seleucid era, Greek became the common tongue of diplomacy and literature throughout the empire

Parthian Empire (248 BC–224 AD)

The Parthian Empire was the realm of the Arsacid dynasty, who reunited and governed the Iranian plateau after the Parni conquest of Parthia and defeating the Seleucid Empire in the later third century BC, and intermittently controlled Mesopotamia between ca 150 BC and 224 AD. The Parthian Empire quickly included Eastern Arabia.

Parthia was the Eastern arch-enemy of theRoman Empire; and it limited Rome's expansion beyond Cappadocia (central Anatolia). The Parthian armies included two types of cavalry: the heavily armed and armouredcataphracts and lightly-armed but highly-mobile mounted archers.

For the Romans, who relied on heavy infantry, the Parthians were too hard to defeat, as both types of cavalry were much faster and more mobile than foot soldiers. The Parthian shot used by the Parthian cavalry was most notably feared by the Roman soldiers, which proved pivotal in the crushing Roman defeat at the Battle of Carrhae. On the other hand, the Parthians found it difficult to occupy conquered areas as they were unskilled in siege warfare. Because of these weaknesses, neither the Romans nor the Parthians were able completely to annex each other's territory.

The Parthian empire subsisted for five centuries, longer than most Eastern Empires. The end of this empire came at last in 224 AD, when the empire's organization had loosened and the last king was defeated by one of the empire's vassal peoples, the Persians under the Sasanians. However, the Arsacid dynasty continued to exist for centuries onwards in Armenia, theIberia, and the Caucasian Albania, which were all eponymous branches of the dynasty.

Sasanian Empire (224–651 AD)

The first shah of the Sasanian Empire, Ardashir I, started reforming the country both economically and militarily. For a period of more than 400 years, Iran was once again one of the leading powers in the world, alongside its neighboring rival, the Roman and then Byzantine Empires. The empire's territory, at its height, encompassed all of today's Iran, Iraq, Azerbaijan, Armenia, Georgia,Abkhazia, Dagestan, Lebanon, Jordan, Palestine, Israel, parts of Afghanistan,Turkey, Syria, parts of Pakistan, Central Asia, Eastern Arabia, and parts ofEgypt.

Most of the Sassanian empire's lifespan it was overshadowed by the frequentByzantine–Sasanian wars, a continuation of the Roman–Parthian Wars and the all-comprising Roman–Persian Wars; the last was the longest-lasting conflict in human history. Started in the first century BC by their predecessors, the Parthians and Romans, the last Roman–Persian War was fought in the seventh century. The Persians defeated the Romans at the Battle of Edessa in 260 and took emperorValerian prisoner for the remainder of his life.

Eastern Arabia was conquered early on. During Khosrow II's rule in 590–628, Egypt, Jordan, Palestine and Lebanon were also annexed to the Empire. The Sassanians called their empire *Erânshahr* ("Dominion of the Aryans", i.e. of Iranians).

A chapter of Iran's history followed after roughly six hundred years of conflict with the Roman Empire. During this time, the Sassanian and Romano-Byzantine armies clashed for influence in Anatolia, the western Caucasus (mainly Lazica and theKingdom of Iberia; modern-day Georgia and Abkhazia),Mesopotamia, Armenia and the Levant. Under Justinian I, the war came to an uneasy peace with payment of tribute to the Sassanians.

However the Sasanians used the deposition of the Byzantine emperor Maurice as a *casus belli* to attack the Empire. After many gains, the Sassanians were defeated at Issus, Constantinople and finally Nineveh, resulting in peace. With the conclusion of the over 700 years lasting Roman-Persian Wars through the climactic Byzantine-Sasanian War of 602–628, which included the very siege of the Byzantine capital of Constantinople, the war-exhausted Persians lost the Battle of al-Qâdisiyyah (632) in Hilla (present day Iraq) to the invading Muslim forces.

The Sasanian era, encompassing the length of Late Antiquity, is considered to be one of the most important and influential historical periods in Iran, and had a major impact on the world. In many ways the Sassanian period witnessed the highest achievement of Persian civilization, and constitutes the last great Iranian Empire before the adoption of Islam. Persia influenced Roman civilization considerably during Sassanian times, their cultural influence extending far beyond the empire's territorial borders, reaching as far as Western Europe, Africa, China and India and also playing a prominent role in the formation of both European and Asiatic medieval art.

This influence carried forward to the Muslim world. The dynasty's unique and aristocratic culture transformed the Islamic conquest and destruction of Iran into a Persian Renaissance. Much of what later became known as Islamic culture, architecture, writing and other contributions to civilization, were taken from the Sassanian Persians into the broader Muslim world.

Medieval Iran

Caliphate and Sultanate era

Islamic conquest of Persia (633–651)

In 633, when the Sasanian king Yazdegerd IIIwas ruling over Iran, the Muslims under Umarinvaded the country right after it had been in a bloody civil war. Several Iranian nobles and families such as king Dinar of the House of Karen, and later Kanarangiyans of Khorasan, mutinied against their Sasanian overlords. Although the House of Mihran had claimed the Sasanian throne under the two prominent generals Bahrâm Chôbin and Shahrbaraz, it remained loyal to the Sasanians during their struggle against the Arabs, but the Mihrans were eventually betrayed and defeated by their own kinsmen, the House of Ispahbudhan, under their leader Farrukhzad, who had mutinied against Yazdegerd III.

Yazdegerd III, fled from one district to another until a local miller killed him for his purse at Merv in 651. By 674, Muslims had conquered Greater Khorasan (which included modern Iranian Khorasan province and modern Afghanistan and parts ofTransoxiana).

The Muslim conquest of Persia ended the Sasanian Empire and led to the eventual decline of the Zoroastrian religion in Persia. Over time, the majority of Iranians converted to Islam. Most of the aspects of the previous Persian civilizations were not discarded, but were absorbed by the new Islamic polity. As Bernard Lewis has commented:

These events have been variously seen in Iran: by some as a blessing, the advent of the true faith, the end of the age of ignorance and heathenism; by others as a humiliating national defeat, the conquest and subjugation of the country by foreign invaders. Both perceptions are of course valid, depending on one's angle of vision.

The Umayyad Caliphate and its incursions into the Caspian coast

After the fall of the Sasanian Empire in 651, the Arabs of the Umayyad Caliphate adopted many Persian customs, especially the administrative and the court mannerisms. Arab provincial governors were undoubtedly either Persianized Arameans or ethnic Persians; certainly Persian remained the language of official business of the caliphate until the adoption of Arabic toward the end of the seventh century, when in 692 minting began at the capital, Damascus. The new Islamic coins evolved from imitations of Sasanian coins (as well as Byzantine), and the Pahlavi script on the coinage was replaced withArabic alphabet.

During the Umayyad Caliphate, the Arab conquerors imposed Arabic as the primary language of the subject peoples throughout their empire. Al-Hajjaj ibn Yusuf, who was not happy with the prevalence of the Persian language in the divan, ordered the official language of the conquered lands to be replaced by Arabic, sometimes by force. In al-Biruni's *From The Remaining Signs of Past Centuries* for example it is written:

When Qutaibah bin Muslim under the command of Al-Hajjaj bin Yousef was sent to Khwarazmia with a military expedition and conquered it for the second time, he swiftly killed whomever wrote the Khwarazmian native language that knew of the Khwarazmian heritage, history, and culture. He then killed all their Zoroastrian priests and burned and wasted their books, until gradually the illiterate only remained, who knew nothing of writing, and hence their history was mostly forgotten."

There are a number of historians who see the rule of the Umayyads as setting up the "dhimmah" to increase taxes from the*dhimmis* to benefit the Muslim Arab community financially and by discouraging conversion. Governors lodged complaints with the caliph when he enacted laws that made conversion easier, depriving the provinces of revenues.

In the 7th century, when many non-Arabs such as Persians entered Islam, they were recognized as mawali ("clients") and treated as second-class citizens by the ruling Arab elite until the end of the Umayyad Caliphate. During this era, Islam was initially associated with the ethnic identity of the Arab and required formal association with an Arab tribe and the adoption of the client status of*mawali*. The half-hearted policies of the late Umayyads to tolerate non-Arab Muslims and Shias had failed to quell unrest among these minorities.

However, all of Iran was still not under Arab control, and the region of Daylamwas under the control of the Daylamites, while Tabaristan was under Dabuyidand Paduspanid control, and the Mount Damavand region under Masmughans of Damavand. The Arabs had invaded these regions several times, but achieved no decisive result because of the inaccessible terrain of the regions. The most prominent ruler of the Dabuyids, known as Farrukhan the Great (r. 712–728), managed to hold his domains during his long struggle against the Arab general Yazid ibn al-Muhallab, who was defeated by a combined Dailamite-Dabuyid army, and was forced to retreat from Tabaristan.

With the death of the Umayyad Caliph Hisham ibn Abd al-Malik in 743, the Islamic world was launched into civil war. Abu Muslim was sent to Khorasan by the Abbasid Caliphate initially as a propagandist and then to revolt on their behalf. He tookMerv defeating the Umayyad governor there Nasr ibn Sayyar. He became the de facto Abbasid governor of Khurasan. During the same period, the Dabuyid ruler Khurshid declared independence from the Umayyads, but was shortly forced to recognize Abbasid authority. In 750, Abu Muslim became leader of the Abbasid army and defeated the Umayyads at theBattle of the Zab. Abu Muslim stormed Damascus, the capital of the Umayyad caliphate, later that year.

The Abbasid Caliphate and Iranian semi-independent governments

The Abbasid army consisted primarily of Khorasanians and was led by an Iranian general, Abu Muslim Khorasani. It contained both Iranian and Arab elements, and the Abbasids enjoyed both Iranian and Arab support. The Abbasids overthrew the Umayyads in 750.

According to Amir Arjomand, theAbbasid Revolution essentially marked the end of the Arab empire and the beginning of a more inclusive, multiethnic state in the Middle East.

One of the first changes the Abbasids made after taking power from the Umayyads was to move the empire's capital from Damascus, in the Levant, to Iraq. The latter region was influenced by Persian history and culture, and moving the capital was part of the Persian mawali demand for Arab influence in the empire. The city of Baghdad was constructed on the Tigris River, in 762, to serve as the new Abbasid capital.

The Abbasids established the position of vizierlike Barmakids in their administration, which was the equivalent of a "vice-caliph", or second-in-command. Eventually, this change meant that many caliphs under the Abbasids ended up in a much more ceremonial role than ever before, with the vizier in real power. A new Persian bureaucracy began to replace the old Arab aristocracy, and the entire administration reflected these changes, demonstrating that the new dynasty was different in many ways to the Umayyads.

By the 9th century, Abbasid control began to wane as regional leaders sprang up in the far corners of the empire to challenge the central authority of the Abbasid caliphate. The Abbasid caliphs began enlisting *mamluks*, Turkic-speaking warriors, who had been moving out of Central Asia into Transoxiana as slave warriors as early as the 9th century. Shortly thereafter the real power of the Abbasid caliphs began to wane; eventually they became religious figureheads while the warrior slaves ruled.

As the power of the Abbasid caliphs diminished, a series of dynasties rose in various parts of Iran, some with considerable influence and power. Among the most important of these overlapping dynasties were the Tahirids in Khorasan (821–873); the Saffarids in Sistan (861–1003, their rule lasted as maliks of Sistan until 1537); and the Samanids (819–1005), originally at Bukhara. The Samanids eventually ruled an area from central Iran to Pakistan.

By the early 10th century, the Abbasids almost lost control to the growing Persian faction known as the Buyid dynasty (934–1062). Since much of the Abbasid administration had been Persian anyway, the Buyids were quietly able to assume real power in Baghdad. The Buyids were defeated in the mid-11th century by the Seljuq Turks, who continued to exert influence over the Abbasids, while publicly pledging allegiance to them. The balance of power in Baghdad remained as such – with the Abbasids in power in name only – until the Mongol invasion of 1258 sacked the city and definitively ended the Abbasid dynasty.

During the Abbassid period an enfranchisement was experienced by the *mawali* and a shift was made in political conception from that of a primarily Arab empire to one of a Muslim empire and c. 930 a requirement was enacted that required all bureaucrats of the empire be Muslim.

Islamic golden age, Shu'ubiyya movement and Persianization process

Islamization was a long process by which Islam was gradually adopted by the majority population of Iran. Richard Bulliet's "conversion curve" indicates that only about 10% of Iran converted to Islam during the relatively Arab-centric Umayyad period. Beginning in theAbassid period, with its mix of Persian as well as Arab rulers, the Muslim percentage of the population rose. As Persian Muslims consolidated their rule of the country, the Muslim population rose from approximately 40% in the mid-9th century to close to 100% by the end of the 11th century. Seyyed Hossein Nasr suggests that the rapid increase in conversion was aided by the Persian nationality of the rulers.

Although Persians adopted the religion of their conquerors, over the centuries they worked to protect and revive their distinctive language and culture, a process known asPersianization. Arabs and Turks participated in this attempt.

In the 9th and 10th centuries, non-Arab subjects of the Ummah created a movement calledShu'ubiyyah in response to the privileged status of Arabs. Most of those behind the movement were Persian, but references to Egyptians, Berbers and Aramaeans are attested. Citing as its basis Islamic notions of equality of races and nations, the movement was primarily concerned with preserving Persian culture and protecting Persian identity, though within a Muslim context. The most notable effect of the movement was the survival of the Persian language to the present day.

The Samanid dynasty led the revival of Persian culture and the first important Persian poet after the arrival of Islam, Rudaki, was born during this era and was praised by Samanid kings. The Samanids also revived many ancient Persian festivals. Their successor, the Ghaznawids, who were of non-Iranian Turkic origin, also became instrumental in the revival of Persian. The culmination of the Persianization movement was the *Shahnameh*, the national epic of Iran, written almost entirely in Persian. This voluminous work, reflects Iran's ancient history, its unique cultural values, its pre-Islamic Zoroastrian religion, and its sense of nationhood.

According to Bernard Lewis:"Iran was indeed Islamized, but it was not Arabized. Persians remained Persians. And after an interval of silence, Iran reemerged as a separate, different and distinctive element within Islam, eventually adding a new element even to Islam itself. Culturally, politically, and most remarkable of all even religiously, the Iranian contribution to this new Islamic civilization is of immense importance. The work of Iranians can be seen in every field of cultural endeavor, including Arabic poetry, to which poets of Iranian origin composing their poems in Arabic made a very significant contribution. In a sense, Iranian Islam is a second advent of Islam itself, a new Islam sometimes referred to as Islam-i Ajam. It was this Persian Islam, rather than the original Arab Islam, that was brought to new areas and new peoples: to the Turks, first in Central Asia and then in the Middle East in the country which came to be called Turkey, and of course to India. The Ottoman Turks brought a form of Iranian civilization to the walls of Vienna..."

The Islamization of Iran was to yield deep transformations within the cultural, scientific, and political structure of Iran's society: The blossoming of Persian literature,philosophy, medicine and art became major elements of the newly forming Muslim civilization. Inheriting a heritage of thousands of years of civilization, and being at the "crossroads of the major cultural highways", contributed to Persia emerging as what culminated into the "Islamic Golden Age". During this period, hundreds of scholars and scientists vastly contributed to technology, science and medicine, later influencing the rise of European science during the Renaissance.

The most important scholars of almost all of the Islamic sects and schools of thought were Persian or lived in Iran, including the most notable and reliable Hadith collectors of Shia and Sunni like Shaikh Saduq, Shaikh Kulainy, Hakim al-Nishaburi,Imam Muslim and Imam Bukhari, the greatest theologians of Shia and Sunni like Shaykh Tusi, Imam Ghazali, Imam Fakhr al-Razi and Al-Zamakhshari, the greatest physicians, astronomers, logicians, mathematicians, metaphysicians, philosophersand scientists like Avicenna, and Nasîr al-Dîn al-Tûsî, the greatest Shaykh of Sufism like Rumi, Abdul-Qadir Gilani.

Persianate states and dynasties (977–1219)

In 977 a Turkic governor of the Samanids, Sabuktigin, conquered Ghazna (in present-day Afghanistan) and established a dynasty, the Ghaznavids, that lasted to 1186.The Ghaznavid empire grew by taking all of the Samanid territories south of the Amu Darya in the last decade of the 10th century, and eventually occupied parts of Eastern Iran, Afghanistan, Pakistan and northwest India.

The Ghaznavids are generally credited with launching Islam into a mainly Hindu India. The invasion of India was undertaken in 1000 by the Ghaznavid ruler, Mahmud, and continued for several years. They were unable to hold power for long, however, particularly after the death of Mahmud in 1030. By 1040 the Seljuqs had taken over the Ghaznavid lands in Iran.

The Seljuqs, who like the Ghaznavids were Persianate in nature and of Turkic origin, slowly conquered Iran over the course of the 11th century. The dynasty had its origins in the Turcoman tribal confederations of Central Asia and marked the beginning of Turkic power in the Middle East.

They established a Sunni Muslim rule over parts of Central Asia and the Middle East from the 11th to 14th centuries. They set up an empire known as Great Seljuq Empire that stretched fromAnatolia in the west to western Afghanistan in the east and the western borders of (modern-day) China in the northeast; and was the target of the First Crusade. Today they are regarded as the cultural ancestors of the Western Turks, the present-day inhabitants of Azerbaijan, Turkey, and Turkmenistan, and they are remembered as great patrons of Persian culture, art,literature, and language.

The dynastic founder, Tughril Beg, turned his army against the Ghaznavids in Khorasan. He moved south and then west, conquering but not wasting the cities in his path. In 1055 the caliph in Baghdad gave Tughril Beg robes, gifts, and the title King of the East. Under Tughril Beg's successor, Malik Shah (1072–1092), Iran enjoyed a cultural and scientific renaissance, largely attributed to his brilliant Iranian vizier, Nizam al Mulk. These leaders established the observatory whereOmar Khayyám did much of his experimentation for a new calendar, and they built religious schools in all the major towns. They brought Abu Hamid Ghazali, one of the greatest Islamic theologians, and other eminent scholars to the Seljuq capital at Baghdad and encouraged and supported their work.

When Malik Shah I died in 1092, the empire split as his brother and four sons quarrelled over the apportioning of the empire among themselves. In Anatolia, Malik Shah I was succeeded by Kilij Arslan I who founded the Sultanate of Rûm and in Syria by his brother Tutush I. In Persia he was succeeded by his son Mahmud I whose reign was contested by his other three brothers Barkiyaruq in Iraq, Muhammad I in Baghdad and Ahmad Sanjar in Khorasan. As Seljuq power in Iran weakened, other dynasties began to step up in its place, including a resurgent Abbasid caliphate and the Khwarezmshahs. The Khwarezmid Empire was a Sunni Muslim Persianate dynasty, of East Turkic origin, that ruled in Central Asia. Originally vassals of the Seljuqs, they took advantage of the decline of the Seljuqs to expand into Iran. In 1194 the Khwarezmshah Ala ad-Din Tekish defeated the Seljuq sultan Toghrul III in battle and the Seljuq empire in Iran collapsed. Of the former Seljuq Empire, only the Sultanate of Rum in Anatolia remained.

A serious internal threat to the Seljuqs during their reign came from the Ismailis, a secret sect with headquarters at Alamutbetween Rasht and Tehran. They controlled the immediate area for more than 150 years and sporadically sent out adherents to strengthen their rule by murdering important officials. Several of the various theories on the etymology of the word *assassin* derive from these killers.

Parts of northwestern Iran were conquered in the early 13th century AD by the Kingdom of Georgia, led by Tamar the Great.

Mongol invasion (1219–1221)

The Khwarezmid Empire only lasted for a few decades, until the arrival of the Mongols. Genghis Khan had unified the Mongols, and under him the Mongol Empire quickly expanded in several directions, until by 1218 it bordered Khwarezm. At that time, the Khwarezmid Empire was ruled by Ala ad-Din Muhammad (1200–1220). Muhammad, like Genghis, was intent on expanding his lands and had gained the submission of most of Iran. He declared himself shah and demanded formal recognition from the Abbasid caliph an-Nasir. When the caliph rejected his claim, Ala ad-Din Muhammad proclaimed one of his nobles caliph and unsuccessfully tried to depose an-Nasir.

The Mongol invasion of Iran began in 1219, after two diplomatic missions to Khwarezm sent by Genghis Khan had been massacred. During 1220–21 Bukhara, Samarkand, Herat, Tus and Nishapur were razed, and the whole populations were slaughtered. The Khwarezm-

Shah fled, to die on an island off the Caspian coast. During the invasion of Transoxania in 1219, along with the main Mongol force, Genghis Khan used a Chinese specialist catapult unit in battle, they were used again in 1220 in Transoxania. The Chinese may have used the catapults to hurl gunpowder bombs, since they already had them by this time.

While Genghis Khan was conquering Transoxania and Persia, several Chinese who were familiar with gunpowder were serving in Genghis's army. "Whole regiments" entirely made out of Chinese were used by the Mongols to command bomb hurling trebuchets during the invasion of Iran. Historians have suggested that the Mongol invasion had brought Chinese gunpowder weapons to Central Asia. One of these was the huochong, a Chinese mortar. Books written around the area afterward depicted gunpowder weapons which resembled those of China.

Destruction under the Mongols

Before his death in 1227, Genghis had reached western Azerbaijan, pillaging and burning cities along the way.

The Mongol invasion was disastrous to the Iranians. Although the Mongol invaders were eventually converted to Islam and accepted the culture of Iran, the Mongol destruction of the Islamic heartland marked a major change of direction for the region. Much of the six centuries of Islamic scholarship, culture, and infrastructure was destroyed as the invaders burned libraries, and replaced mosques with Buddhist temples.

The Mongols killed many Iranian civilians. Destruction of qanat irrigation systems destroyed the pattern of relatively continuous settlement, producing numerous isolated oasis cities in a land where they had previously been rare. A large number of people, particularly males, were killed; between 1220 and 1258, 90% of the total population of Iran may have been killed as a result of mass extermination and famine.

Ilkhanate (1256–1335)

After Genghis's death, Iran was ruled by several Mongol commanders. Genghis' grandson, Hulagu Khan, was tasked with the westward expansion of Mongol dominion. However, by time he ascended to power, the Mongol Empire had already dissolved, dividing into different factions. Arriving with an army, he established himself in the region and founded the Ilkhanate, a breakaway state of the Mongol Empire, which would rule Iran for the next eighty years and become Persianate in the process.

Hulagu Khan seized Baghdad in 1258 and put the last Abbasid caliph to death. The westward advance of his forces was stopped by theMamelukes, however, at the Battle of Ain Jalut in Palestine in 1260. Hulagu's campaigns against the Muslims also enraged Berke, khan of the Golden Horde and a convert to Islam. Hulagu and Berke fought against each other, demonstrating the weakening unity of the Mongol empire.

The rule of Hulagu's great-grandson, Ghazan Khan (1295–1304) saw the establishment of Islam as the state religion of the Ilkhanate. Ghazan and his famous Iranian vizier, Rashid al-Din, brought Iran a partial and brief economic revival. The Mongols lowered taxes for artisans, encouraged agriculture, rebuilt and extended irrigation works, and improved the safety of the trade routes. As a result, commerce increased dramatically.

Items from India, China, and Iran passed easily across the Asian steppes, and these contacts culturally enriched Iran. For example, Iranians developed a new style of painting based on a unique fusion of solid, two-dimensional Mesopotamian painting with the feathery, light brush strokes and other motifs characteristic of China. After Ghazan's nephew Abu Said died in 1335, however, the Ilkhanate lapsed into civil war and was divided between several petty dynasties – most prominently theJalayirids, Muzaffarids, Sarbadars and Kartids.

The mid-14th-century Black Death killed about 30% of the country's population.

Sunnism and Shiism in pre-Safavid Iran

Prior to the rise of the Safavid Empire, Sunni Islam was the dominant religion, accounting for around 90% of the population at the time. According to Mortaza Motahhari the majority of Iranian scholars and masses remained Sunni until the time of the Safavids. The domination of Sunnis did not mean Shia were rootless in Iran. The writers of The Four Books of Shia were Iranian, as well as many other great Shia scholars.

The domination of the Sunni creed during the first nine Islamic centuries characterized the religious history of Iran during this period. There were however some exceptions to this general domination which emerged in the form of the Zaydîs of Tabaristan, the Buyids, theKakuyids, the rule of Sultan Muhammad Khudabandah (r. Shawwal 703-Shawwal 716/1304-1316) and the Sarbedaran.

Apart from this domination there existed, firstly, throughout these nine centuries, Shia inclinations among many Sunnis of this land and, secondly, original Imami Shiism as well as Zaydî Shiism had prevalence in some parts of Iran. During this period, Shia in Iran were nourished from Kufah, Baghdad and later from Najaf and Hillah. Shiism was the dominant sect inTabaristan, Qom, Kashan, Avaj and Sabzevar. In many other areas merged population of Shia and Sunni lived together.

During the 10th and 11th centuries, Fatimids sent Ismailis Da'i (missioners) to Iran as well as other Muslim lands. When Ismailis divided into two sects, Nizaris established their base in Iran. Hassan-i Sabbah conquered fortresses and capturedAlamut in 1090 AD. Nizaris used this fortress until a Mongol raid in 1256.

After the Mongol raid and fall of the Abbasids, Sunni hierarchies faltered. Not only did they lose the caliphate but also the status of official madhhab. Their loss was the gain of Shia, whose center wasn't in Iran at that time. Several local Shia dynasties like Sarbadars were established during this time.

The main change occurred in the beginning of the 16th century, when Ismail I founded the Safavid dynasty and initiated a religious policy to recognize Shi'a Islam as the official religion of the Safavid Empire, and the fact that modern Iran remains an officially Shi'ite state is a direct result of Ismail's actions.

Timurid Empire (1370–1507)

Iran remained divided until the arrival of Timur, who is variously described as of Mongol or Turkic origin belonging to the Timurid dynasty. Like its predecessors, the Timurid Empire was also part of the Persianate world. After establishing a power base in Transoxiana, Timur invaded Iran in 1381 and eventually conquered most of it. Timur's campaigns were known for their brutality; many people were slaughtered and several cities were destroyed.

His regime was characterized by its inclusion of Iranians in administrative roles and its promotion of architecture and poetry. His successors, the Timurids, maintained a hold on most of Iran until 1452, when they lost the bulk of it toBlack Sheep Turkmen. The Black Sheep

Turkmen were conquered by the White Sheep Turkmen under Uzun Hasan in 1468; Uzun Hasan and his successors were the masters of Iran until the rise of the Safavids.

Early modern era (1502–1925)

Persia underwent a revival under the Safavid dynasty (1502-1736), the most prominent figure of which was Shah Abbas I. Some historians credit the Safavid dynasty for founding the modern nation-state of Iran. Iran's contemporary Shia character, and significant segments of Iran's current borders take their origin from this era (*e.g. Treaty of Zuhab*).

Safavid Empire (1501–1736)

The Safavid dynasty was one of the most significant ruling dynasties of Persia (modern Iran), and "is often considered the beginning of modern Persian history". They ruled one of the greatest Persian empires after the Muslim conquest of Persia and established the Twelver school of Shi'a Islam as the official religion of their empire, marking one of the most important turning points in Muslim history. The Safavids ruled from 1501 to 1722 (experiencing a brief restoration from 1729 to 1736) and at their height, they controlled all of modernIran, Azerbaijan and Armenia, most of Georgia, the North Caucasus, Iraq, Kuwait and Afghanistan, as well as parts ofTurkey, Syria, Pakistan, Turkmenistan and Uzbekistan. Safavid Iran was one of the Islamic "gunpowder empires", along with its neighbours, its archrival and principal enemy the Ottoman Empire, as well as the Mughal Empire.

The Safavid ruling dynasty was founded by Ismâil, who styled himself Shâh Ismâil I.Practically worshipped by his Qizilbâsh followers, Ismâil invaded Shirvan to avenge the death of his father, Shaykh Haydar, who had been killed during his siege of Derbent, inDagestan. Afterwards he went on a campaign of conquest, and following the capture ofTabriz in July 1501, he enthroned himself as the Shâh of Azerbaijan, minted coins in this name, and proclaimed Shi'ism the official religion of his domain.

Although initially the masters of Azerbaijan and southern Dagestan only, the Safavids had, in fact, won the struggle for power in Persia which had been going on for nearly a century between various dynasties and political forces following the fragmentation of the Kara Koyunlu and the Aq Qoyunlu. A year after his victory in Tabriz, Ismâil proclaimed most of Persia as his domain, and quickly conquered and unified Iran under his rule. Soon afterwards, the new Safavid Empire rapidly conquered regions, nations, and peoples in all directions, including Armenia, Azerbaijan, parts of Georgia, Mesopotamia (Iraq), Kuwait, Syria,Dagestan, large parts of what is now Afghanistan, parts of Turkmenistan, and large chunks of Anatolia, laying the foundation of its multi-ethnic character which would heavily influence the empire itself (most notably the Caucasus and its peoples).

During Tahmasp' reign, he carried out multiple invasions in the Caucasus which had been incorporated in the Safavid empire since Shah Ismail I and for many centuries afterwards, and started with the trend of deporting and moving hundreds of thousands of Circassians, Georgians, and Armenians to Iran's heartlands. Initially only solely put in the royal harems, royal guards, and minor other sections of the Empire, Tahmasp believed he could eventually reduce the power of the Qizilbash, by creating and fully integrating a new layer in Iranian society. As *Encyclopædia Iranica* states, for Tahmãsp, the problem circled around the military tribal elite of the empire, the Qezelbâð, who believed that physical proximity to and control of a member of the immediate Safavid family guaranteed spiritual advantages, political fortune, and material advancement. With this new Caucasian layer in Iranian society, the indisputed might of the Qizilbash (who functioned much like the *ghazis* of the neighboring Ottoman Empire) would be questioned and fully diminished as society would become fully meritocratic.

Shah Abbas I and his successors would significantly expand this policy and plan initiated by Tahmasp, deporting during his reign alone around some 200,000 Georgians, 300,000 Armenians and 100,000–150,000 Circassians to Iran, completing the foundation of a new layer in Iranian society. With this, and the complete systematic disorganisation of the Qizilbash by his personal orders, he eventually fully succeeded in replacing the power of the Qizilbash, with that of the Caucasian ghulams. These new Caucasian elements (the so-called *ghilman* / Ûöáúãó*Çä* / *"servants"*), almost always after conversion to Shi'ismdepending on given function would be, were unlike the Qizilbash, fully loyal only to the Shah. The other masses of Caucasians were deployed in all other possible functions and positions available in the empire, as well as in the harem, regular military, craftsmen, farmers, etc. This system of mass usage of Caucasian subjects remained to exist until the fall of the Qajar Dynasty.

Rostom (also known as*Rustam Khan*), viceroy of*Kartli*, eastern

Georgia, from 1633–1658.

The greatest of the Safavid monarchs, Shah Abbas I the Great (1587–1629) came to power in 1587 aged 16. Abbas I first fought the Uzbeks, recapturing Herat and Mashhad in 1598, which had been lost by his predecessor Mohammad Khodabanda by the Ottoman-Safavid War (1578–1590). Then he turned against the Ottomans, the Safavids their archrivals, recapturing Baghdad, eastern Iraq and the Caucasian provinces and beyond by 1618. Between 1616–1618, following the disobedience of his most loyal Georgian subjectsTeimuraz I and Luarsab II, Abbas carried out a punitive campaign in his territories of Georgia, devastating Kakheti and Tbilisi and carrying away 130,000 – 200,000Georgian captives towards mainland Iran. His new army, which had dramatically been improved with the advent of Robert Shirley and his brothers following the first diplomatic mission to Europe, pitted the first crushing victory over the Safavids' archrivals, the Ottomans in the abovementioned 1603–1618 war and would surpass the Ottomans in military strength. He also used his new force to dislodge the Portuguese from Bahrain (1602) and Hormuz (1622) with aid of the English navy, in the Persian Gulf.

He expanded commercial links with the Dutch East India Company and established firm links with the European royal houses, which had been initiated by Ismail I earlier on by theHabsburg-Persian alliance. Thus Abbas I was able to break the dependence on the Qizilbash for military might and therefore was able to centralize control. The Safavid dynasty had already established itself during Shah Ismail I, but under Abbas I it really became a major power in the world along with its archrival the Ottoman Empire, against whom it became able to compete with on equal foot. It also started the promotion of tourism in Iran. Under their rule Persian Architecture flowered again and saw many new monuments in various Iranian cities, of which Isfahan is the most notable example.

Except for Shah Abbas the Great, Shah Ismail I, Shah Tahmasp I, and Shah Abbas II, many of the Safavid rulers were ineffectual, often being more interested in their women, alcohol and other leisure activities. The end of Abbas II's reign in 1666, marked the beginning of the end of the Safavid dynasty. Despite falling revenues and military threats, many of the later shahs had lavish lifestyles. Shah Soltan Hosain (1694–1722) in particular was known for his love of wine and disinterest in governance.

The declining country was repeatedly raided on its frontiers. Finally, Ghilzai Pashtun chieftain named Mir Wais Khan began a rebellion in Kandahar and defeated the Safavid army under the Iranian Georgian governor over the region, Gurgin Khan. In 1722, Peter the Great of neighbouring Imperial Russia launched the Russo-Persian War (1722–1723), capturing many of Iran's Caucasian territories, including Derbent, Shaki, Baku, but also Gilan, Mazandaran and Astrabad. At the mids of all chaos, in the same year 1722 an Afghan army led by Mir Wais' son Mahmud marched across eastern Iran, besieged and took Isfahan. Mahmud proclaimed himself 'Shah' of Persia. Meanwhile, Persia's imperial rivals, the Ottomans and the Russians, took advantage of the chaos in the country to seize more territory for themselves. By these events, the Safavid dynasty had effectively ended. In 1724, conform the Treaty of Constantinople, the Ottomans and the Russians agreed to divide the newly conquered territories of Iran amongst themselves.

Nader Shah and his successors

Iran's territorial integrity was restored by a native Iranian Turkic Afshar warlord from Khorasan, Nader Shah. He defeated and banished the Afghans, defeated the Ottomans, reinstalled the Safavids on the throne, and negotiated Russian withdrawal from Irans Caucasian territories, by the Treaty of Resht and Treaty of Ganja. By 1736, Nader had become so powerful he was able to depose the Safavids and have himself crowned shah. Nader was one of the last great conquerors of Asia and briefly possessed over what was probably the most powerful empire in the world.

To financially aid his wars against Persia's archrival, the Ottoman Empire, he fixated his mind on the weak but rich Mugal Empire to the east. In 1739, accompanied by his loyal Caucasian subjects including Erekle II, he invaded Mughal India, defeated a numerically superior Mughal army in less than three hours, and completely sacked and looted Delhi, bringing back immense wealth to Persia. On his way back, he also conquered all Uzbek khanates – except Kokand – and made the Uzbeks his vassals.

He also firmly reestablished Persian rule over the entire Caucasus, Bahrain, as well as large parts of Anatolia and Mesopotamia. Undefeated for years, his defeat in Dagestan, following guerrilla rebellions by theLezgins and the assassination attempt on him near Mazandaran is often marked as the turning point in Naders impressive career. Frustratingly for him, the Dagestanis resorted to guerrilla warfare and Nader with his standard army could make little headway against them. At the Battle of Andalal and the Battle of Avaria, Nader's army was crushingly defeated and he lost half of his entire force, as well forcing him to flee for the mountains.

Though Nader managed to take most ofDagestan during his campaign, the effective guerrilla warfare as deployed by the Lezgins, but also the Avars and Laks made the Iranian re-conquest of the particular North Caucasian region this time a short lived one; several years later, Nader was forced to withdraw. Around the same time, the assassination attempt was made on him near Mazandaran which accelerated the course of history; he slowly grew ill and megalomaniac, blinding his sons whom he suspected of the assassination attempts, and increasing cruelty against his subjects and officers. In his later years this eventually provoked multiple revolts and, ultimately, Nader's assassination in 1747.

Nader's death was followed by a period of anarchy in Iran as rival army commanders fought for power. Nader's own family, the Afsharids, were soon reduced to holding on to a small domain in Khorasan. Many of the Caucasian territories broke away in various Caucasian khanates. Ottomans regained lost territories in Anatolia and Mesopotamia. Oman and the Uzbek khanates of Bukhara and Khiva regained independence. Ahmad Shah Durrani, one of Nader's officers, founded an independent state which eventually became modern Afghanistan. Erekle II and Teimuraz II, who, in 1744, had been made the kings of Kakheti and Kartli respectively by Nader himself for their loyal service, capitalized on the eruption of instability, and declared *de facto* independence. Erekle II assumed control over Kartli after Teimuraz II's death, thus unifying the two as the Kingdom of Kartli-Kakheti, becoming the first Georgian ruler in three centuries to preside over a politically unified eastern Georgia, and due to the frantic turn of events in mainland Iran he would be able to remain *de facto*autonomous through the Zand period. From his capital Shiraz, Karim Khan of the Zand dynasty ruled "an island of relative calm and peace in an otherwise bloody and destructive period," however the extent of Zand power was confined to contemporary Iran and parts of the Caucasus. Karim Khan's death in 1779 led to yet another civil war in which the Qajar dynasty eventually triumphed and became kings of Iran. During the civil war, Iran permanently lost Basra in 1779 to the Ottomans, which had been captured during the Ottoman-

Persian War (1775–76), and Bahrain to Al Khalifa family afterBani Utbah invasion in 1783.

Qajar dynasty (1796–1925)

Agha Mohammad Khan emerged victorious out of the civil war that commenced with the death of the last Zand king. His reign is noted for the reemergence of a centrally led and united Iran. After the death of Nader Shah and the last of the Zands, most of Iran's Caucasian territories had broken away into various Caucasian khanates. Agha Mohammad Khan, like the Safavid kings and Nader Shah before him, viewed the region as no different than the territories in mainland Iran. Therefore, his first objective after having secured mainland Iran, was to reincorpate the Caucasus region into Iran. Georgia was seen as one of the most integral territories. For Agha Mohammad Khan, the resubjugation and reintegration of Georgia into the Iranian Empire was part of the same process that had brought Shiraz, Isfahan, andTabriz under his rule.

As the *Cambridge History of Iran* states, its permanent secession was inconceivable and had to be resisted in the same way as one would resist an attempt at the separation of Fars or Gilan. It was therefore natural for Agha Mohammad Khan to perform whatever necessary means in the Caucasus in order to subdue and reincorporate the recently lost regions following Nader Shah's death and the demise of the Zands, including putting down what in Iranian eyes was seen as treason on the part of the *wali* (viceroy) of Georgia, namely the Georgian king Erekle II (Heraclius II) who was appointed viceroy of Georgia by Nader Shah himself.

Agha Mohammad Khan subsequently demanded Heraclius II to renounce the treaty with Russia of several years earlier, and to reaccept Persian suzerainty, in return for peace and the security of his kingdom. The Ottomans, Iran's neighboring rival, recognized the latters rights over Kartli and Kakheti for the first time in four centuries. Heraclius appealed then to his theoretical protector, Empress Catherine II of Russia, pledging for at least 3,000 Russian troops, but he was ignored, leaving Georgia to fend off the Persian threat alone. Nevertheless, Heraclius II still rejected the Khan's ultimatum. As a response, Agha Mohammad Khan invaded the Caucasus region after crossing the Aras river, and, while on his way to Georgia, he re-subjugated Iran's territories of the Erivan Khanate, Shirvan, Nakhchivan Khanate,Ganja khanate, Derbent Khanate, Baku khanate, Talysh Khanate, Shaki

Khanate,Karabakh Khanate, which comprise modern-day Armenia, Azerbaijan, Dagestan, andIgdir. Having reached Georgia with his large army, it culminated in the Battle of Krtsanisi, which resulted in the capture, and sack of Tbilisi, as well as the effective resubjugation of Georgia into Iran. Upon his return from his successful campaign in Tbilisi and in effective control over Georgia, together with some 15,000Georgian captives that were moved back to mainland Iran, Agha Mohammad was formally crowned Shah in 1796 in the Mughan plain, just like his predecessor Nader Shah was about sixty years earlier.

Agha Mohammad Shah was later assassinated while preparing a second expedition against Georgia in 1797 in Shusha (nowadays part of the Republic of Azerbaijan) and the seasoned king Heraclius died early in 1798. Reassessment of Iranian hegemony over Georgia did not last long; in 1799 the Russians marched into Tbilisi.The Russians were already actively occupied with an expansionistic policy towards its neighboring empires to its south, namely the Ottoman Empire and the successive Iranian kingdoms since the late 17th/early 18th century. The next two years following Russia's entrance into Tbilisi were a time of muddle and confusion, and the weakened and devastated Georgian kingdom, with its capital half in ruins, was easily absorbed by Russia in 1801. As Iran could not permit or allow the cession of Transcaucasiaand Dagestan, which had made an integral part of Iran for centuries, it would lead directly to the wars of several years later, namely the Russo-Persian Wars of 1804-1813 and 1826-1828. The outcome of these two wars (Treaty of Gulistan and theTreaty of Turkmenchay, respectively) proved for the irrevocable forced cession and loss of what is nowadays eastern Georgia, Dagestan, Armenia, and Azerbaijan to Imperial Russia.

The area to the North of the river Aras, among which the territory of the contemporary republic of Azerbaijan, eastern Georgia, Dagestan, and Armenia were Iranian territory until they were occupied by Russia in the course of the 19th century.

Migration of Caucasian Muslims

Following the official losing of the aforementioned vast territories in the Caucasus, major demographic shifts were bound to take place. Solidly Persian-speaking territories of Iran were lost, with all its inhabitants in it. Following the 1804–1814 War, but also per the 1826–1828 war which ceded the last territories, large migrations, so called

Caucasian Muhajirs, set off to migrate to mainland Iran. Some of these groups included the Ayrums, Qarapapaqs, Circassians, Shia Lezgins, and other Transcaucasian Muslims.

Through the Battle of Ganja of 1804 during the Russo-Persian War (1804–13), many thousands of Ayrums and Qarapapaqs were settled in Tabriz. During the remaining part of the 1804–1813 war, as well as through the 1826–1828 war, the absolute bulk of the Ayrums and Qarapapaqs that were still remaining in newly conquered Russian territories were settled in and migrated to Solduz (in modern-day Iran's West Azerbaijan province). As the *Cambridge History of Iran* states; "The steady encroachment of Russian troops along the frontier in the Caucasus, GeneralYermolov's brutal punitive expeditions and misgovernment, drove large numbers of Muslims, and even some GeorgianChristians, into exile in Iran."

In 1864 until the early 20th century, another mass expulsion took place of Caucasian Muslims as a result of the Russian victory in the Caucasian War. Others simply voluntarily refused to live under Christian Russian rule, and thus disembarked for Turkey or Iran. These migrations once again, towards Iran, included masses of Caucasian Azerbaijanis, other Transcaucasian Muslims, as well as many North Caucasian Muslims, such as Circassians, Shia Lezgins and Laks.Many of these migrants would prove to play a pivotal role in further Iranian history, as they formed most of the ranks of thePersian Cossack Brigade, which was also to be established in the late 19th century. The initial ranks of the brigade would be entirely composed of Circassians and other Caucasian Muhajirs. This brigade would prove decisive in the following decades to come in Qajar history.

Furthermore, the 1828 Treaty of Turkmenchay included the official rights for the Russian Empire to encourage settling ofArmenians from Iran in the newly conquered Russian territories. This also helped in changing the demographics of the regions considerably. The Treaty of Adrianople, concluded with Turkey in 1829 granted for more mass settling of Armenians in the newly incorporated territories. Slowly but surely, the number of Christians, that formerly made out since the 17th century a relatively small minority in the region (except for Georgia), were starting to compose an ever-growing number of the total population, especially in the former Iranian-ruled Armenian and Georgian territories.

Following the resettlement of Persian Armenians in the newly conquered Russian territories after 1828, thus significant demographic shifts were bound to take place. The Armenian-American historian George Bournoutian gives a summary of the ethnic makeup prior to the events of 1828 just for the territory of the Erivan administrative division as an example: "In the first quarter of the 19th century the Khanate of Erevan included most of Eastern Armenia and covered an area of approximately 7,000 square miles. The land was mountainous and dry, the population of about 100,000 was roughly 80 percent Muslim (Persian, Azeri, Kurdish) and 20 percent Christian (Armenian)."

After the incorporation of the Erivan khanate into the Russian Empire, Muslim majority of the area gradually changed, at first the Armenians who were left captive were encouraged to return. As a result of which an estimated 57,000 Armenian refugees from Persia returned to the territory of the Erivan khanates after 1828, while about 35,000 Muslims (Persians, Turkic groups, Kurds, Lezgis, etc.) out total population of over 100,000 left the region.

Fath Ali Shah's reign saw increased diplomatic contacts with the West and the beginning of intense European diplomatic rivalries over Iran. His grandson Mohammad Shah, who fell under the Russian influence and made two unsuccessful attempts to capture Herat, succeeded him in 1834. When Mohammad Shah died in 1848 the succession passed to his son Nasser-e-Din, who proved to be the ablest and most successful of the Qajar sovereigns.

Constitutional Revolution and deposement

The Great Persian Famine of 1870–1871 is believed to have caused the death of 2 million persons.

A new era in the history of Persia dawned with the Persian Constitutional Revolution against the Shah in the late 19th and early 20th centuries. The Shah managed to remain in power, granting a limited constitution in 1906 (making the country aconstitutional monarchy). The first Majlis (parliament) was convened on October 7, 1906.

The discovery of petroleum in 1908 by the British in Khuzestan spawned intense renewed interest in Persia by the British Empire. Control of Persia remained contested between the United Kingdom and Russia, in what became known as The Great Game, and codified in the Anglo-Russian Convention of 1907, which divided Persia into spheres of influence, regardless of her national sovereignty.

During World War I, the country was occupied by British, Ottoman and Russian forces but was essentially neutral (seePersian Campaign). In 1919, after the Russian revolution and their withdrawal, Britain attempted to establish a protectoratein Persia, which was unsuccessful.

Finally, the Constitutionalist movement of Gilan and the central power vacuum caused by the instability of the Qajar government resulted in the rise of Reza Khan, who was later to become Reza Shah Pahlavi, and the subsequent establishment of the Pahlavi dynasty in 1925. In 1921, a military coup established Reza Khan, an officer of the Persian Cossack Brigade, as the dominant figure for the next 20 years. Seyyed Zia'eddin Tabatabai was also a leader and important figure in the perpetration of the coup. The coup was not actually directed at the Qajar monarchy; according to *Encyclopædia Iranica*, it was targeted at officials who were in power and actually had a role in controlling the government; the cabinet and others who had a role in governing Persia. In 1925, after being prime minister for two years, Reza Khan became the first shah of the Pahlavi dynasty.

PAHLAVI ERA (1925–1979)

Reza Shah (1925–1941)

Reza Shah ruled for almost 16 years until September 16, 1941, when he was forced to abdicate by the Anglo-Soviet invasion of Iran. He established an authoritarian government that valued nationalism, militarism, secularism and anti-communism combined with strict censorship and state propaganda. Reza Shah introduced many socio-economic reforms, reorganizing the army, government administration, and finances.

To his supporters his reign brought "law and order, discipline, central authority, and modern amenities – schools, trains, buses, radios, cinemas, and telephones". However, his attempts of modernisation have been criticised for being "too fast" and "superficial", and his reign a time of "oppression, corruption, taxation, lack of authenticity" with "security typical of police states."

Many of the new laws and regulations created resentment among devout Muslims and the clergy. For example, mosques were required to use chairs; most men were required to wear western clothing, including a hat with a brim; women were encouraged to discard the hijab; men and women were allowed to freely congregate, violating Islamic mixing of the sexes. Tensions boiled over in 1935, when bazaaris and villagers rose up in rebellion at the Imam Reza shrine in Mashhad, chanting slogans such as 'The Shah is a new Yezid.' Dozens were killed and hundreds were injured when troops finally quelled the unrest.

World War II

German interests held great influence within Iran in 1941, with the Germans staging a coup in an attempt to overthrow the Pahlavi dynasty. With German armies highly successful against Russia, the Iranian government expected Germany to win the war and establish a powerful force on its borders. It rejected British and Russian demands to expel the Germans. In response the Allies invaded in August 1941, and easily overwhelmed the weak Iranian army in *Operation Countenance*. Iran became the major conduit of Allied Lend-Lease aid to the Soviet Union. The purpose was to secure Iranian oil fields and ensure Allied supply lines. Iran remained officially neutral. Its monarch Rezâ Shâh was deposed during the subsequent occupation and replaced with his young son Mohammad Reza Pahlavi.

At the Tehran Conference of 1943, the Allies issued the Tehran Declarationguaranteed the post-war independence and boundaries of Iran. However, when the war actually ended, Soviet troops stationed in northwestern Iran not only refused to withdraw but backed revolts that established short-lived, pro-Soviet separatist national states in the northern regions of Azerbaijan and Iranian Kurdistan, theAzerbaijan People's Government and the Republic of Kurdistan respectively, in late 1945. Soviet troops did not withdraw from Iran proper until May 1946 after receiving a promise of oil concessions. The Soviet republics in the north were soonoverthrown and the oil concessions were revoked.

Mohammad-Reza Shah (1941–1979)

Initially there were hopes that post-occupation Iran could become a constitutional monarchy. The new, young Shah Mohammad Reza Shah Pahlavi initially took a very hands-off role in government, and allowed parliament to hold a lot of power. Some elections were held in the first shaky years, although they remained mired in corruption. Parliament became chronically unstable, and from the 1947 to 1951 period Iran saw the rise and fall of six different prime ministers.

Pahlavi increased his political power by convening the Iran Constituent Assembly, 1949, which finally formed the Senate of Iran—a legislative upper house allowed for in the 1906 constitution but never brought into being. The new senators were largely supportive of Pahlavi, as he had intended.

In 1951 Prime Minister Mohammed Mosaddeq received the vote required from the parliament tonationalize the British-owned oil industry, in a situation known as the Abadan Crisis. Despite British pressure, including an economic blockade, the nationalization continued. Mosaddeq was briefly removed from power in 1952 but was quickly re-appointed by the shah, due to a popular uprising in support of the premier and he, in turn, forced the Shah into a brief exile in August 1953 after a failed military coup by Imperial Guard Colonel Nematollah Nassiri.

1953: U.S. organized coup removes Mosaddeq

Shortly thereafter on August 19 a successful coup was headed by retired army generalFazlollah Zahedi, organized by the United States (CIA) with the active support of the British (MI6) (known as Operation Ajax and Operation Boot to the respective agencies). The coup—with a black propaganda campaign designed to turn the population against Mosaddeq—forced Mosaddeq from office. Mosaddeq was arrested and tried for treason. Found guilty, his sentence reduced to house arrest on his family estate while his foreign minister, Hossein Fatemi, was executed. Zahedi succeeded him as prime minister, and suppressed opposition to the Shah, specifically the National Front and Communist Tudeh Party.

Iran was ruled as an autocracy under the shah with American support from that time until the revolution. The Iranian government entered into agreement with an international consortium of foreign companies which ran the Iranian oil facilities for the next 25 years splitting profits fifty-fifty with Iran but not allowing Iran to audit their accounts or have members on their board of directors. In 1957 martial law was ended after 16 years and Iran became closer to the West, joining the Baghdad Pactand receiving military and economic aid from the US. In 1961, Iran initiated a series of economic, social, agrarian and administrative reforms to modernize the country that became known as the Shah's White Revolution.

The core of this program was land reform. Modernization and economic growth proceeded at an unprecedented rate, fueled by Iran's vast petroleum reserves, the third-largest in the world. However the reforms, including the White Revolution, did not greatly improve economic conditions and the liberal pro-Western policies alienated certain Islamic religious and political groups. In early June 1963 several days of massive rioting occurred in support of Ayatollah Ruhollah Khomeini following the cleric's arrest for a speech attacking the shah.

Two years later, premier Hassan Ali Mansur was assassinated and the internal security service, SAVAK, became more violently active. In the 1970s leftist guerilla groups such as Mujaheddin-e-Khalq (MEK), emerged and attacked regime and foreign targets.

Nearly a hundred Iran political prisoners were killed by the SAVAK during the decade before the revolution and many more were arrested and tortured. The Islamic clergy, headed by the Ayatollah Ruhollah Khomeini (who had been exiled in 1964), were becoming increasingly vociferous.

Iran greatly increased its defense budget and by the early 1970s was the region's strongest military power. Bilateral relations with its neighbor Iraq were not good, mainly due to a dispute over the Shatt al-Arab waterway. In November 1971, Iranian forces seized control of three islands at the mouth of the Persian Gulf; in response, Iraq expelled thousands of Iranian nationals. Following a number of clashes in April 1969, Iran abrogated the 1937 accord and demanded a renegotiation.

In mid-1973, the Shah returned the oil industry to national control. Following the Arab-Israeli War of October 1973, Iran did not join the Arab oil embargo against the West and Israel. Instead, it used the situation to raise oil prices, using the money gained for modernization and to increase defense spending.

A border dispute between Iraq and Iran was resolved with the signing of the Algiers Accord on March 6, 1975.

IRANIAN REVOLUTION AND THE ISLAMIC REPUBLIC (1979)

The Iranian Revolution, also known as the Islamic Revolution, was therevolution that transformed Iran from an absolute monarchy under Shah Mohammad Reza Pahlavi, to an Islamic republic under Ayatollah Ruhollah Khomeini, one of the leaders of the revolution and founder of the Islamic Republic. Its time span can be said to have begun in January 1978 with the first major demonstrations, and concluded with the approval of the new theocratic Constitution—

whereby Ayatollah Khomeini became Supreme Leader of the country – in December 1979.

In between, Mohammad Reza Pahlavi left the country for exile in January 1979 after strikes and demonstrations paralyzed the country, and on February 1, 1979 Ayatollah Khomeini returned to Tehran to a greeting of several million Iranians. The final collapse of the Pahlavi dynasty occurred shortly after on February 11 when Iran's military declared itself "neutral" after guerrillas and rebel troops overwhelmed troops loyal to the Shah in armed street fighting. Iran officially became an Islamic Republic on April 1, 1979, when Iranians overwhelmingly approved a national referendum to make it so.

Ideology of the 1979 Iranian Revolution

The ideology of revolutionary government was populist, nationalist and most of all Shi'a Islamic. Its unique constitution is based on the concept of *velayat-e faqih* the idea advanced by Khomeini that Muslims – in fact everyone – requires "guardianship", in the form of rule or supervision by the leading Islamic jurist or jurists. Khomeini served as this ruling jurist, or supreme leader, until his death in 1989.

Iran's rapidly modernising, capitalist economy was replaced by populist and Islamic economic and cultural policies. Much industry was nationalized, laws and schools Islamicized, and Western influences banned.

The Islamic revolution also created great impact around the world. In the non-Muslim world it has changed the image of Islam, generating much interest in the politics and spirituality of Islam, along with "fear and distrust towards Islam" and particularly the Islamic Republic and its founder.

Khomeini Takes Power (1979–1989)

Khomeini served as leader of the revolution or as Supreme Leader of Iran from 1979 to his death on June 3, 1989. This era was dominated by the consolidation of the revolution into a theocratic republic under Khomeini, and by the costly and bloodywar with Iraq.

The consolidation lasted until 1982–3, as Iran coped with the damage to its economy, military, and apparatus of government, and protests and uprisings by secularists, leftists, and more traditional Muslims – formerly ally revolutionaries but now rivals – were effectively suppressed. Many political opponents were executed by the new regimes. Following the events of the revolution, Marxist guerrillas and federalist parties revolted in some regions comprising Khuzistan, Kurdistanand Gonbad-e Qabus, which resulted in severe fighting between rebels and revolutionary forces. These revolts began in April 1979 and lasted between several months to over a year, depending on the region. The Kurdish uprising, led by the KDPI, was the most violent, lasting until 1983 and resulting in 10,000 casualties.

In the summer of 1979 a new constitution giving Khomeini a powerful post as guardian jurist Supreme Leader and a clerical Council of Guardians power over legislation and elections, was drawn up by an Assembly of Experts for Constitution. The new constitution was approved by referendum in December 1979.

Iran hostage crisis (1979–1981)

An early event in the history of the Islamic republic that had a long-term impact was the Iran hostage crisis. Following the admitting of the former Shah of Iran into the United States for cancer treatment, on November 4, 1979, Iranian studentsseized US embassy personnel, labeling the embassy a "den of spies." Fifty-two hostages were held for 444 days until January 1981. An American military attempt to rescue the hostages failed.

The takeover was enormously popular in Iran, where thousands gathered in support of the hostage takers, and it is thought to have strengthened the prestige of the Ayatollah Khomeini and consolidated the hold of anti-Americanism. It was at this time that Khomeini began referring to America as the "Great Satan." In America, where it was considered a violation of the long-standing principle of international law that diplomats may be expelled but not held captive, it created a powerful anti-Iranian backlash. Relations between the two countries have remained deeply antagonistic and American international sanctions have hurt Iran's economy.

Iran–Iraq War (1980–1988)

During this political and social crisis, Iraqi leader Saddam Hussein attempted to take advantage of the disorder of the Revolution, the weakness of the Iranian military and the revolution's antagonism with Western governments. The once-strong Iranian military had been disbanded during the revolution, and with the Shah ousted, Hussein had ambitions to position himself as the new strong man of the Middle East, and sought to expand Iraq's access to the Persian Gulf by acquiring territories that Iraq had claimed earlier from Iran during the Shah's rule.

Of chief importance to Iraq was Khuzestan which not only boasted a substantial Arab population, but rich oil fields as well. On the unilateral behalf of the United Arab Emirates, the islands of Abu Musa and the Greater and Lesser Tunbsbecame objectives as well. With these ambitions in mind, Hussein planned a full-scale assault on Iran, boasting that his forces could reach the capital within three days. On September 22, 1980, the Iraqi army invaded Iran at Khuzestan, precipitating the Iran–Iraq War. The attack took revolutionary Iran completely by surprise.

Although Saddam Hussein's forces made several early advances, Iranian forces had pushed the Iraqi army back into Iraq by 1982. Khomeini sought to export his Islamic revolution westward into Iraq, especially on the majority Shi'a Arabs living in the country. The war then continued for six more years until 1988, when Khomeini, in his words, "drank the cup of poison" and accepted a truce mediated by the United Nations.

Tens of thousands of Iranian civilians and military personnel were killed when Iraq used chemical weapons in its warfare. Iraq was financially backed by Egypt, the Arab countries of the Persian Gulf, the Soviet Union and the Warsaw Pact states, the United States (beginning in 1983), France, the United Kingdom, Germany, Brazil, and the People's Republic of China (which also sold weapons to Iran).

There were more than 100,000 Iranian victims of Iraq's chemical weapons during the eight-year war. The total Iranian casualties of the war were estimated to be between 500,000 and 1,000,000. Almost all relevant international agencies have confirmed that Saddam engaged in chemical warfare to blunt Iranian human wave attacks; these agencies unanimously confirmed that Iran never used chemical weapons during the war.

Starting on 19 July 1988 and lasting about five months the government systematically executed thousands of political prisoners across Iran. This is commonly referred to as the 1988 executions of Iranian political prisoners or the 1988 Iranian Massacre. The main target was the membership of the People's Mojahedin Organization of Iran (PMOI), although a lesser number of political prisoners from other leftist groups were also included such as the Tudeh Party of Iran (Communist Party). Estimates of the number executed vary from 1,400 to 30,000.

Rule under Khamenei (1989–present)

The first eight years (1989–1997)

On his deathbed in 1989, Khomeini appointed a 25-man Constitutional Reform Council which named then president Ali Khamenei as the next Supreme Leader, and made a number of changes to Iran's constitution. A smooth transition followed Khomeini's death on June 3, 1989. While Khamenei lacked Khomeini's "charisma and clerical standing", he developed a network of supporters within Iran's armed forces and its economically powerful religious foundations. Under his reign Iran's regime is said – by at least one observer – to resemble more "a clerical oligarchy ... than an autocracy."

Succeeding Khamenei as president was pragmatic conservative Ali-Akbar Hashemi Rafsanjani, who served two four-year terms and focused his efforts on rebuilding Iran's economy and war-damaged infrastructure though low oil prices hampered this endeavor. He sought to restore confidence in the government among the general population by privatizing the companies that had been nationalized in the first few years of the Islamic Republic, as well as by bringing in qualified technocrats to manage the economy. The state of their economy also influenced the government to move towards ending their diplomatic isolation. This was achieved through the reestablishment of normalized relations with neighbors such asSaudi Arabia and an attempt to improve its reputation in the region with assertions that its revolution was not exportable to other states. During the Persian Gulf War in 1991 the country remained neutral, restricting its action to the condemnation of the U.S. and allowing fleeing Iraqi aircraft and refugees into the country.

Iran in the 1990s had a greater secular behavior and admiration for Western popular culture than in the previous decades, it had become a way in which the urban population expressed their resentment at the invasive Islamic policies of the government. The pressures from the population placed on the new Supreme Leader, Ayatollah Ali Khamenei led to an uneasy alliance between him and President Akbar Hashemi Rafsanjani. Through this alliance they attempted to hinder theulama's ability to gain further control of the state. In 1989, they created a sequence of constitutional amendments that removed the office of prime minister and increased the scope of presidential power. However, these new amendments did not curtail the powers of the Supreme Leader of Iran in any way; this position still contained the ultimate authority over the armed forces, the making of war and peace, the final say in foreign policy, and the right to intervene in the legislative process whenever he deemed it necessary.

Reforms and consequences (1997–2005)

President Rafsanjani's economic policies that led to greater relations with the outside world and his government's relaxation on the enforcement certain regulations on social behavior were met with some responses of widespread disenchantment among the general population with the ulama as rulers of the country. This led to the defeat of the government's candidate for president in 1997, who had the backing of the supreme Islamic jurist. He was beaten by an independent candidate from the reformist, Mohammad Khatami.

He received 69% of the vote and enjoyed particular support from two groups of the population that had felt ostracized by the practices of the state: women and youth. The younger generations in the country had been too young to experience the shah's regime or the revolution that ended it, and now they resented the restrictions placed on their daily lives under the Islamic Republic.

Mohammad Khatami's presidency was soon marked by tensions between thereform-minded government and an increasingly conservative and vocal clergy. This rift reached a climax in July 1999 when massive anti-government protests erupted in the streets of Tehran. The disturbances lasted over a week before police and pro-government vigilantes dispersed the crowds.

Khatami was re-elected in June 2001 but his efforts were repeatedly blocked by the conservatives in the parliament. Conservative elements within Iran's government moved to undermine the reformist movement, banning liberal newspapers and disqualifying candidates for parliamentary elections.

This clampdown on dissent, combined with the failure of Khatami to reform the government, led to growing political apathy among Iran's youth.

In June 2003, anti-government protests by several thousand students took place in Tehran. Several human rightsprotests also occurred in 2006.

2005 presidential election and consequences (2005–2009)

In 2005 Iranian presidential election, Mahmoud Ahmadinejad, mayor of Tehran, became the sixth president of Iran, after winning 62 percent of the vote in the run-off poll, against former president Ali-Akbar Hashemi Rafsanjani. During the authorization ceremony he kissed Khamenei's hand in demonstration of his loyalty to him.

During this time, the American invasion of Iraq, overthrow of Saddam Hussein's regime and empowerment of its Shi'amajority, all strengthened Iran's position in the region particularly in the mainly Shi'a south of Iraq, where a top Shia leader in the week of September 3, 2006 renewed demands for an autonomous Shi'a region. At least one commentator (Former U.S. Defense Secretary William S. Cohen) has stated that as of 2009 Iran's growing power has eclipsed anti-Zionism as the major foreign policy issue in the Middle East.

During 2005 and 2006, there were claims that the United States and Israel were planning to attack Iran, with the most cited reason being Iran's civilian nuclear energy program which the United States and some other states fear could lead to a nuclear weapons program. China and Russia opposed military action of any sort and opposed economic sanctions. Supreme Leader Ali Khamenei issued a fatwa forbidding the production, stockpiling and use of nuclear weapons. The fatwa was cited in an official statement by the Iranian government at an August 2005 meeting of the International Atomic Energy Agency (IAEA) in Vienna.

In 2009, Ahmadinejad's reelection was hotly disputed and marred by large protests that formed the "greatest domestic challenge" to the leadership of the Islamic Republic "in 30 years". The resulting social unrest is widely known as the Iranian Green Movement. Reformist opponent Mir-Hossein Mousavi and his supporters alleged voting irregularities and by 1 July 2009, 1000 people had been arrested and 20 killed in street demonstrations. Supreme Leader Ali Khamenei and other Islamic officials blamed foreign powers for fomenting the protest.

2013 presidential election and improving US–Iran relations (2013–present)

On 15 June 2013, Hassan Rouhani won the presidential election in Iran, with a total number of 36,704,156 ballots cast; Rouhani won 18,613,329 votes. In his press conference one day after election day, Rouhani reiterated his promise to recalibrate Iran's relations with the world.

On April 2, 2015, following eight days of tortuous discussions in Switzerland, which lasted through the night to Thursday, Iran and six world powers (United States, United Kingdom, France, China and Russia plus Germany) agreed on the outlines of an understanding to limit Iran's nuclear programs, negotiators indicated, as both sides prepared for announcements. Iranian Foreign Minister Mohammad Javad Zarif tweeted: "Found solutions. Ready to start drafting immediately." European Union foreign policy chief Federica Mogherini tweeted that she would meet the press with Zarif after a final meeting of the seven nations in the nuclear talks. She wrote: "Good news."

Reading out a joint statement, European Union foreign policy chief Federica Mogherini hailed what she called a "decisive step" after more than a decade of work. Iranian Foreign Minister Mohammad Javad Zarif followed with the same statement inPersian. U.S. Secretary of State John Kerry and the top diplomats of Britain, France and Germany also briefly took the stage behind them.

The deal is intended to be a provisional framework for a comprehensive agreement that is not due to be signed until the end of June, but if it includes concrete facts and figures, it will mark a significant breakthrough in the 12-year history of negotiations with Iran over its nuclear programme.

3

Geography

Geographically, Iran is located in West Asia and borders the Caspian Sea,Persian Gulf, and Gulf of Oman. Its mountains have helped to shape both the political and the economic history of the country for several centuries. The mountains enclose several broad basins, on which major agricultural and urban settlements are located. Until the 20th century, when majorhighways and railroads were constructed through the mountains to connect the population centers, these basins tended to be relatively isolated from one another.

Typically, one major town dominated each basin, and there were complex economic relationships between the town and the hundreds of villages that surrounded it. In the higher elevations of the mountains rimming the basins, tribally organized groups practiced transhumance, moving with their herds of sheep and goats between traditionally established summer and winterpastures. There are no major river systems in the country, and historically transportation was by means of caravans that followed routes traversing gaps and passes in the mountains. The mountains also impeded easy access to the Persian Gulf and the Caspian Sea.

With an area of 1,648,000 square kilometres (636,000 sq mi), Iran ranks eighteenth in size among the countries of the world. Iran shares its northern borders with three post-Soviet states: Armenia, Azerbaijan, andTurkmenistan. These borders extend for more than 2,000 kilometres (1,200 mi), including nearly 650 kilometres (400 mi) of water along the southern shore of the Caspian Sea. Iran's western borders are with Turkeyin the north and Iraq in the south, terminating at the Arvand Rud.

The Persian Gulf and Gulf of Oman littorals form the entire 1,770 kilometres (1,100 mi) southern border. To the east lie Afghanistan on the north andPakistan on the far south. Iran's diagonal distance from Azerbaijan in the northwest to Sistan and Baluchestan Province in the southeast is approximately 2,333 kilometres (1,450 mi).

TOPOGRAPHY

The topography of Iran consists of rugged, mountainous rims surrounding high interior basins. The main mountain chain is the Zagros Mountains, a series of parallel ridges interspersed with plains that bisect the country from northwest to southeast. Many peaks in the Zagros exceed 3,000 metres (9,843 ft) above sea level, and in the south-central region of the country there are at least five peaks that are over 4,000 metres (13,123 ft).

As the Zagros continue into southeastern Iran, the average elevation of the peaks declines dramatically to under 1,500 metres (4,921 ft). Rimming the Caspian Sea littoral is another chain of mountains, the narrow but high Alborz Mountains. VolcanicMount Damavand, 5,610 metres (18,406 ft), located in the center of the Alborz, is not only the country's highest peak but also the highest mountain on the Eurasian landmass west of the Hindu Kush.

The center of Iran consists of several closed basins that collectively are referred to as the Central Plateau. The average elevation of this plateau is about 900 metres (2,953 ft), but several of the mountains that tower over the plateau exceed 3,000 metres (9,843 ft). The eastern part of the plateau is covered by two salt deserts, theDasht-e Kavir (Great Salt Desert) and the Dasht-e Lut. Except for some scatteredoases, these deserts are uninhabited.

Parts of northwestern Iran are part of the Armenian highlands, which adjoins it topographically with other parts of neighbouring Turkey, Armenia, Azerbaijan, andGeorgia.

Iran has only two expanses of lowlands: the Khuzestan Plain in the southwest and the Caspian Sea coastal plain in the north. The former is a roughly triangular-shaped extension of the Mesopotamia plain and averages about 160 kilometres (99 mi) in width. It extends for about 120 kilometres (75 mi) inland, barely rising a few meters above sea level, then meets abruptly with the first foothills of the Zagros. Much of the Khuzestan plain is covered with marshes. The Caspian plain is both longer and narrower. It extends for some 640 kilometres (400 mi) along the Caspian shore, but its widest point is less than 50 kilometres (31 mi), while at some places less than 2 kilometres (1.2 mi) separate the shore from the Alborz foothills. The Persian Gulf coast south of Khuzestan and the Gulf of Oman coast have no real plains because the Zagros in these areas come right down to the shore.

There are no major rivers in the country. Of the small rivers and streams, the only one that is navigable is the 830 kilometres (520 mi)-long Karun, which shallow-draft boats can negotiate from Khorramshahr to Ahvaz, a distance of about 180 kilometres (110 mi). Other major rivers include the Karkheh, spanning 700 kilometres (430 mi) and joining the Tigris; and the Zayandeh River, which is 300 kilometres (190 mi) long. Several other permanent rivers and streams also drain into the Persian Gulf, while a number of small rivers that originate in the northwestern Zagros or Alborz drain into the Caspian Sea.

On the Central Plateau, numerous rivers—most of which have dry beds for the greater part of the year—form from snow melting in the mountains during the spring and flow through permanent channels, draining eventually into salt lakes that also tend to dry up during the summer months. There is a permanent salt lake, Lake Urmia (the traditional name, also cited as Lake Urmiyeh, to which it has reverted after being called Lake Rezaiyeh under Mohammad Reza Shah), in the northwest, whose brine content is too high to support fish or most other forms of aquatic life. There are also several connected salt lakes along the Iran-Afghanistan border in the province of Baluchestan va Sistan.

CLIMATE

Iran has a variable climate. In the northwest, winters are cold with heavy snowfall and subfreezing temperatures during December and January. Spring and fall are relatively mild, while summers are dry and hot. In the south, winters are mild and the summers are very hot, having average daily temperatures in July exceeding 38 °C (100.4 °F). On the Khuzestan Plain, summer heat is accompanied by high humidity.

In general, Iran has an arid climate in which most of the relatively scant annual precipitation falls from October through April. In most of the country, yearly precipitation averages 250 millimetres (9.8 in) or less. The major exceptions are the higher mountain valleys of the Zagros and the Caspian coastal plain, where precipitation averages at least 500 millimetres (19.7 in) annually. In the western part of the Caspian, rainfall exceeds 1,000 millimetres (39.4 in) annually and is distributed relatively evenly throughout the year. This contrasts with some basins of the Central Plateau that receive ten centimeters or less of precipitation.

Flora and fauna

7% of the country is forested. The most extensive growths are found on the mountain slopes rising from the Caspian Sea, with stands of oak, ash, elm,cypress, and other valuable trees. On the plateau proper, areas of scrub oak appear on the best-watered mountain slopes, and villagers cultivate orchards and grow the plane tree, poplar, willow, walnut, beech, maple, and mulberry. Wild plants and shrubs spring from the barren land in the spring and afford pasturage, but the summer sun burns them away. According to FAO reports,the major types of forests that exist in Iran and their respective areas are:

1. Caspian forests of the northern districts – 19,000 km^2 (7,300 sq mi)

2. Limestone mountainous forests in the northeastern districts (*Juniperus*forests) – 13,000 km^2 (5,000 sq mi)

3. Pistachio forests in the eastern, southern and southeastern districts – 26,000 km^2 (10,000 sq mi)

4. Oak forests in the central and western districts – 35,000 km^2(14,000 sq mi)

5. Shrubs of the Kavir (desert) districts in the central and northeastern part of the country – 10,000 km^2 (3,900 sq mi)

6. Sub-tropical forests of the southern coast, like the Hara forests – 5,000 km^2 (1,900 sq mi)

Wildlife of Iran is diverse and composed of several animal species including bears, gazelles, wild pigs, wolves, jackals, panthers, Eurasian lynx, and foxes. Domestic animals include, sheep, goats, cattle, horses, water buffalo, donkeys, and camels. The pheasant, partridge, stork, eagles and falcon are also native to Iran.

As of 2001, 20 of Iran's mammal species and 14 bird species are endangered. Among them are the Baluchistan bear (*Ursus thibetanus gedrosianus*), a subspecies of Asian black bear, Persian fallow deer, Siberian crane, hawksbill turtle, green turtle,Oxus cobra, Latifi's viper, dugong and dolphins. The Asiatic cheetah is a critically endangered species which is extinct elsewhere and now can only be found in central to northeastern parts of Iran.

Iran lost all its Asiatic lions and Caspian tigers by the earlier part of the 20th century. The Syrian wild ass has become extinct. Syrian brown bears in the mountains, wild sheep and goats, gazelles, Persian onagers, wild pigs, Persian leopards, and foxes abound. Domestic animals include sheep, goats, cattle, horses, water buffalo, donkeys, and camels. Thepheasant, partridge, stork, and falcon are native to Iran.

The Persian leopard is said to be the largest of all the subspecies of leopards in the world. The main range of this species in Iran closely overlaps with that of bezoar ibex. Hence, it is found throughout Alborz and Zagros mountain ranges, as well as smaller ranges within the Iranian plateau.

The leopard population is very sparse, due to loss of habitat, loss of natural prey, and population fragmentation. Apart from bezoar ibex, wild sheep, boar, deer, (either Caspian red deer or roe deer), and domestic animals constitute leopards' diet in Iran.

Ecosystem and biosphere

Iran's bio-diversity ranks 13th in the world. There are 272 conservation areas around Iran for a total of 17 million hectares under the supervision of the Department of Environment (Iran), variously named national parks, protected areas, and natural wildlife refuges, all meant to protect the genetic resources of the country. There are only 2,617 rangers and 430 environmental monitoring nits engaged in protecting these vast areas, which amounts to 6,500 hectares to cover for each ranger.

Environmental concerns

Natural hazards: periodic droughts, floods; dust storms, sandstorms; earthquakes along western border and in the northeast.

Environment – current issues: air pollution, especially in urban areas, from vehicle emissions, refinery operations, and industrial effluents; deforestation; desertification; oil pollution in the Persian Gulf; wetland losses from drought; soil degradation (salination); inadequate supplies of potable water in some areas; water pollution from raw sewage and industrial waste; urbanization.

Resources and land use

Natural resources: petroleum, natural gas, coal, chromium, copper, iron ore, lead,manganese, zinc, sulfur

arable land: 10.87%

permanent crops: 1.19%

other: 87.93% (2012 est.)

Irrigated land: 87,000 km^2 (34,000 sq mi) (2009)

Total renewable water resources: 137 km^3 (2011)

Freshwater withdrawal (domestic/industrial/agricultural):

total: 93.3 km^3/yr (7%/1%/92%)

per capita: 1,306 m^3/yr (2004)

Area and boundaries

Area:

total: 1,648,195 km^2 (636,372 sq mi)

land: 1,531,595 km^2 (591,352 sq mi)

water: 116,600 km^2 (45,000 sq mi)

Land boundaries:

total: 5,894 kilometres (3,662 mi)

border countries: Afghanistan 921 kilometres (572 mi), Armenia 44 kilometres (27 mi), Azerbaijan-proper 432 kilometres (268 mi), Azerbaijan-Nakhchivan exclave 179 kilometres (111 mi), Iraq 1,599 kilometres (994 mi), Pakistan 959 kilometres (596 mi), Turkey 534 kilometres (332 mi), Turkmenistan 1,148 kilometres (713 mi).

Maritime boundaries: Qatar, Saudi Arabia, United Arab Emirates, Bahrain, Kuwait, Oman

Coastline: 2,440 kilometres (1,520 mi)

note: Iran also borders the Caspian Sea, for 740 kilometres (460 mi)

Maritime claims:

territorial sea: 12 nmi (22.2 km; 13.8 mi)

contiguous zone: 24 nmi (44.4 km; 27.6 mi)

exclusive economic zone: bilateral agreements, or median lines in the Persian Gulf

continental shelf: natural prolongation

Elevation extremes:

lowest point: Caspian Sea "28 metres ("92 ft)

highest point: Mount Damavand 5,610 metres (18,410 ft)

International territorial disputes

Iran is currently engaged in international territorial disputes with several neighbouring countries.

The country protests Afghanistan's limiting flow of dammed tributaries to the Helmand River in periods of drought. The lack of a maritime boundary in the Persian Gulf with Iraq also prompts jurisdictional disputes beyond the mouth of the Aravnd Rud. Iran and the United Arab Emirates have a territorial dispute over the Greater and Lesser Tunbs and Abu Musa islands, which are administered by Iran. Iran currently insists on dividing the Caspian Sea resources equally among the five littoral states, after the Russian-backed former soviet breakaway republics refused to respect the 50-50 agreements between Iran and the Soviet Union (despite their international obligation). Russia, Azerbaijan, Kazakhstan and Turkmenistan continue to claim territorial waters thus regarding the Caspian Sea as open international body of water, dismissing its geographically lake nature.

GEOGRAPHY

Location

Iran is situated in south-western Asia and borders Armenia, Azerbaijan and Turkmenistan, as well as the Caspian Sea to the north, Turkey and Iraq to the west, the Persian Gulf and the Gulf of Oman to the south and Pakistan and Afghanistan to the east.

Landscape

A series of massive, heavily eroded mountain ranges surround Iran's high interior basin. Most of the country is above 1,500 feet, one-sixth of it over 6,500 high. In sharp contrast are the coastal regions outside the mountain ring. In the north, the 400-mile strip along the Caspian Sea, never more than 70 miles wide and frequently narrowing to 10, falls sharply from the 10,000-foot summit to 90 feet below sea level. In the south, the land drops away from a 2,000 foot plateau, backed by a rugged escarpment three times as high, to meet the Persian Gulf and the Gulf of Oman.

Mountains

The Zagros range stretches from the border with Armenia in the north-west to the Persian Gulf, and then eastward into Baluchistan. As it moves southward, it broadens into a 125-mile-wide band of parallel, alternating mountains lying between the plains of Mesopotamia and the great central plateau of Iran. It is drained on the west by streams that cut deep, narrow gorges and water fertile valleys. The land is extremely hard, difficult to access, and populated largely by pastoral nomads.

The Alborz mountain range, narrower than the Zagros but equally forbidding, runs along the Zagros but equally forbidding, runs along the southern shore of the Caspian to meet the border ranges of Khorassan to the east. The highest of its volcanic peaks is 18,600-foot, snow-covered Mt. Damavand. On the border of Afghanistan, the mountains fall away, to be replaced by barren sand dunes.

The arid interior plateau, which extends into Central Asia, is cut by two smaller mountain ranges. Parts of this desert region, known as dasht, are covered by loose stones and sand, gradually merging into fertile soil on the hillsides. Where fresh water can be held, oases have existed from time immemorial, marking the ancient caravan routes. The most remarkable feature of the plateau is a salt waste 200 miles long and half as wide, knows as the kavir (deserts). It remains unexplored, since its treacherous crust has been formed by large, sharp-edged salt masses which cover mud. Cut by deep ravines, it is virtually impenetrable.

Deserts

The vast deserts of Iran stretch across the plateau from the north-west, close to Tehran and Qom, for a distance of about 400 miles to the south-east and beyond the frontier. Approximately one-sixth of the total area of Iran is barren desert.

The two largest desert areas are known as the Kavir-e-Lut and the Dasht-e-Kavir. Third in size of these deserts is the Jazmurian. It is often said that the Kavir-e-Lut and Dasht-e-Kavir are impossible to cross except by the single road which runs from Yazd to Ferdows, but in recent years, heavy trucks and other vehicles have travelled over long stretches of these deserts which contain extensive mineral deposits - chlorides, sulphates and carbonates - and it is only a matter of time before they are exploited.

Lakes & Seas :

The Caspian Sea: The Caspian Sea, which is the largest landlocked body of water in the world (424,240 sq. km.), lies some 85 feet below the sea level. It is comparatively shallow, and for some centuries has been slowly shrinking in size. Its salt content is considerably less than that of the oceans and though it abounds with fish, its shelly coasts do not offer any good natural harbours, and sudden and violent storms make it dangerous for small boats. The important ports on the Caspian coast are: Bandar Anzali, Noshahr, and Bandar Turkman.

The Persian Gulf: the shallow marginal part of the Indian Ocean that lies between the Arabian Peninsula and south-east Iran. The sea has an area of 240,000 square kilometres. Its length is 990 kilometres, and its width varies from a maximum of 338 kilometres to a minimum of 55 kilometres in the Strait of Hormuz. It is bordered on the north, north-east and east by Iran, on the north-west by Iraq and Kuwait, on the west and south-west by Saudi Arabia, Bahrain and Qatar, and on the south and south-east by the United Arab Emirates and partly Oman. The term Persian Gulf is often used to refer not only proper to the Persian Gulf but also to its outlets, the Strait of Hormuz and the Gulf of Oman, which open into the Arabian Sea.

The most important islands of the Persian Gulf on the Iranian side are: Minoo, Kharg, Sheikh Saas, Sheikh Sho'ayb, Hendurabi, Kish, Farur, Sirri, Abu Mussa, the Greater and Lesser Tunb Qeshm, Hengam, Larak, Farsi, Hormuz, Lavan, The notable ports on the Persian Gulf coast are: Abadan, Khorramshahr, Bandar Iman Khomeini, Mahshahr, Deilam, Gonaveh, Rig, Bushehr, Bandar Lengeh, Bandar Abbas.

The Iranian shore is mountainous, and there are often cliffs, elsewhere a narrow coastal plain with beaches, intertidal flats, and small estuaries borders the gulf. The coastal plain widens north of Bushehr on the eastern shore of the gulf and passes into the broad deltaic plain of the Tigris, Euphrates and Karun rivers. It is noticeably asymmetrical in profile, with the deepest water occurring along the Iranian coast and a broad shallow area, which is usually less than 120 feet deep, along the Arabian coast.

There are some ephemeral streams on the Iranian coast south of Bushehr, but virtually no fresh water flows into the gulf on its south-west side. Large quantities of fine dust are, however, blown into the sea by predominant north-west winds from the desert areas of the surrounding lands. The deeper parts of the Persian Gulf adjacent to the Iranian coast and the are around the Tigris-Euphrates Delta are mainly floored with grey-green muds rich in calcium carbonate.

The Persian Gulf has a notoriously bad climate. Temperatures are high, though winters may be quite cool at the north-western extremities. The sparse rainfall occurs mainly as sharp down pours between November and April and is heavier in the north-east. Humidity is high. The little cloud cover is more prevalent in winter than in summer. Thunderstorms and fog are rare, but dust storms and haze occur frequently in summer.

Until the discovery of oil in Iran in 1908, the Persian Gulf area was important mainly for fishing, pearling, the building of dhows, sailcloth making, camel breeding, reed mat making, date cultivating, and the production of other minor products, such as red ochre from the islands in the south. Today these traditional industries have declined, and the economy of the region is dominated by the production of oil.

The Persian Gulf and the surrounding countries produce approximately 31 per cent of the world's total oil production and have 63 per cent of the world's proven reserves. The Persian Gulf area will probably remain and important source of world oil for a long period.

Other Lakes: Along the frontier between Iran and Afghanistan there are several marshy lakes which expand and contract according to the season of the year. The largest of these, the Seestan (Hamun-Sabari), in the north of the Seestan &Y Baluchistan province, is alive with wild fowl.

Real fresh water lakes are exceedingly rare in Iran. There probably are no more than 10 lakes in the whole country, most of them brackish and small in size. The largest are: Lake Urmiya (area: 3,900-6,000 sq. km. depending on season) in Western Azerbaijan, Namak (1,806 sq. km.) in the Central province, Bakhtegan (750 sq. km.) in Fars province, Tasht (442 sq. km.) in fars province, Moharloo (208 sq. km.) in Fars province, Howz Soltan (106.5 sq. km.) in Central province.

Drainage & Soil

The few streams that empty into the desiccated central plateau dissipate themselves in saline marshes. There are several large rivers, the only navigable one of which is Karun. Others are too steep and irregular. The largest rivers are: the Karun (890 km.), Sefidrood (765), Karkheh (755), Mand (685), Qara-Chay (540), Atrak (535), Dez (515),

Hendijan (488), Jovein (440), Jarahi (438), Zayandehrood (405). All streams are seasonal and variable, spring floods do enormous damage, and there is little water flow in summer when many streams disappear. Water is however stored naturally underground, finding its outlet in subterranean water canals (qanat), springs and being tapped by wells.

Dams: Dams have always played an important role in harnessing Iran's precious water reserves. The Amir Kabir dam on the Karaj river is a multi-purpose dam that supplies Tehran with hydroelectric power and much needed water.

With its sailing and water-skiing facilities, the dam is a popular weekend summer resort. Among others, the Manjil dam on the Sefidrood, the Mahabad dam on the Mahabad river (which supplies water for irrigation of 2,000 hectares of land, as well as domestic water and hydroelectric power), the Martyr Abbaspur dam on the Karun, and the Dez dam on the Dez river to the north of Dezful are noteworthy.

Soil Patterns: The abundant subtropical vegetation of the Caspian's coastal region is supported by rich brown forest soils. Mountain soils are shallow layers over bedrock, with a high proportion of unweathered fragments. Natural erosion moves the finer textured soils into the valleys. These alluvial deposits are mostly chalky, and many are used for pottery.

The semi-aired plateaus lying above 3,000 feet are covered by brown or chestnut-coloured soil that supports grassy vegetation. The soil is slightly alkaline and contains three to four per cent of organic material. The saline and alkaline soils in the arid regions are light coloured and infertile. The sand dunes are composed of loose quartz and fragments of other minerals. Except where protect by vegetation, they are in almost constant motion, driven by high winds.

Rural settlement

Plain villages follow an ancient rectangular pattern. High mud walls with towers from the outer face of the houses, which have flat roofs of mud and straw supported by wooden rafters. In the open centre of the village is an occasional mosque, sometimes serving as a school, too.

The cattle that used to be herded there are now usually kept outside. Mountain villages are situated on the rocky slopes above the valley floor, they are surrounded by terraced fields, usually irrigated, of grain and lucerne (alfalfa). The houses are square, mud-brick, windowless buildings with flat or domed roofs. The stable is usually under the house.

Caspian villages are completely different. Here, where there is an abundance of water, the scattered hamlets have two-story wooden houses, frequently built on pilings, with a gallery around the upper floor. Separate out-buildings (barns, hen-houses, silk worm houses) surround an open courtyard.

Urban settlement

Urban settlement has a long precedent in Iran. At present, around 50 per cent of the population lives in the big and medium-size cities. The biggest city of all is the capital, Tehran. Other big cities are Mashhad, Shiraz, Rasht, Isfahan, Tabriz, followed by the medium-size cities like Ahvaz, Sari, Kermanshah, Hamadan, Kerman, Yazd and others. Traditional architecture and town planning have undergone notable changes in the last few decades. The European designs have largely replaced the old ones. Nevertheless, old buildings are still around in the medium-size cities, but fewer can be found in the big ones.

4

Government and Politics

GOVERNMENT OF ISLAMIC REPUBLIC OF IRAN

Government of Islamic Republic of Iran is the name given to the Iranian government after the Islamic revolution. Two months after the victory of Iranian revolution in a referendum more than 98% of Iranian voters approved this name for their government. This government is one of the kinds of Islamic republic and it political structure includes the supreme leader, and theexecutive , legislative and the Judicial system and Assembly of Experts,Expediency Discernment Council and City and Village Councils of Iran are other institutes of this government. The Supreme Leader is the commander-in-chief of Iran.

The Constitution of Islamic Republic of Iran ratified by referendum in 1979 and was amended on 28 July 1989.

CREATION

Islamic Republic of Iran created with the Iranian Revolution. The first major demonstrations to overthrow Mohammad Reza Pahlavi began in January 1978. The new theocratic Constitution was approved in December 1979. In between, the Shah fled Iran in January 1979 after strikes and demonstrations paralyzed the country, and on February 1, 1979 Ayatollah Khomeini returned to Tehran to a greeting by several million Iranians. The final collapse of thePahlavi dynasty occurred shortly after on February 11 when Iran's military declared itself "neutral" after guerrillas and rebel troops overwhelmed troops loyal to the Shah in armed street fighting.

Iranian Islamic Republic referendum

After the victory of Iranian revolution, a referendum was held by Interim Government of Iran on 30 and 31 March (10 and 11 Farvardin 1358) and asked people to vote *Yes or No* to an Islamic Republic. The referendum results was announced that 98.2 percent of the Iranian people voted to Islamic Republic and this result officially proclaimed by Ayatollah Khomeini in the night between April 1 and 2, 1979.

Constitution

On 2-3 December 1979, The constitution of Islamic Republic of Iran was ratified by referendum. In this referendum 99.5 present of Iranian voters approved the constitution. Ten years later, in the summer of 1989, Iranian voters approved the amendments to the constitution of 1979 in a referendum. The constitution has been called a "hybrid" of "theocratic and democratic elements". While articles One and Two vest sovereignty in God, article six "mandates popular elections for the presidency and the Majlis, or parliament." However all democratic procedures and rights are subordinate to the Guardian Counciland the Supreme Leader, whose powers are spelled out in Chapter Eight (Articles 107-112). The Constitution of 1989 has 175 articles.

The principles of government

The government of Islamic Republic of Iran is a theocratic republic. The article two of Constitution explains the principle of government of Islamic Republic of Iran:

Article 2 :The Islamic Republic is a system based on belief in: 1.the One God (as stated in the phrase "There is no god except Allah"), His exclusive sovereignty and the right to legislate, and the necessity of submission to His commands; 2.Divine revelation and its fundamental role in setting forth the laws; 3.the return to God in the Hereafter, and the constructive role of this belief in the course of man's ascent towards God; 4.the justice of God in creation and legislation; 5.continuous leadership (imamah) and perpetual guidance, and its fundamental role in ensuring the uninterrupted process of the revolution of Islam; 6.the exalted dignity and value of man, and his freedom coupled with responsibility before God; in which equity, justice, political, economic, social, and cultural independence, and national solidarity are secured by recourse to: 1.continuous ijtihad of the fuqaha' possessing necessary qualifications, exercised on the basis off the Qur'an and the Sunnah of the Ma'sumun, upon all of whom be peace; 2.sciences and arts and the most advanced results of human experience, together with the effort to advance them further; 3.negation of all forms of oppression, both the infliction of and the submission to it, and of dominance, both its imposition and its acceptance.

THE POLITICAL STRUCTURE

Leadership

The leader of Islamic Republic of Iran called Supreme Leadership Authority officially in Iran. This post was established by the Article 5 of Constitution of the Islamic Republic of Iran in accordance with the concept of the Guardianship of the Islamic Jurist. This post is a life tenure post. Article 109 is about *the Leadership Qualifications* and Article 110 mentions to*Functions and duties of the Supreme Leader*. According to this article he is the commander-in-chief of the Armed Forces. Also according to Article 57 the Legislature, the Executive and the Judiciary system shall operate under the superintendence of Supreme leader. The Islamic Republic has had two Supreme Leaders: Ayatollah Ruhollah Khomeini, who held the position from Iranian revolution in 1979 until his death in 1989, and Ayatollah Ali Khamenei, who has held the position since Khomeini's death.

Legislature

The Legislature of Islamic Republic of Iran has two parts: Islamic Consultative Assembly and Guardian Council. The Article 62-99 are about Legislature of Islamic Republic of Iran.

Consultative Assembly

The Articles 62-90 of Constitution of Islamic Republic of Iran are about Islamic Consultative Assembly.In Article 71 is mentioned that The Islamic Consultative Assembly can establish laws on all matters, within the limits of its competence as laid down in the Constitution. According to Article 62 The Islamic consultative Assembly is constituted by the representatives of the people elected directly and by secret ballot. Article 64 notes There are to be two hundred seventy members of the Islamic Consultative Assembly which, keeping in view the human, political, geographic and other similar factors, may increase by not more than twenty for each ten-year period from the date of the national referendum of the year 1368 of the solar Islamic calendar. The Parliament currently has 290 representatives, changed from the previous 272 seats since the18 February 2000 election. The most recent election took place on 26 February 2016 and the new parliament was opened on 28 May 2016.

Guardian Council

Guardian Council is a part of legislative that acts in many ways as an upper Consultative Assembly.This council reviews the legislation by Consultative Assembly to examine its compatibility with Islam and Constitution.

The articles 91-99 are about Guardian Council. According to article 91 it has 12 members, Half its members are faqihs that are chosen by Supreme Leader and the other six members are jurists who are elected by the Islamic Consultative Assembly from among the Muslim jurists nominated-by the Chief Justice of Iran.

The current Faqihs members of this council are: Ahmad Jannati (council chairman), Mohammad Momen, Mohammad-Reza Modarresi Yazdi, Mehdi Shab Zende Dar Jahromi, Mahmoud Hashemi Shahroudi and Mohammad Yazdi and the jurists are: Mohammad Reza Alizadeh (deputy chairman), Nejatollah Ebrahimian (Spokesman), Mohsen Esmaili, Siamak Rahpeyk,Mohammad Salimi and Sam Savadkouhi.

Executive

President

In Islamic Republic of Iran President is the second person of government and the head of government. The President is the highest popularly elected official in Iran, although the President answers to the Supreme Leader of Iran, who functions as the country's head of state. Chapter 9 (Articles 133-142) of the Constitution of the Islamic Republic of Iran sets forth the qualifications for presidential candidates and procedures for election, as well as the President's powers and responsibilities as "functions of the executive". These include signing treaties and other agreements with foreign countries and international organizations; administering national planning, budget, and state employment affairs; and appointing ministers subject to the approval of Parliament.

According to article 114 the President of Iran is elected for a four-year term by the direct vote of the people and may not serve for more than two consecutive terms or more than 8 years. The current President of Iran is Hassan Rouhani, who assumed office on August 3, 2013, after the 2013 Iranian presidential election. He succeeded Mahmoud Ahmadinejad, who served 8 years in office from 2005 to 2013.

Judicial system

The judiciary of Islamic Republic of Iran is an independent power, the protector of the rights of the individual and society, responsible for the implementation of justice, and entrusted with the following duties:

1. investigating and passing judgement on grievances, violations of rights, and complaints; the resolving of litigation; the settling of disputes; and the taking of all necessary decisions and measures in probate matters as the law may determine;

2. restoring public rights and promoting justice and legitimate freedoms;

3. supervising the proper enforcement of laws;

4. uncovering crimes; prosecuting, punishing, and chastising criminals; and enacting the penalties and provisions of the Islamic penal code;

5. taking suitable measures to prevent the occurrence of crime and to reform criminals. (Article 156 of Constitution)

Other institution

Assembly of Experts

Assembly of Experts or Assembly of Experts of the Leadership is a deliberative body of eighty eight (88) Mujtahids. The members are elected by direct public voting for eight years.

According to article 107, 109 and 111 the duties of this assembly are electing and removing the Supreme Leader of Iran and supervising his activities.

The last voting took place on 26 February 2016. The new assembly was opened on 24 May 2016 and selected Ahmad Jannati as chairman of the Fifth Assembly.

Expediency Discernment Council

The Expediency Discernment Councilis an administrative assembly appointed by the Supreme Leader and was created upon the revision to the Constitution of the Islamic Republic of Iran on 6 February 1988. According to article 112 of Constitution It was originally set up to resolve differences or conflicts between the Consultative Assembly and theGuardian Council, but "its true power lies more in its advisory role to the Supreme Leader."

Members of the council are chosen by the Supreme Leader every five years. Akbar Hashemi Rafsanjani is the chairman of this Council.

Councils of Iran

According to article 7 the city and village Councils are one of the decision-making and administrative organs of the country. The chapter seven (article 100-106) of Iran's constitution is about these local Councils. According to article 100: In order to expedite social, economic, development, public health, cultural, and educational programmes and facilitate other affairs relating to public welfare with the cooperation of the people according to local needs, the administration of each village, division, city, municipality, and province will be supervised by a council to be named the Village, Division, City, Municipality, or Provincial Council. Members of each of these councils will be elected by the people of the locality in question. Qualifications for the eligibility of electors and candidates for these councils, as well as their functions and powers, the mode of election, the jurisdiction of these councils, the hierarchy of their authority, will be determined by law, in such a way as to preserve national unity, territorial integrity, the system of the Islamic Republic, and the sovereignty of the central government.

Islamic Republic of Iran Broadcasting

The Islamic Republic of Iran Broadcasting (IRIB) according to Constitution is the only radio and television services in Iran.According to article 175 of Constitution the appointment and dismissal of the head of Islamic Republic of Iran Broadcasting rests with the Leader. A council consisting of two representatives each of the President, the head of the judiciary branch and the Islamic Consultative Assembly shall supervise the functioning of this organization.

ARMED FORCES

General Staff of Armed Forces of the Islamic Republic of Iran

General staff of Armed forces of the Islamic Republic of Iran is the highest military body in Iran, with an aim to implement policy, monitor and coordinate activities within Armed Forces of the Islamic

Republic of Iran. Major general Mohammad Hossein Bagheri is the current chief of this staff.

Islamic Republic of Iran Army

Islamic Republic of Iran Army is the "conventional military of Iran" and part of Armed Forces of the Islamic Republic of Iran. The army is tasked to protect the territorial integrity of Iranian state from external and internal threats and to project power. According to article 143 of Constitution the Army of the Islamic Republic of Iran is responsible for guarding the independence and territorial integrity of the country, as well as the order of the Islamic Republic. Artesh has its own Joint Staff which coordinates its four separate service branches: Ground Forces, Air Force, Navy and Air Defense Base.The current chief of Army is MG Ataollah Salehi.

Army of the Guardians of the Islamic Revolution

The Army of the Guardians of the Islamic Revolution (Sepah) is a branch of Iran's Armed Forces, established after the Islamic revolution on 5 May 1979. Article 150 says about Sepah that The Islamic Revolution Guards Corps, organized in the early days of the triumph of the Revolution, is to be maintained so that it may continue in its role of guarding the Revolution and its achievements. MG Mohammad Ali Jafari is the current commander of the Army of the Guardians of the Islamic Revolution.

Law Enforcement Force of Islamic Republic of Iran

Law Enforcement Force of Islamic Republic of Iran is the uniformed police force in Iran. It established in 1992 by merging theShahrbani , Gendarmerie and Committee of Iran into a single force, it has more than 60,000 police personnel served under the Ministry of Interior, including border patrol personnel. Brigadier General Hossein Ashtari is the current commander of this force.

Islamic political culture

It is said that there are attempts to incorporate modern political and social concepts into Islamic canon since 1950. The attempt was a reaction to the secular political discourse namely Marxism, liberalism and nationalism. However we could observe the great influence of western culture in Iran after coup d'etat in 1953. Following the death of Ayatollah Boroujerdi, some of the scholars like Murtaza Mutahhari, Muhammad Beheshti and Muhmud Talighani found new opportunity to change the condition. Before them, Boroujerdi considered as conservative Marja. They try to reforms the conditions after the death of ayatollah. They presented their arguments by rendering lectures in 1960 and 1963 in Tehran. The result of the lectures was the book of An inquiry into principles of Mar'jaiyat. Some of the major issues are to the government in Islam, the need for the clergy's independent financial organization, Islam as a way of life, advising and guiding youth and necessity of being community. Allameh Tabatabei refers to velayat as a political philosophy for Shia and velayat faqih for Shia community. There are also other attempts to formulate new attitude of Islam such as the publication of three volumes of Maktab Tashayyo. Also somebodies believe that it is indispensable to revive the religious gathered in Hoseyniyeh-e-Ershad.

POLITICS OF IRAN

The politics of Iran take place in a framework of a theocracy in a format ofsyncretic politics that is guided by a repressive, non-secular Islamic ideology. The December 1979 constitution, and its 1989 amendment, define the political, economic, and social order of the Islamic Republic of Iran, declaring that Shia Islam of the Twelver school of thought is Iran's official religion.

Iran has an elected president, parliament (or Majlis), "Assembly of Experts" (which elects the Supreme Leader), and local councils. According to the constitution all candidates running for these positions must be vetted by the Guardian Council before being elected.

In addition, there are representatives elected from appointed organizations (usually under the Supreme Leader's control) to "protect the state's Islamic character".

POLITICAL CONDITIONS

The early days of the revolutionary government were characterized by political tumult. In November 1979 the American embassy was seized and its occupants taken hostage and kept captive for 444 days because of support of the American Government to the King of Iran (Shah of Iran). The eight-year Iran–Iraq War killed hundreds of thousands and cost the country billions of dollars. By mid-1982, a succession of power struggles eliminated first the center of political spectrum and then the Republicans leaving the revolutionary leader Ayatollah Khomeini and his supporters in power.

Iran's post-revolution challenges have included the imposition of economic sanctions and suspension of diplomatic relations with Iran by the United States because of the hostage crisis, political support to Iraq and other acts of terrorism that the U.S. government and some others have accused Iran of sponsoring. Emigration has lost Iran millions of entrepreneurs, professionals, technicians, and skilled craftspeople and their capital." For this and other reasons Iran's economy has not prospered. Poverty rose in absolute terms by nearly 45% during the first 6 years since Iraqi invasion on Iran started and per capita income has yet to reach pre-revolutionary levels when Iraqi invasion ended in 1988.

The Islamic Republic Party was Iran's ruling political party and for years its only political party until its dissolution in 1987. After the war, new reformist/progressive parties had started to form. The country had no functioning political parties until theExecutives of Construction Party formed in 1994 to run for the fifth parliamentary elections, mainly out of executive body of the government close to the then-president Akbar Hashemi-Rafsanjani. After the election of Mohammad Khatami in 1997, more parties started to work, mostly of the reformist movement and opposed by hard-liners. This led to incorporation and official activity of many other groups, including hard-liners. After the war ended in 1988, reformist and progressive candidates won four out of six presidential elections in Iran and Right-wing nationalist party of Mahmoud Ahmadinejad won twice.

The Iranian Government is opposed by several Militias, including the Mojahedin-e-Khalq, the People's Fedayeen, and theKurdish Democratic Party.

Supreme Leader

The Supreme Leader of Iran is the head of state and highest ranking political and religious authority in the Islamic Republic of Iran (above the President). The armed forces, judicial system, state television, and other key governmental organizations are under the control of the Supreme Leader. There have been only two Supreme Leaders since the founding of the Islamic Republic, and the current leader (Ali Khamenei), has been in power since 1989. His powers extend to issuing decrees and making final decisions on the economy, environment, foreign policy, education, national planning of population growth, the amount of transparency in elections in Iran, and who is to be fired and reinstated in the Presidential cabinet. This compares against America's Supreme Court, who are also selected not elected, serve for life, and have supreme moral and judicial authority over other parts of the government.

The Supreme Leader is appointed and supervised by the Assembly of Experts. However, all candidates to the Assembly of Experts, the President and the Majlis (Parliament), are selected by the Guardian Council, half of whose members are selected by the Supreme Leader of Iran. Also, all directly-elected members after the vetting process by the Guardian Council still have to be approved by the Supreme Leader. As such, the Assembly has never questioned the Supreme Leader.

Guardian Council

The Guardian Council is an appointed and constitutionally mandated 12-member council with considerable power. It approves or vetoes legislative bills from the Islamic Consultative Assembly (the Iranian Parliament), and approves or forbids candidates seeking office to the Assembly of Experts, the Presidency and the parliament, Six of the twelve members are Islamic faqihs (expert in Islamic Law) selected by the Supreme Leader of Iran, and the other six are jurists nominated by the Head of the Judicial system (who is also appointed by the Supreme Leader),, and approved by the Iranian Parliament.

POLITICAL PARTIES AND ELECTIONS

These are the most recent elections that have taken place.

Political pressure groups and leaders

Active student groups include the pro-reform "Office for Strengthening Unity" and "the Union of Islamic Student Societies';

- Groups that generally support the Islamic Republic include Ansar-e Hizballah, The Iranian Islamic Students Association, Muslim Students Following the Line of the Imam, Islam's Students, and the Islamic Coalition Association. The conservative power base has been said to be made up of a "web of Basiji militia members, families of war martyrs, some members of the Revolutionary Guard, some government employees, some members of the urban and rural poor, and conservative-linked foundations."

- opposition groups include the Freedom Movement of Iran and the Nation of Iran party;

- armed political groups that have been almost completely repressed by the government include Mojahedin-e Khalq Organization (MEK), People's Fedayeen, Democratic Party of Iranian Kurdistan; the Society for the Defense of Freedom.

MILITARY

The military and the Corps of the Guardians (often mistranslated as *guards*) of the Islamic Revolution (or *Sepaah* in Persian meaning *the Corps*) are charged with defending Iran's borders and *Baseej* (Persian for *Mobilization*) militia are charged with maintaining both external and internal security.

Public finance and fiscal policy

Budget

Iran's fiscal year goes from 21 to 20 March of the following year.

Iran has two types of budget:

1. Public or "General" Government Budget
2. Overall or "Total" Government Budget; which includes state-owned companies

Iran's budget is established by the Management and Planning Organization of Iran and then *proposed* by the government to the parliament/Majlis. Once approved by Majlis, the bill still needs to be ratified by the Guardian Council. The bill will be sent back to the parliament for amendments if it is voted down by the Guardian Council. The Expediency Council acts as final arbiter in any dispute.

Following annual approval of the government's budget by Majlis, the central bank presents a detailed monetary and credit policy to the Money and Credit Council (MCC) for approval. Thereafter, major elements of these policies are incorporated into the five-year economic development plan. The 5-year plan is part of "Vision 2025", a strategy for long-term sustainable growth.

A unique feature of Iran's economy is the large size of the religious foundations(called *Bonyads*) whose combined budgets make up more than 30% that of thecentral government.

Setad, another organization worth more than $95 billion, has been described as "secretive" and "little known". It is not overseen by the Iranian Parliament, as that body voted in 2008 to "prohibit itself from monitoring organizations that the supreme leader controls, except with his permission". It is, however, an important factor in the Supreme Leader's power, giving him financial independence from parliament and the national budget.

The National Development Fund of Iran (NDFI) does not depend on Iran's budget.But according to the Santiago Principles, NDFI must coordinate its investment decisions and actions with the macro-economic and monetary policies of the government of Iran.

Revenues

Officials in Iran estimate that Iran's annual oil and gas revenues could reach $250 billion by 2015 once the current projects come on stream.

In 2004, about 45 percent of the government's budget came from exports of oil and natural gas revenues, although this varies with the fluctuations in world petroleum markets and 31 percent came from taxes and fees. Overall, an estimated 50 percent of Iran's GDP was exempt from taxes in FY 2004.

As of 2010, oil income accounts for 80% of Iran's foreign currency revenues and 60% of the nation's overall budget. Any surplus revenues from the sale of crude oil and gas are to be paid into the Oil Stabilization Fund (OSF). The approved *"total budget"*, including state owned commercial companies, was $295 billion for the same period.

The Government seeks to increase the share of tax revenue in the budget through the implementation of the economic reform plan through more effective tax collection from businesses.

As of 2016, the formula set by law is that, for sales of oil at or below the budget's price assumption, 14.5% remains with theNational Iranian Oil Company (NIOC), 20% goes to the National Development Fund (NDF), 2% goes to deprived and oil-producing provinces, and 63.5% goes to the government treasury.

Expenditures

Because of changes in the classification of budgetary figures, comparison of categories among different years is not possible. However, since the Revolution the government's general budget payments have averaged:

- 59 percent for social affairs,
- 17 percent for economic affairs,
- 15 percent for national defense, and

- 13 percent for general affairs.

For a breakdown of expenditures for social and economic purposes, see attached chart.

In FY 2004, central government expenditures were divided as follows:

- current expenditures, 59 percent, and
- capital expenditures, 32 percent.
- Other items (earmarked expenditures, foreign-exchange losses, coverage of liabilities of letters of credit, and net lending) accounted for the remainder.

Among current expenditures, wages and salaries accounted for 36 percent; subsidies and transfers to households accounted for 22 percent (not including *indirect* subsidies). Earmarked expenditures totaled 13 percent of the central government total. Between FY 2000 and FY 2004, total expenditures and net lending accounted for about 26 percent of GDP. According to the Vice President for Parliamentary Affairs, Iran's subsidy reformswould save 20 percent of the country's budget.

According to the head of the Department of Statistics of Iran, if the rules of budgeting were observed in this structure, the government could save at least 30 to 35 percent on its expenses.

External debts

In 2013 Iran's external debts stood at $7.2 billion compared with $17.3 billion in 2012. Meanwhile, Iran's banks and financial institutions total claims on the public sector (government and governmental institutions) amounted to 929 trillion IRR ($34.8 billion) in 2014, which must be reduced according to the IMF. IMF estimates that public debt could be as high as 40% of GDP once government arrears to the private sector are recognized.

2009–10

In Iran's state budget for the Iranian calendar year 1388 (2009–2010), of the $102 billion earmarked for government spending,

- 53% will be funded through revenues from the sale of crude oil and gas,
- 28% will come from taxes and the remaining
- 19% from other sources such as the privatization program.

Oil revenues are calculated based on the average price of $37.50 per barrel at the US Dollar conversion rate of 9,500 Rials. Iran balances its external accounts around $75 per barrel.

2010–11

The budget for Iranian year 1389 (2010–2011), which starts on 21 March, amounts to $368.4bn, representing an increase of 31 per cent on the previous year and is based on a projected oil price of $60 a barrel compared with just $37.50 last year.

2011–12

The public budget was $165 billion (1,770 trillion rials) in Iranian year 2011-2012. The Iranian Parliament also approved a total budget of $500 billion (5,170 trillion rials) that factors in $54 billion from price hikes and subsidy cuts and aside from the government (or public budget) also includes spending for state-owned companies. The budget is based on an oil price of $80 per barrel. The value of the US dollar is estimated at IRR 10,500 for the same period. the 2011-total budget shows a 45-percent increase compared with that of 2011 which stood at $368 billion.

2012–13

The proposed budget for 2011–2012 amounts to 5.1 quadrillion rials (approximately $416 billion). The funding for running the government has been decreased by 5.6 percent and the government's tax revenues have been envisaged to rise by 20 percent. The defense budget shows an increase of 127 percent. The government also is seeking higher sums for development, research, and health projects. Approved budget of 5,660 trillion Rials $477 billion is based on an oil price of $85 per barrel and the average value of the U.S. dollar for the fiscal year has been projected to be 12,260 rials, allowing the government to gain $53.8 billion from subsidy cut. The approved total state budget figure shows an 11% increase in Rial terms, in comparison to the previous year's budget. Of this amount, $134 billion relates to the government's general budget and the remaining $343 billion relates to state-owned companies and organizations. Of the $134 billion for the government's general budget, $117 billion relates to operating expenditure and $17 billion is for infrastructure developments. The government's general budget for 2012–13 shows a 3.5% decline in comparison to the previous year, while the budget for state-owned companies and organisations has risen by 18.5%. Revenues from crude oil make up 37% of the state's total revenues in the budget. Revenues from taxes have been projected at 458 trillion Rials ($37 billion), which shows a 10% increase year-on-year. In the first half of 2012, Iran announced in Majlis that it has taken in only 25% of its budgeted annual revenue. According to Apicorp, Iran needs oil to average $127 a barrel in 2012 for its fiscal budget to break even.

2013–14

In May 2013, the Iranian parliament approved a 7.27-quadrillion-rial (about $593 billion) national budget bill for 2013–14. The new national budget has forecast a 40% drop in oil revenues compared to the previous year's projected figure. The bill has set the price of oil at $95 per barrel, based on the official exchange rate of 12,260 rials for a U.S. dollar, which has been fixed by the Central Bank of Iran. The budget law also includes income of 500 trillion Rials from the subsidies reform plan. Out of this amount, 410 trillion Rials is allocated for direct cash handouts to those eligible who have registered and for social funds.

2014–15

Iran's earmarked government spending for the year starting in March 2014 at $75 billion, calculated on an open-market exchange rate, with an overall/"total" budget ceiling estimated at about $265 billion. The draft budget estimates oil exports at about 1.1 million barrels per day (bpd). The 2014 budget assumes an average oil price of $100 per barrel, inflation at 21%, GDP growth at 3% and the official USD/IRR exchange rate at 26,000 Iranian rials. The budget bill permits the government to use more than $35 billion in foreign finance. Capital expenditure is set to rise by 9.7%. The administration has set the goal of 519 trillion rials, (about $20.9 billion) government's income from implementation of thesubsidy reform plan in budget bill and will be likely forced to double fuel prices. In February 2014, Parliament approved a *total* budget bill worth 7,930 trillion rials ($319 billion at the official exchange rate). The International Monetary Fund has estimated Iran needs an oil price above $130 a barrel to balance its 2015-state budget; Brent crude was below $80 a barrel in November 2014. The IMF estimated in October 2014 that Iran would run a general government deficit of $8.6 billion in 2015, at the official exchange rate, to be compensated by drawing on the National Development Fund.

2015–16

Iran's 2015 proposed budget is nearly $300 billion. The overall/ "total" budget shows a 4% growth compared with the 2014 budget. The budget assumes that the country exports 1 million barrels per day of crude oil and 0.3 million barrels per day of gas condensates at an average price of $72 per barrel of crude. The official exchange rate is projected to be on average 28,500 USD/IRR. Dependency on oil exports in this overall budget bill has dropped to 25% (down from over 30% of government revenues in 2014.) The plan is to increase taxation on large organizations by reducing tax evasion/exemption. The Iranian state is the biggest player in the economy, and the annual budget strongly influences the outlook of local industries and the stock market. The 2015 budget is not expected to bring much growth for many of the domestic industries. An average oil price of $50 for the coming year would result in a deficit of $7.5 billion. The government can lower this deficit by increasing the official exchange rate but this will trigger higher inflation. The proposed expenses are $58 billion including $39 billion is salary and pension payments to government employees. Proposed development expenditure amounts to $17 billion. R&D's share in the GNP is at 0.06% (where it should be 2.5% of GDP) and industry-driven R&D is almost non existent.

2016-17

Proposed government budget is 9.52-quadrillion Iranian rials (about 262 billion US dollars). Assumptions made in the budget are $50 billion in foreign investment and foreign loans, 5-6% GDP growth and 11% inflation. Sixty-five percent of the budget is to be financed through taxation and the remaining 35% from oil sales, based on 2.25 million barrels of oil sales per day, an average oil price of 40 dollars a barrel and US dollar-Iranian rial exchange rate at 29,970.

According to the sixth five-year development plan (2016-2021), the subsidy reform plan is to continue until 2021. An amendment to the budget was passed in August 2016. This amendment allows the government to issue debt based instruments and the use of forex reserves in an attempt to clear its debt to the private sector, including contractors, banks and insurers.

COMPLEXITY OF THE SYSTEM

According to the constitution, the Guardian Council oversees and approves electoral candidates for most national elections in Iran. The

Guardian Council has 12 members, six clerics, appointed by theSupreme Leader and six jurists, elected by the Majlis from among the Muslim jurists nominated by the Head of the Judicial System, who is appointed by the Supreme Leader. According to the current law, the Guardian Council approves the Assembly of Experts candidates, who in turn supervise and elect the Supreme Leader.

The reformists say this system creates a closed circle of power.Iranian reformists, such as Mohammad-Ali Abtahi have considered this to be the core legal obstacle for the reform movement in Iran.

CABINET OF IRAN

The Cabinet of Iran is a formal body composed of government officials, ministers, chosen and led by a President. Its composition must be approved by a vote in the Parliament. According to the Constitution of the Islamic Republic of Iran, the President may dismiss members of the cabinet, but must do so in writing, and new appointees must again be approved by the Parliament. The cabinet meets weekly on Saturdays in Tehran. There may be additional meetings if circumstances require it. The president chairs the meetings.

History

From 1699 until 1907 the Iranian cabinet was led by Premiers who were appointed by the Shah of Iran.

The Persian Constitutional Revolution of 1905 led to the creation of the Persian Constitution of 1906 and the establishment of the Iranian parliament, whose members were elected from the general population. The position of premier was abolished and replaced by the Prime Minister of Iran. The constitution stipulated that all Prime Minister must be subject to a vote in parliament for both approval and removal.

During the period 1907 to 1951 all Prime Ministers were selected by the Shah and subject to a vote-of-confidence by the Iranian Parliament. From 1951 to 1953, the members of parliament elected the Prime Minister among themselves (the head of the party holding the majority of seats), through a vote-of-confidence. The Shah, as the head of state, then appointed the parliament's selection to the position of Prime Minister, in accordance with the Westminster system of parliamentary democracy. Following the removal of Prime Minister Mohammad Mosaddegh via the 1953 Iranian coup d'état, this practice was abolished and the selection of Prime Minister reverted to the process in effect before 1951.

Following the Iranian Revolution of 1979, the position of Shah was removed as the head of state, effectively ending Iran's history of monarchy. Iran's new Islamic constitution stipulated that the President of Iran would nominate the Iranian cabinet, including the Prime Minister, which was to be approved by a vote-of-confidence in the Iranian parliament. The constitutional amendment of 1989 effectively ended the position of Prime Minister and transferred its powers to that of the president andvice president.

2009 appointments

President Ahmadinejad announced controversial ministerial appointments for his second term. Esfandiar Rahim Mashaeiwas briefly appointed as first vice president, but opposed by a number of Majlis members and by the intelligence minister,Gholam-Hossein Mohseni-Eje'i. Mashaei followed orders to resign. Ahmadinejad then appointed Mashaei as chief of staff, and fired Mohseni-Eje'i.

On 26 July 2009, Ahmadinejad's government faced a legal problem after he sacked four ministers. Iran's constitution (Article 136) stipulates that, if more than half of its members are replaced, the cabinet may not meet or act before the Majlis approves the revised membership. The Vice Chairman of the Majlis announced that no cabinet meetings or decisions would be legal, pending such a reapproval.

The main list of 21 cabinet appointments was announced on 19 August 2009. On 4 September, Parliament of Iran approved 18 of the 21 candidates and rejected three of them, including two women. Sousan Keshavarz, Mohammad Aliabadi, and Fatemeh Ajorlou were not approved by Parliament for the Ministries of Education, Energy, and Welfare and Social Security respectively. Marzieh Vahid Dastjerdi is the first woman approved by Parliament as a minister in the Islamic Republic of Iran.

2011 merges and dismissals

On 9 May, Ahmedinejad announced Ministries of Petroleum and Energy would merge, as would Industries and Mines with Commerce, and Welfare with Labour. On 13 May, he dismissed Masoud Mir Kazemi (Minister of Petroleum), Aliakbar Mehrabian (Minister Industry and Mines) and Sadeq Mahsouli (Minister of Welfare). On 15 May, he was announced he would be caretaker minister of the Petroleum

Ministry. From August 2009 to February 2013, a total of nine ministers in the cabinet was dismissed by the Majlis, the last of who was labor minister, Reza Sheykholeslam at the beginning of February 2013.

Rouhani's cabinet

Hassan Rouhani was elected as President of Iran in 2013 presidential election and took office on 3 August 2013. He nominated his coalition cabinet members to the parliament for vote of confidence on the next day. 15 out of 18 designated ministers was confirmed by the parliament.

5

Foreign Relations and Policy

FOREIGN RELATIONS OF IRAN

Foreign relations of Iran refers to inter-governmental relationships betweenthe Islamic Republic of Iran and other countries. Geography is a very significant factor in informing Iran's foreign policy. Following the 1979 Iranian Revolution, the newly born Islamic Republic, under the leadership of Ayatollah Khomeini, dramatically reversed the pro-American foreign policy of the lastShah of Iran Mohammad Reza Pahlavi. Since then the country's policies have oscillated between the two opposing tendencies of revolutionary ardour, which would eliminate Western and non-Muslim influences while promoting the Islamic revolution abroad, and pragmatism, which would advance economic development and normalization of relations. Iran's bilateral dealings are accordingly sometimes confused and contradictory.

Iran currently maintains full diplomatic relations with 97 countries worldwide.

History

Iranians have traditionally been highly sensitive to foreign interference in their country, pointing to such events as theRussian conquest of northern parts of the country in the course of the 19th century, the tobacco concession, the British and Russian occupations of the First and Second World Wars, and the CIA plot to overthrow Prime Minister Mohammed Mosaddeq. This suspicion manifests itself in attitudes that many foreigners might find incomprehensible, such as the "fairly common" belief that the Iranian Revolution was actually the work of a conspiracy between Iran's Shi'a clergy and the British government. This may have been a result of the anti-Shah bias in BBC Radio's influential Persian broadcasts into Iran: a BBC report of 23 March 2009 explains that many in Iran saw the broadcaster and the government as one, and interpreted the bias for Khomeini as evidence of weakening British government support for the Shah. It is entirely plausible that the BBC did indeed help hasten revolutionary events.

REVOLUTIONARY PERIOD UNDER KHAMENEI

Under the Khamenei government Iran's foreign policy often emphasized the elimination of foreign influence and the spread of Islamic revolution over state-to-state relations or the furtherance of trade. In Khamenei's own words,

We shall export our revolution to the whole world. Until the cry"There is no God but God" resounds over the whole world, there will be struggle.

The Islamic Republic's effort to spread the revolution is considered to have begun in earnest in March 1982, when 380 men from more than 25 Arab and Islamic nations met at the former Tehran Hilton Hotel for a "seminar" on the "ideal Islamic government" and, less academically, the launch of a large-scale offensive to cleanse the Islamic world of the satanic Western and Communist influences that were seen to be hindering the Islamic world's progress. The gathering of militants, primarily Shi'a but including some Sunnis, "with various religious and revolutionary credentials," was hosted by the Association of Militant Clerics and the Pasdaran Islamic Revolutionary Guards. The nerve centre of the revolutionary crusade, operational since shortly after the 1979 revolution, was located in downtown Tehran and known to outsiders as the "Taleghani Centre". Here the groundwork for the gathering was prepared: the establishment of Arab cadres, recruited or imported from surrounding countries to spread the revolution, and provision of headquarters for such groups as the Islamic Front for the Liberation of Bahrain, the Iraqi Shi'a movement, and Philippine Moro, Kuwaiti, Saudi, North African and Lebanese militant clerics.

These groups came under the umbrella of the "Council for the Islamic Revolution", which was supervised by AyatollahHussein Ali Montazeri, the designated heir of Ayatollah Khomeini. Most of the council's members were clerics, but they also reportedly included advisors from the Syrian and Libyan intelligence agencies. The council apparently received more than $1 billion annually in contributions from the faithful in other countries and in funds allocated by the Iranian government.

Its strategy was two-pronged: armed struggle against what were perceived as Western imperialism and its agents; and an internal purifying process to free Islamic territory and Muslim minds of non-Islamic cultural, intellectual and spiritual influences, by providing justice, services, resources to the *mustazafin* (weak) masses of the Muslim world. These attempts to spread its Islamic revolution strained the country's relations with many of its Arab neighbours, and the extrajudicial execution of Iranian dissidents in Europe unnerved European nations, particularly France and Germany. For example, the Islamic Republic expressed its opinion of Egypt's secular government by naming a street in Tehran after Egyptian President Anwar Sadat's killer, Khalid al-Istanbuli. At this time Iran found itself very isolated, but this was a secondary consideration to the spread of revolutionary ideals across the Persian Gulf and confrontation with the US (or "Great Satan") in the 1979-1981hostage crisis.

Training volunteers

Arab and other Muslim volunteers who came to Iran were trained in camps run by the Revolutionary Guards. There were three primary bases in Tehran, and others in Ahvaz, Isfahan, Qom, Shiraz, and Mashad, and a further facility, converted in 1984, near the southern naval base at Bushire.

In 1981 Iran supported an attempt to overthrow the Bahraini government, in 1983 expressed political support for Shi'ites who bombed Western embassies in Kuwait, and in 1987 Iranian pilgrims rioted at poor living conditions and treatment during theHajj (pilgrimage) in Mecca, Saudi Arabia, and were consequently massacred. Nations with strong fundamentalist movements, such as Egypt and Algeria, also began to mistrust Iran. With the Israeli invasion of Lebanon, Iran was thought to be supporting the creation of the Hizballah organization. Furthermore, Iran went on to oppose the Arab–Israeli peace process, because it saw Israel as an illegal country.

Iran–Iraq War

Relations with Iraq had never been good historically; however, they took a turn for the worse in 1980, when Iraq invaded Iran. The stated reason for Iraq's invasion was the contested sovereignty over the Shatt al-Arab waterway (*Arvand Rud* in Persian). Other reasons, unstated, were probably more significant: Iran and Iraq had a history of interference in each other's affairs by supporting separatist movements, and although this interference had ceased since the Algiers Agreement (1975), after the Revolution Iran resumed support for Kurdish guerrillas in Iraq.

Iran demanded the withdrawal of Iraqi troops from Iranian territory and the return to the *status quo ante* for the Shatt al-Arab, as established under the Algiers Agreement. This period saw Iran become even more isolated, with virtually no allies. Exhausted by the war, Iran signed UN Security Council Resolution 598 in July 1988, after the United States and Germany began supplying Iraq with chemical weapons.

The ceasefire resulting from the UN resolution was implemented on 20 August 1988. Neither nation had made any real gains in the war, which left one million dead and had a dramatic effect on the country's foreign policy. From this point on, the Islamic Republic recognized that it had no choice but to moderate its radical approach and rationalize its objectives. This was the beginning of what Anoushiravan Ehteshami calls the "reorientation phase" of Iranian foreign policy.

Pragmatism

Like other revolutionary states, practical considerations have sometimes led the Islamic Republic to inconsistency and subordination of such ideological concerns as pan-Islamic solidarity. One observer, Graham Fuller, has called the Islamic Republic "stunningly silent"

about [Muslim] Chechens in [non-Muslim] Russia, or Uyghurs in China, simply because the Iranian state has important strategic ties with both China and Russia that need to be preserved in the state interest. Iran has astonishingly even supported Christian Armenia against Shi'ite Azerbaijan and has been careful not to lend too much support to Islamic Tajiks in Tajikistan, where the language is basically a dialect of Persian.

In this regard the Islamic Republic resembles another revolutionary state, the old Soviet Union. The USSR was ideologically committed not to Islam but to world proletarian revolution, led by Communist parties under its leadership, but "frequently abandoned support to foreign communist parties when it served Soviet national interests to cooperate with the governments that were oppressing them."

Post-War period (1988–present)

Since the end of the Iran–Iraq War, Iran's new foreign policy has had a dramatic effect on its global standing. Relations with the European Union have dramatically improved, to the point where Iran is a major oil exporter and a trading partner with such countries as Italy, France, and Germany. China and India have also emerged as friends of Iran; these three countries face similar challenges in the global economy as they industrialize, and consequently find themselves aligned on a number of issues.

Iran maintains regular diplomatic and commercial relations with Russia and theformer Soviet Republics. Both Iran and Russia believe they have important national interests at stake in developments in Central Asia and the Transcaucasus, particularly concerning energy resources from the Caspian Sea.

Significant historical treaties

- Treaty of Zuhab by which Iran irrevocably lost Mesopotamia (Iraq) to the Ottomans. Roughly settled the modern-day Iran-Iraq-Turkey borders
- Treaty of Gulistan 1813, by which Iran irrevocably lost Georgia, Dagestan, and most of Azerbaijan.
- Treaty of Turkmenchay 1828, by which Iran irrevocably lost Armenia and the remainder of the contemporary Republic of Azerbaijan (comprising the Lankaran and Nakchivan khanates.
- Treaty of Akhal
- Treaty of Paris (1857) (by which Iran renounced claims over Herat and parts of Afghanistan)
- Anglo-Russian Convention of 1907

CURRENT POLICIES

The Islamic Republic of Iran accords priority to its relations with the other states in the region and with the rest of the Islamic world. This includes a strong commitment to the Organisation of Islamic Cooperation (OIC) and the Non-Aligned Movement. Relations with the states of the Arab Gulf Cooperation Council (GCC), especially with Saudi Arabia, have improved in recent years. However, an unresolved territorial dispute with the United Arab Emirates concerning three islands in the Persian Gulf continues to mar its relations with these states. Iran has close relations with Kuwait.

Iran is seeking new allies around the world due to its increasing political and economic isolation in the international community. This isolation is evident in the various economic sanctions and the EU oil embargo that have been implemented in response to questions that have been raised over the Iranian nuclear program (*Iran's Nuclear Program*).

Tehran supports the Interim Governing Council in Iraq, but it strongly advocates a prompt and full transfer of state authority to the Iraqi people. Iran hopes for stabilization in Afghanistan and supports the reconstruction effort so that the Afghan refugees in Iran (which number approximately 2.5 million.) can return to their homeland and the flow of drugs from Afghanistan can be stemmed. Iran is also pursuing a policy of stabilization and cooperation with the countries of theCaucasus and Central Asia, whereby it is seeking to capitalise on its central location to establish itself as the political and economic hub of the region.

On the international scene, it has been argued by some that Iran has become, or will become in the near future, a superpower due to its ability to influence international events. Others, such as Robert Baer, have argued that Iran is already an energy superpower and is on its way to becoming an empire.

Flynt Leverett calls Iran a rising power that might well become a nuclear power in coming years — if the US does not prevent Iran from acquiring nuclear technology, as part of a grand bargain under which Iran would cease its nuclear activities in exchange for a guarantee of its borders by the US.

Current territorial disputes

- Iran and Iraq restored diplomatic relations in 1990, but they are still trying to work out written agreements settling outstanding disputes from their eight-year war concerning border demarcation, prisoners of war, and freedom of navigation in and sovereignty over the Shatt al-Arab waterway.

- Iran governs and possesses two islands in the Persian Gulf claimed by theUAE: Lesser Tunb (which the UAE calls *Tunb as Sughra* in Arabic, and Iran calls *Jazireh-ye Tonb-e Kuchek* in Persian) and Greater Tunb (Arabic *Tunb al Kubra*, Persian *Jazireh-*

ye Tonb-e Bozorg).

- Iran jointly administers with the UAE an island in the Persian Gulf claimed by the UAE (Arabic *Abu Musa*, Persian, *Jazireh-ye Abu Musa*), over which Iran has taken steps to exert unilateral control since 1992, including access restrictions.

- The Caspian Sea borders between Azerbaijan, Iran, and Turkmenistan are not yet determined, although this problem is set to be resolved peacefully in the coming years through slow negotiations. After the breakup of the USSR, the newly independent republics bordering the Caspian Sea claimed shares of territorial waters and the seabed, thus unilaterally abrogating the existing half-and-half USSR-Iran agreements which, like all other Soviet treaties, the republics had agreed to respect upon their independence. It has been suggested by these countries that the Caspian Sea should be divided in proportion to each bordering country's shoreline, in which case Iran's share would be reduced to about 13%. The Iranian side has expressed eagerness to know if this means that all Irano–Russian and –Soviet agreements are void, entitling Iran to claim territorial sovereignty over lands lost to Russia by treaties that the parties still consider *vivant*. Issues between Russia, Kazakhstan, and Azerbaijan were settled in 2003, but Iran does not recognize these agreements, on the premise that the international law governing open water can not be applied to the Caspian Sea, which is in fact a lake (a landlocked body of water). Iran has not pressed its Caspian territorial claims in recent years because it relies heavily on Russia's support in its nuclear-development battle with the West.

INDIA–IRAN RELATIONS

India–Iran relations refers to the bilateral relations between the countries India and Iran. Independent India and Iran established diplomatic relations on 15 March 1950. During much of the Cold War period, relations between the Republic of India and the erstwhile Imperial State of Iran suffered due to different political interests—non-aligned India fostered strong military links with the Soviet Union while Iran enjoyed close ties with the United States.Following the 1979 revolution, relations between Iran and India strengthened momentarily. However, Iran's continued support for Pakistan and India's close relations with Iraq during the Iran–Iraq War impeded further development of Indo–Iranian ties. In the 1990s, India and Iran supported the Northern Alliance in Afghanistan against the Taliban regime. They continue to collaborate in supporting the broad-based anti-Taliban government led byAshraf Ghani and backed by the United States. The two countries signed a defence cooperation agreement in December 2002.

Even though the two countries share some common strategic interests, India and Iran differ significantly on key foreign policy issues. India has expressed strong opposition against Iran's nuclear programme and whilst both the nations continue to oppose the Taliban, India supports the presence of NATO forces in Afghanistan unlike Iran. Iran is the second largest supplier of crude oil to India, supplying more than 425,000 barrels of oil per day, and consequently India is one of the largest foreign investors in Iran's oil and gas industry.

In 2011, the US$12 billion annual oil trade between India and Iran was halted due to extensive economic sanctions against Iran, forcing the Indian oil ministry to pay off the debt through a banking system through Turkey.

According to a BBC World Service Poll conducted at the end of 2005, 71% of Iranians viewed India's influence positively, with 21% viewing it negatively, the most favourable rating of India for any country in the world. Also, due to Iran being on good terms with both India and Pakistan, Iran has offered to serve as a mediator between the two.

CURRENT RELATIONS

India and Iran have friendly relations in many areas, despite India not welcoming the 1979 Revolution. There are significant trade ties, particularly in crude oil imports into India and diesel exports to Iran. Iran frequently objected to Pakistan's attempts to draft anti-India resolutions at international organisations such as the OIC and theHuman Rights Commission. India welcomed Iran's inclusion as an observer state in the SAARC regional organisation.

A growing number of Iranian students are enrolled at universities in India, most notably in Pune and Bengaluru. The clerical government in Tehran sees itself as a leader of Shiites worldwide including India. Indian Shiites enjoy state support such as a recognised national holiday for Muharram. Lucknow continues to be a major centre of Shiite culture and Persian study in the subcontinent.

In the 1990s, India and Iran supported the Northern Alliance in Afghanistan against the Taliban regime. They continue to collaborate in supporting the broad-based anti-Taliban government led by Ashraf Ghani and backed by the United States. The two countries signed a defence cooperation agreement in December 2002.

In August 2013, while carrying oil in the Persian Gulf, Iran detained India's largest ocean liner Shipping Corporation (SCI)'s vessel MT Desh Shanti carrying crude oil from Iraq . Iran was resolute, and insited the detention of the tanker was "a technical and non-political issue".

On 22 May 2016, Prime minister Narendra Modi paid an official visit to Iran. The visit focused on bilateral connectivity and infrastructure, an energy partnership, and trade.

Just before Prime Minister Narendra Modi's visit to Israel in July 2017, Iran's Supreme Leader Ayatollah Khamenei, urged Muslims in Kashmir to 'repudiate oppressors'.

Economic relations

Iran's trade with India exceeded US$13 billion in 2007, an 80% increase in trade volume within a year. Via third party countries such as UAE this figure reaches $30 billion.

Oil and Gas

In 2008–09, Iranian oil accounted for nearly 16.5% of India's crude oil imports. Indian oil imports from Iran increased by 9.5% in 2008–09 due to which Iran emerged as India's second largest oil supplier. About 40% of the refined oil consumed by India is imported from Iran. In June 2009, Indian oil companies announced their plan to invest US$5 billion in developing an Iranian gas field in the Persian Gulf. In September 2009, the Mehr news agency reported a Pakistani diplomat as saying "India definitely quitted the IPI (India-Pakistan-Iran) gas pipeline deal", in favour of Indo-US civilian nuclear agreement for energy security. Iranian officials however said India is yet to make an official declaration. In 2010, US officials warned New Delhi that Indian companies using the Asian Clearing Union for financial transactions with Iran run the risk of violating a recent US law that bans international firms from doing business with Iranian banks and Tehran's oil and gas sector, and that Indian companies dealing with Iran in this manner may be barred from the US. The United States criticises the ACU of being insufficiently transparent in its financial dealings with Iran and suspects that much of their assets are funnelled to blacklisted repressive organisations in Iran such as the Army of the Guardians of the Islamic Revolution.The United States Department of the Treasury also believes that Iran uses the ACU to bypass the US banking system. On 27 November 2010, the Indian government, through the Reserve Bank of India, instructed the country's lenders to stop processing current-account transactions with Iran using the Asian Clearing Union, and that further deals should be settled without ACU involvement. RBI also declared that they will not facilitate payments for Iranian crude imports as global pressure on Tehran grows over its nuclear programme. This move by the Indian government will make clear to Indian companies that working through the ACU "doesn't necessarily mean an Iranian counterpart has an international seal of approval". As of December 2010, neither Iran nor the ACU have responded to this development. India objected to further American sanctions on Iran in 2010. An Indian foreign policy strategist, Rajiv Sikri, dismissed the idea that a nuclear armed Iran was a threat to India, and said that India would continue to invest in Iran and do business. Despite increased pressure by the US and Europe, and a significant reduction in oil imports from Persian oil fields in 2012, leading political figures in India have clearly stated that they are not willing to stop trade relations altogether. To the contrary, they aim at expanding the commodity trade with the Islamic republic.

Renewed increase in oil imports

While overall, India's total volume of imported crude has only been rising slightly from 3.2 million b/d in 2009-10 to 3.44 million b/d in 2012-13, imports from Iran have basically been fluctuating around 250,000 b/d from 2012 to 2013 and thus rising proportionally due to a halt for Iranian exports to Europe. The recent detainment of an Indian tanker by Iranian officials is unrelated to the oil embargo, but in an effort to save over USD 8.5 billion in hard currency, and realising a 180-day waiver from US sanctions, India plans to increase Iranian imports by 11 million tons for 2014, in addition to the two million tons of crude oil shipped from Iran by June 2013, up 21.1% from last year.

Iran's Nuclear Interests

India, despite close relations and convergence of interests with Iran, voted against Iran in the International Atomic Energy Agency in 2005, which took Iran by surprise. A "welcoming prospect" Ali Larijani was reported as saying: "India was our friend". Stephen Rademaker also acknowledged that India's votes against Iran at the International Atomic Energy Agency were "coerced":

"The best illustration of this is the two votes India cast against Iran at the IAEA. I am the first person to admit that the votes were coerced."

The USA considers support from India – which is on 35-member board of Governors at the International Atomic Energy Agency – crucial in getting a sizeable majority for its proposal to refer the matter to the Security Council for positive punitive action against Iran. Greg Schulte, US ambassador to the IAEA, said *"India's voice will carry particular weight...I hope India joins us in making clear our collective concerns about Iran's nuclear programme"*. Schulte did not deny that the Indo-US nuclear deal was conditional to India supporting the US on the Iran issue. Appraising of the situation vis-a-vis Iran, a senior US official told the New York Times that *The Indians are emerging from their non-aligned status and becoming a global power, and they have to begin to think about their responsibilities. They have to make a basic choice..* The Bush administration, however, recognised India's close relations with Iran and tempered its position, stating that India can "go ahead with a pipeline deal involving Iran and Pakistan. Our beef with Iran is not the pipeline."

Infrastructure

A highway between Zaranj and Delaram (Zaranj-Delaram Highway) is being built with financial support from India. TheChabahar port has also been jointly financed by Iran and India. India is helping develop the Chabahar Port, which will give it access to the oil and gas resources in Iran and the Central Asian states. By so doing, India hopes to compete with the Chinese, who are building Gwadar Port, in Pakistani Baluchistan. Iran plans to use Chabahar for transshipment to Afghanistan and Central Asia, while keeping the port of Bandar Abbas as a major hub mainly for trade with Russia and Europe. India, Iran and Afghanistan have signed an agreement to give Indian goods, heading for Central Asia and Afghanistan, preferential treatment and tariff reductions at Chabahar.

Work on the Chabahar-Milak-Zaranj-Delaram route from Iran to

Afghanistan is in progress. Iran is, with Indian aid, upgrading the Chabahar-Milak road and constructing a bridge on the route to Zaranj. India's BRO is laying the 213 km Zaranj-Delaram road. It is a part of India's USD 750 million aid package to Afghanistan. The Chabahar port project is Iran's chance to end its US-sponsored economic isolation and benefit from the resurgent Indian economy. Along with Bandar Abbas, Chabahar is the Iranian entrepot on the North-South corridor. A strategic partnership between India, Iran and Russia is intended to establish a multi-modal transport link connecting Mumbai with St Petersburg, providing Europe and the former Soviet republics of Central Asia access to Asia and vice versa.

North-South Transport Corridor

The North–South Transport Corridor is the ship, rail, and road route for moving freight between India, Russia, Iran, Europe and Central Asia. The route primarily involves moving freight from India, Iran, Azerbaijan and Russia via ship, rail and road. The objective of the corridor is to increase trade connectivity between major cities such asMumbai, Moscow, Tehran, Baku, Bandar Abbas, Astrakhan, Bandar Anzali and etc.Dry runs of two routes were conducted in 2014, the first was Mumbai to Baku via Bandar Abbas and the second was Mumbai to Astrakhan via Bandar Abbas, Tehran and Bandar Anzali. The objective of the study was to identify and address keybottlenecks. The results showed transport costs were reduced by "$2,500 per 15 tons of cargo". Other routes under consideration include via Armenia, Kazakhstanand Turkmenistan.

Education

There are about 8,000 Iranian students studying in India. India provides 67 scholarships every year to Iranian students under ITEC, ICCR, Colombo Plan and IOR-ARC schemes. every year around 40,000 Iranians visit India for various purposes. Kendriya Vidyalaya Tehran, the Embassy of India School, serves Indian citizens living in Tehran.

Religion

The world's largest population of Zoroastrians are the Parsi community in India. When the Islamic Arabs invaded Persia, the local population which was unwilling to convert to Islam or accept *dhimmi* status were persecuted to different regions of the world with western India being the most significant. They sought refuge in the western coast of India and subsequent the country has the largest population of Zoroastrians in the world. In the modern era, the Parsi community have contributed significantly to India and Pakistan in the areas of politics, industry, science and culture. Prominent Indian Parsis includeDadabhai Naoroji (three times president of Indian National Congress), Field Marshal Sam Manekshaw, nuclear energy scientist Homi Bhabha, industrialist JRD Tata and the Tata family. The Queen rock star Freddie Mercury was an Indian Parsi born in Zanzibar. Zubin Mehta, a conductor of Western classical music orchestras is also a Parsi originally from Mumbai.

IRAN–PAKISTAN RELATIONS

After Pakistan gained its independence in August 1947, Iran was the first country to recognize its sovereign status. Iran supported Pakistan in itsconflicts with India, while Pakistan in turn supported Iran militarily during theIran–Iraq War in the 1980s. Pakistan's relations with Iran grew strained at times due to sectarian tensions, as Pakistani Shias claimed that they were being discriminated against under the Pakistani government's Islamisationprogramme.

Iran and Saudi Arabia used Pakistan as a battleground for their proxy sectarian war, and by the 1990s Pakistan's support for the Sunni Taliban organisation in Afghanistan became a problem for Shia Iran, which opposed a Taliban-controlled Afghanistan.

Nevertheless, economic and trade relations continued to expand in both absolute and relative terms, leading to the signing of a Free Trade Agreement between the two countries in 1999. Both countries are founding members of the Economic Cooperation Organization (ECO). At present, both countries are cooperating and forming alliances in a number of areas of mutual interest, such as fighting the drug trade along their common border and combating the Balochistan insurgency along their border. Iran has expressed an interest joining the China-Pakistan Economic Corridor.

Polls have consistently shown that a very high proportion of Pakistanis view their western neighbor positively. Ayatollah Khamenei has also called for the sympathy and assistance of many Muslim nations, including Pakistan. However, on the same time, a growing portion of Pakistanis also resent Iran for what had happened since 1979.

Relations during the Cold War

Iran maintained close relations with Pakistan during much of the Cold War. Iran was the first country to recognise Pakistan as an independent state, and the Shah of Iran was the first head of state to come on a state visit to Pakistan (in March 1950).Since 1947, Mohammad Ali Jinnah, the founder of Pakistan, had successfully advocated a policy of fostering cordial relations with Iran in particular and the Muslim world in general. Despite Shia-Sunni divisions, Islamic identity became an important factor in shaping Iranian–Pakistani relations, especially after the Islamic Revolution in Iran.

In May 1950, a treaty of friendship was signed by Prime Minister Liaquat Ali Khan and the Shah of Iran. Some of the clauses of the treaty of friendship had wider geopolitical significance. Pakistan found a natural partner in Iran after the Indian government chose to support Egyptian President Gamal Abdel Nasser, who was seeking to export apan-Arab ideology that threatened many of the more traditional Arab monarchies, a number of which were allied with the Shah. Harsh V. Pant, a foreign policy writer, noted that Iran was a natural ally and model for Pakistan for other reasons as well. Both countries granted each other MFN status for trade purposes; the shah offered Iranian oil and gas to Pakistan on generous terms, and the Iranian and Pakistani armies cooperated to suppress the rebel movement in Baluchistan. During the Shah's era, Iran moved closer to Pakistan in many fields. Pakistan, Iran, and Turkey joined the United States-sponsored Central Treaty Organisation, which extended a defensive alliance along the Soviet Union's southern perimeter. Iran played an important role in the Indo-Pakistani war of 1965, providing Pakistan with nurses, medical supplies, and a gift of 5,000 tons of petroleum. Iran also indicated that it was considering an embargo on oil supplies to India for the duration of the fighting. The Indian government believed that Iran had blatantly favored Pakistan. After the suspension of United States military aid to Pakistan, Iran was reported to have purchased ninety Sabre jet fighter planes from West Germany, and to have sent them on to Pakistan.

Although Pakistan's decision to join the Central Treaty Organisation (CENTO) in 1955 was largely motivated by its security imperatives regarding India, Pakistan did not sign on until Iran was satisfied that the British Government was not going to obstruct the nationalization of British oil companies in Iran. According to Dr. Mujtaba Razvi, Pakistan likely would not have joined CENTO had Iran not decided to do so.

Iran again played a vital role in Pakistan's 1971 conflict with India, this time supplying military equipment as well as diplomatic support against India. The Shah described the Indian attack as aggression and interference in Pakistan's domestic affairs;in an interview with a Parisian newspaper he openly acknowledged that "We are one hundred percent behind Pakistan".Iranian Prime Minister Amir-Abbas Hoveida followed suit, saying that "Pakistan has been subjected to violence and force."The Iranian leadership repeatedly expressed its opposition to the dismemberment of Pakistan, fearing it would adversely affect the domestic stability and security of Iran by encouraging Kurdish separatists to rise up against the Iranian government. In the same vein, Iran attempted to justify its supplying arms to Pakistan on the grounds that, in its desperation, Pakistan might fall into the Chinese lap. On the other hand, Iran changed its foreign priorities after making a move to maintain good relations with India.

The breakup of Pakistan in December 1971 convinced Iran that extraordinary effort was needed to protect the stability and territorial integrity of its eastern flank. With the emergence of Bangladesh as a separate State, the *"Two-nations theory"* received a severe blow and questions arose in the Iranian establishment as to whether the residual western part of Pakistan could hold together and remain a single country. Events of this period caused significant perceptional changes in Tehran regarding Pakistan.

When widespread armed insurgency broke out in Pakistan's Balochistan Province in 1973, Iran, fearing the insurgency might spill over into its own Balochistan Province, offered large-scale support. The Iranians provided Pakistan with military hardware (including thirty Huey cobra attack helicopters), intelligence sharing, and $200 million in aid. The government of Prime Minister Zulfikar Ali Bhutto declared its belief that, as in the 1971 Bangladesh Liberation War, India was behind the unrest. However, the Indian government denied any involvement, and claimed that it was fearful of further balkanisation of the subcontinent. After three years of fighting the uprising was suppressed.

In addition to military aid, the Shah of Iran offered considerable developmental aid to Pakistan, including oil and gas on preferential terms. Pakistan was a developing countryand small power, while Iran, in the 1960-70s, had the world's fifth largest military and a strong industrial base, and was the clear, undisputed regional superpower.

However, Iran's total dependence on the United States at that time for its economic development and military build-up had won it the hostility of Arab world. Tensions arose in 1974, when Mohammad Reza Pahlavi refused to attend the Islamic Conference in Lahore because Libyan leaderMuammar Gaddafi had been invited to it, despite the known hostility between the two. In 1976, Iran again played a vital and influential role by facilitating a rapprochement between Pakistan and Afghanistan.

Iran's reaction to India's 1974 surprise nuclear test detonation (codenamed *Smiling Buddha*) was muted. During a state visit to Iran in 1977, Bhutto tried to persuade Pahlavi to support Pakistan's own clandestine atomic bomb project. Although the Shah's response is not known, there are indications that he refused to oblige Bhutto.

In July 1977, following political agitation by an opposition alliance, Bhutto was forced out of office in a military coup d'état. The new military government, under General Zia-ul-Haq, was ideologically ultraconservative and Islamically oriented in its nature and approach.

Iranian revolution

The 1979 Iranian Revolution transformed Pakistan and Iran into rivals instead of partners. Bhutto's ouster was followed a half year later by the Iranian Revolution and overthrow of the Shah of Iran. Iran's new Supreme Leader, the Ayatollah Khomeini, withdrew the country from CENTO and ended its association with the United States. The religiously influenced military government of Zia-ul-Haq and the Islamic Revolution in Iran suited one another well, and as such there was no diplomatic and political cleavage between them. In 1979, Pakistan was one of the first countries in the world to recognize the revolutionary regime in Iran. Responding swiftly to this revolutionary change, Foreign Minister of Pakistan Agha Shahiimmediately undertook a state visit to Tehran, meeting with his Iranian counterpart Karim Sanjabi on 10 March 1979. Both expressed confidence that Iran and Pakistan were going to march together to a brighter future. The next day, Agha Shahi held talks with the Ayatollah Ruhollah Khomeini, in which developments in the region were discussed. On 11 April 1979, Zia famously declared that "Khomeini is a symbol of Islamic insurgence". Reciprocating President Zia's sentiments, Imam Khomeini, in his letter, called for Muslim unity. He declared: "Ties with Pakistan are based on Islam." By 1981, however, Pakistan, under Zia-ul-Haq, had once again formed close ties with the United States, a position it has remained in since.

Pakistani support for Iran during the Iran–Iraq war

While Pakistan remained neutral during the Iran-Iraq War, Ayatollah Ruhollah Khomeini's attempts to export the Iranian revolution fueled tensions between Pakistan's Sunnis and Shias. The militancy of Shia inspired by revolutionary Iran left many Pakistani Sunni feeling deeply threatened. President Zia, despite his pro-Saudi and anti-Shia sentiments, had to manage his country's security carefully, knowing that Pakistan risked being dragged into a war with its closest neighbor because of its alliance with the United States. In support of the Gulf Cooperation Council, formed in 1981, around 40,000 personnel of the Pakistan Armed Forces were stationed in Saudi Arabia to reinforce the internal and external security of the region. Although high-ranking members of Pakistan Armed Forces strongly objected to the killing of Shia pilgrims in the1987 Mecca incident in Saudi Arabia, Zia did not issue any orders to Pakistan Armed Forces-Arab Contingent Forces to engage any country militarily. Many Stinger missiles shipped to Pakistan for use by Afghan mujahideen were instead sold to Iran, which proved to be a defining factor for Iran in the Tanker war.

Soviet integration and Afghan civil war

In December 1979, the Soviet Union invaded fragile Communist Afghanistan to protect its interests in Central Asia and as response to American dominance in the Middle East, in notably Israel, Iran, and many Arab states. In 1980, the Iraqi attackon Iran, and subsequent Soviet support for Iraq, improved Iranian ties with Pakistan. Pakistan focused its covert support on the sectarian Pashtun groups while Iran largely supported the Tajik groups, though they all fought as Afghan mujahideen.

After the Soviet withdrawal from Afghanistan, the rivalry between Iran and Pakistan intensified. After 1989, both state's policies in Afghanistan became even more divergent as Pakistan, under Benazir Bhutto, explicitly supported Taliban forces in Afghanistan. This resulted in a major breach, with Iran becoming closer to India. Pakistan's support for the SunniTaliban organisation in Afghanistan became a problem for Shia Iran which opposed a Taliban-controlled Afghanistan. The Pakistani backed Taliban fought the Iranian backed Northern Alliance in Afghanistan and gained control of 90 percent of that country. As noted by a Pakistani foreign service officer, it was difficult to maintain good relations with Israel, Saudi Arabia, the United States, and Iran at the same time, given Iran's long history of rivalry with these states. In 1995 Bhutto paid a lengthy state visit to Iran, which greatly relaxed relations. At a public meeting she spoke highly of Iran and Iranian society. However, increasing activity by Shia militants in Pakistan strained relations further. This was followed by the Taliban's capture of the city of Mazar-i-Sharif in 1998, in which thousands of Shias were massacred, according to Amnesty International. The most serious breach in relations came in 1998, after Iran accused Taliban Afghanistan of taking 11 Iranian diplomats, 35 Iranian truck drivers and an Iranian journalist hostage, and later killing them all.

Iran massed over 300,000 troops on the Afghan border and threatened to attack the Taliban government, which it had never recognized.This strained relations with Pakistan, as the Taliban were seen as Pakistan's key allies. In May 1998, Iran criticised Pakistan for its nuclear testing in the Chagai region, and held Pakistan accountable for global "atomic proliferation".

New Prime Minister Nawaz Sharif acknowledged his country's nuclear capability on 7 September 1997. Before making the announcement, Sharif directed a secret courier to Israel via Pakistan Ambassador to United Nations Inam-ul-Haq andPakistan Ambassador to the United States Dr. Maliha Lodhi, in which Pakistan gave utmost assurance to Israel that Pakistan would not transfer any aspects of its nuclear technology or materials to Iran.

Bilateral and Multilateral visits in the late 1990s

In 1995, Prime Minister Benazir Bhutto paid a state visit to Iran to lay the groundwork for a memorandum on energy, and begin work on an Energy security agreement between the two countries. This was followed by Prime Minister Nawaz Sharif's visit to Tehran for the 8th OIC Summit Conference on 9–11 December 1997. While there Sharif held talks with PresidentKhatami, with a view to improving bilateral relations, as well as finding a solution to the Afghan crisis.

Chief Executive General Pervez Musharraf paid a two-day visit to Tehran on 8–9 December 1999. This was his first visit to Iran (and third international trip) since his military coup d'état of 12 October 1999 and subsequent seizure of power in Pakistan. In Iran, Musharraf held talks with Iranian President Mohammad Khatami and with the Iranian Supreme Leader Ali Khamenei. This visit was arranged to allow Musharraf to explain the reasons for his takeover in Pakistan.

The meetings included discussions on the situation in Afghanistan, which were intended to lead both countries to "coordinate the policies of our two countries for encouraging the peace process through reconciliation and dialogue among the Afghan parties".

In 1998 Iran accused Pakistani troops of war crimes at Bamiyan in Afghanistan and claimed that Pakistani warplanes had, in support of the Taliban, bombarded Afghanistan's last Shia stronghold.

RELATIONS SINCE 2000

Since 2000, relations between Iran and Pakistan have begun to normalize, and economic cooperation has strengthened. The 9/11 terrorist attacks on the United States changed the foreign policy priorities of both Iran and Pakistan. The George W. Bush administration's tough stance forced President Pervez Musharraf to support Washington's War on Terror, which ended Taliban rule in Kabul. Though Iranian officials welcomed the move, they soon found themselves encircled by U.S. forces in Pakistan, Afghanistan, Central Asia, and the Persian Gulf.

President Bush's inclusion of the Islamic Republic as part of an "Axis of Evil" also led some Iranian officials to presume that Tehran might be next in line for regime change, ending whatever *détente* had occurred in Iran–U.S. ties under Khatami. Bush's emphasis on transformative diplomacy and democratization worried Iranian leaders further.

More recently, Iran and Pakistan have joined forces and engaged in co-operation to contain insurgency in Balochistan which has included the severe use of force and been a cause of human rights concern.

Bilateral visits after 2000

In April 2001, the Secretary of Supreme National Security CouncilHassan Rowhani (who is President of Iran since August 2013) paid a state visit to Pakistan and met with Pervez Musharraf and his cabinet.During this visit, Iran and Pakistan agreed to put their differences aside and agree on a broad-based government for Afghanistan.

Iranian Foreign Minister Kamal Kharazi paid a two-day visit to Islamabad from 29–30 November 2001. Kharazi met with Foreign Minister Abdul Sattar and President Musharraf. Iran and Pakistan vowed to improve their relations, and agreed to help establish a broad-based, multi-ethnic government under U.N. auspices.

The President of Iran, Mohammad Khatami, paid a three-day state visit to Pakistan from 23–25 December 2002, the first visit by an Iranian head of government since 1992. It was a high-level delegation, consisting of the Iranian cabinet, members of the Iranian parliament, Iranian Vice-President and President Khatami. This visit was meant to provide a new beginning to Iran–Pakistan relations. It would also allow for high-level discussions on the future of the Iran–Pakistan–India pipeline (IPI) project. Khatami met, and had detailed discussions, with both President Musharraf and the new Prime Minister Zafarullah Khan Jamali.

Several accords were signed between Iran and Pakistan in this visit. Khatami also delivered a talk on "Dialogue Among Civilizations," at The Institute of Strategic Studies. The presidential delegation initially visited Islamabad, and then followed that up with a visit to Lahore, where Khatami also paid his respects at the tomb of Allama Sir Muhammad Iqbal. A Joint communique was issued by Iran and Pakistan on the conclusion of Khatami's visit. On his return to Tehran, Khatami evaluated the trip as "positive and fruitful".

As in return, Jamali paid a state visit in 2003 where he held talks with economic cooperation, security of the region, and better bilateral ties between Pakistan and Iran. During this visit, Jamali gave valuable advises to Iranian leadership on their nuclear programme "against the backdrop of the country's" negotiations with the International Atomic Energy Agency(IAEA), and measures to strengthen economic relations between the two countries.

Military and security

Iranian support for Pakistan dates back to the 1960s when Iran supplied Pakistan with American military weaponry and spare parts after America cut off their military aid to Pakistan. After 1971 Indo-Pakistani War, new Prime minister Zulfikar Ali Bhutto immediately withdrew Pakistan from CENTO and SEATO after Bhutto thought that the military alliances failed to protect or appropriately assist Pakistan and instead alienated the Soviet Union. A serious military cooperation between took place during the Balochistan insurgency phases against the armed separatist movement in 1974–77. Around ~100,000 Pakistan and Iranian troops were involved in quelling the separatist organisations in Balochistan and successfully put the resistance down in 1978–80. In May 2014, the two countries agreed to joint operations against terrorists and drug traffickers in the border regions. In May 2016, Iran warned Pakistan of cross border military action if Pakistan did not reign in militants operating against Iran from its soil.

Iran's view on Kashmir issue

On 19 November 2010 Iran's Supreme Leader Ayatollah Ali Khamenei appealed to Muslims worldwide to back the freedom struggle in Jammu and Kashmir, equating the dispute with the ongoing conflicts of the Greater Middle East region.

"Today the major duty of the elite of the Islamic Ummah is to provide help to the Palestinian nation and the besieged people of Gaza, to sympathize and provide assistance to the nations of Afghanistan, Pakistan, Iraq and Occupied Kashmir, to engage in struggle and resistance against the aggressions of the United States, the Zionist Regime..." He further said that Muslims should be united and "spread awakening and a sense of responsibility and commitment among Muslim youth throughout Islamic communities".

The thrust of his speech was directed at Israel, India, and the US, but also made a veiled reference to Pakistan's nuclear program:

"The US and the West are no longer the unquestionable decision-makers of the Middle East that they were two decades ago. Contrary to the situation 20 years ago, nuclear know-how and other complex technologies are no longer considered inaccessible daydreams for Muslim nations of the region."

He said the US was bogged down in Afghanistan and "is hated more than ever before in disaster-stricken Pakistan".

A former president of Iran (1981–89), Khamenei succeeded Ayatollah Khomeini as the spiritual head of the Iranian people. A staunch supporter of Iranian President Mahmoud Ahmadinejad, Khamenei is believed to be highly influential in Iran's foreign policy.

Khamenei visited Jammu and Kashmir in the early 1980s and delivered a sermon at Srinagar's Jama Masjid mosque.

Atoms for Peace cooperation

Since 1987, Pakistan has steadily blocked any Iranian acquisition of nuclear weapons; however, Pakistan has wholeheartedly supported Iran's viewpoint on the issue of its nuclear energy program, maintaining that "Iran has the right to develop its nuclear program within the ambit of NPT." In 1987 Pakistan and Iran signed an agreement on civil nuclear energy cooperation, with Zia-ul-Haq personally visiting Iran as part of its "Atoms for Peace" program. Internationally, Zia calculated that this cooperation with Iran was purely a "civil matter", necessary for maintaining good relations with Tehran. According to IAEA, Iran wanted to purchase fuel-cycle technology from Pakistan, but was rebuffed. Zia did not approve any further nuclear deals, but one of Pakistan's senior scientists did secretly hand over a sensitive report on centrifuges in 1987–89. In 2005, IAEA evidence showed that Pakistani cooperation with Iran's nuclear program was limited to "non-military spheres", and was peaceful in nature. Tehran had offered as much as $5 billion for nuclear weapons technology in 1990, but had been firmly rejected. Centrifuge technology was transferred in 1989; since then, there have been no further atoms for peace agreements.

In 2005, IAEA evidence revealed that the centrifuge designs transferred in 1989 were based on early commercial power plant technology, and were riddled with technical errors; the designs were not evidence of an active nuclear weapons program.

Non-belligerent policy and official viewpoint

Difficulties have included disputes over trade, and political position. While Pakistan's foreign policy maintains balanced relations with Saudi Arabia, the United States, and the European Union, Iran tends to warn against it, and raised concerns about Pakistan's absolute backing of the Taliban during the fourth phase of civil war in Afghanistan in the last years of the 20th century. Through a progressive reconciliation and chaotic diplomacy, both countries come closer to each other in last few years. In the changing security environment, Pakistan and Iran boosted their ties by maintaining the warmth in the relationship without taking into account the pressures from international actors.

On Iran's nuclear program and its own relations with Iran, Pakistan adopted a policy of neutrality, and played a subsequent non-belligerent role in easing the tension in the region. Since 2006, Pakistan has been strategically advising Iran on multiple occasions to counter the international pressure on its nuclear program to subsequently work on civil nuclear power, instead of active nuclear weapons program. On international front, Pakistan has been a great advocate for Iranian usage of nuclear energy for economics and civil infrastructure while it steadily stop any Iranian acquisition of nuclear weapons, fearing another nuclear armed race with Saudi Arabia.

In a speech at Harvard University in 2010, the Pakistan's foreign minister Shah Mehmood Qureshi justified Iran's nuclear program as peaceful and argued that Iran had "no justification" to pursue nuclear weapons, citing the lack of any immediate threat to Iran, and urged Iran to "embrace overtures" from the United States. Qureshi also observed that Iran had signed theNuclear Non-Proliferation Treaty and should respect the treaty.

Trade and Economics

Relations between Iran and Pakistan improved after the removal of the Taliban in 2002, but tensions remain. Pakistan has been under a strong influence of Saudi Arabia in its competition with Shiite majority Iran for influence across the broader Islamic world, which it already has in its allied nations Lebanon and Syria. Iran considers northern and western Afghanistan as its sphere of influence since its population is Persian Dari speaking. Pakistan considers southern and eastern Afghanistan as its sphere of influence since it is Pashto and Baloch speaking such as the Khyber Pakhtunkhwa and Baluchistan, respectively. Pakistan expressed concern over India's plan to build a highway linking the southern Afghanistan city ofKandahar to Zahidan, since it will reduce Afghanistan's dependence on Pakistan to the benefit of Iran.

Free Trade Agreement

In 2005, Iran and Pakistan had conducted US$500 million of trade. The land border at Taftan is the conduit for trade in electricity and oil. Iran is extending its railway network towards Taftan.

The Iran-Pakistan-India pipeline (IPI Pipeline) is currently under discussion; though India backed out from the project. TheIndian government was under pressure by the United States against the IPI pipeline project, and appears to have heededAmerican policy after India and the United States proceeded to sign the nuclear deal. In addition, the international sanctionson Iran due to its controversial nuclear program could also become a factor in derailing IPI pipeline project altogether.

Trade between the two countries has increased by £1.4 billion in 2009. In 2007-08, annual Pakistan merchandise trade with Iran consisted of $256 million in imports and $218.6 million in export, according to WTO.

Bilateral trade

On 12 January 2001, Pakistan and Iran formed a "Pakistan-Iran Joint Business Council" (PIJB) body on trade disputes.The body works on to encourage the privatization in Pakistan and economic liberalization on both sides of the countries.In 2012, the bilateral trade exceeded $3 billion. Official figures from the State Bank of Pakistan for fiscal year 2011-12 indicate imports of $124 million and exports of $131 million, which had collapsed to $36 million of exports to Iran and less than $1 million of imports for the year to April 2015. In 2011, the trade between Iran and Pakistan stood at less than $1 billion and the common geographical borders as well as religious affinities are among other factors, which give impetus to enhanced level of trade. According to the media reports, Iran is the second-largest market of Basmati rice of Pakistan, ranking after Iraq.

Effects of US sanctions on Iran

The U.S. economic sanctions on Iran regarding their nuclear program generally effected Pakistan's industrial sector. The fruit industry of Pakistan have reportedly lost a lucrative market in Iran, where at least 30,000 tons of mango were exported previously, as a result of the trade embargo imposed by the United States on Tehran. According to the statistics by Pakistan, the fruit industry and the exporters could not export around $10 million worth of mango during the current season. The Ministry of Commerce (MoCom) has been in direct contact with the US Department of Agriculture to resolve the issue through diplomatic channels.

Energy

Iran–Pakistan gas pipeline

Discussions between the governments of Iran and Pakistan started in 1994 for the gas pipelines and energy security. A preliminary agreement was signed in 1995 by Prime Minister Benazir Bhutto and Iranian President Akbar Hashemi Rafsanjani, in which, this agreement foresaw construction of a pipeline from South–North Pars gas field to Karachi in Pakistan. Later, Iran made a proposal to extend the pipeline from Pakistan into India. In February 1999, a preliminary agreement between Iran and India was signed.

Iran has the world's second largest gas reserves, after Russia, but has been trying to develop its oil and gas resources for years, due to sanctions by the West. However, the project could not take off due to different political reasons, including the new gas discoveries in Miano, Sawan and Zamzama gas fields of Pakistan. The Indian concerns on pipeline security and Iranian indecisiveness on different issues, especially prices. The Iran-Pakistan-India (denoted as IPI Pipeline) project was planned in 1995 and after almost 15 years India finally decided to quit the project in 2008 despite severe energy crises in that country.

In February 2007, India and Pakistan agreed to pay Iran US$4.93 per million BTUs (US$4.67/GJ) but some details relating to price adjustment remained open to further negotiation. Since 2008, Pakistan began facing severe criticism from the United States over any kind of energy deal with Iran. Despite delaying for years the negotiations over the IPI gas pipeline project, Pakistan and Iran have finally signed the initial agreement in Tehran in 2009. The project, termed as the peace pipeline by officials from both the countries, was signed by President Zardari and President Mahmoud Ahmadinejad of Iran. In 2009, India withdrew from the project over pricing and security issues, and after signing another civilian nuclear deal with the United States in 2008. However, in March 2010 India called on Pakistan and Iran for trilateral talks to be held in May 2010 in Tehran.

According to the initial design of the project, the 2,700 km long pipeline was to cover around 1,100 km in Iran, 1,000 km in Pakistan and around 600 km in India, and the size of the pipeline was estimated to be 56 inches in diameter. However, as India withdrew from the project the size of the pipeline was reduced to 42 inch. In April 2008, Iran expressed interest in thePeople's Republic of China's participation in the project.

Since as early as in 2005, China and Pakistan are already working on a proposal for laying a trans-Himalayan pipeline to carry Middle Eastern crude oil to western China. Beijing has been pursuing Tehran and Islamabad for its participation in the pipeline project and willing to sign a bilateral agreement with Iran. China and Pakistan are already working on a proposal for laying a trans-Himalayan pipeline to carry Middle Eastern crude oil to western China. In August 2010, Iran invitedBangladesh to join the project.

Power Transmissions

Tehran has provided •50 million for laying of 170Km transmission line for the import of 1000MW of electricity from Iran in 2009. Pakistan is already importing 34MW of electricity daily from Iran. The imported electricity is much cheaper than the electricity produced by the Independent Power Producers (IPPs) because Iran subsidises oil and gas which feed the power plants. Iran has also offered to construct a motorway between Iran and Pakistan connecting the two countries.

DIPLOMACY AND ROLE IN MEDIATION

Since Iran has no diplomatic relations with the United States; the Iranian interests section in the United States is represented by the Embassy of Pakistan Embassy in Washington. Iranian nuclear scientist, Shahram Amiri, thought to have been abducted by CIA from Saudi Arabia, took sanctuary in the Pakistan Embassy in Washington, D.C. The Iranian government claimed the United States has trumped up charges they were involved with the 9/11 attacks.

Diplomatic missions

Iranian missions in Pakistan

Iran's chief diplomatic mission to Pakistan is the Iranian Embassy in Islamabad. The embassy is further supported by many Consulates located throughout in Pakistan.

The Iranian government supports Consulates in several major Pakistan's cities including: Karachi, Lahore, Quetta, Peshawar. Iranian government maintains a cultural consulate-general, Persian Research Center, and *Sada-o-Sima* center, all in Islamabad. Other political offices includes cultural centers inLahore[†], Karachi[†], Rawalpindi[†], Peshawar[†], Quetta[†], Hyderabad[†], and Multan[†].

- [‡] *denotes mission is Consulate General*
- [†] *denotes mission is* Khana-e-Farhang *(lit. culture center)*

There is also an Iran Air corporate office located in Karachi Metropolitan Corporation site.

Immigration

In the Balochistan region of southeastern Iran and western Pakistan, theBalochi people routinely travel the area with little regard for the official border, causing considerable problems for the Iranian Guards Corps and the Frontier Corps of Pakistan. Both countries have ongoing conflicts with Balochi separatistgroups.

Since 2010, there has been an increase in meetings between senior figures of both governments as they attempt to find a regional solution to the Afghan warand continue discussions on a proposed Iran-Pakistan-India gas pipeline and an Economic Cooperation Organization.

Iranian media delegations have been visiting Pakistan annually since 2004, with many journalists settling in Pakistan. These visits have played an effective role in promoting mutual understanding and projecting a positive image of Pakistan in Iran.

Notable Pakistani political figures Benazir, Murtaza, and Shahnawaz Bhutto were half Kurdish-Iranian on their mother's side.

Pakistan missions in Iran

Pakistan's chief diplomatic mission to Iran is the Pakistan Embassy in Tehran. It is further supported by two consulates-general located throughout in Iran. The Pakistan government supports its consulates in Mashhad and Zahidan.

Education

Pakistan International School and College Tehran serves Pakistani families living in Tehran.

6

Military and Defence

ARMED FORCES OF THE ISLAMIC REPUBLIC OF IRAN

The Armed Forces of the Islamic Republic of Iran include the Army (*Artesh*), theRevolutionary Guard Corps (*Sepâh*) and the Law Enforcement Force (Police).

These forces total about 523,000 active personnel (not including theLaw Enforcement Force). All branches of armed forces fall under the command of General Staff of Armed Forces. The Ministry of Defense and Armed Forces Logistics is responsible for planning logistics and funding of the armed forces and is not involved with in-the-field military operational command.

Despite lacking the modern sophisticated military equipment its U.S allied neighbors possess, Iran's military has been described as the Middle East's "most powerful military force" (exempting Israel) by retired US General John Abizaid.

History

With the Iranian revolution in 1979, deteriorating relations with the United States of America resulted in international sanctions led by the USA, including an arms embargo being imposed on Iran.

Revolutionary Iran was taken by surprise, by the Iraqi invasion that began the Iran–Iraq War of 1980–1988. During this conflict, there were several confrontations with the United States. From 1987, theUnited States Central Command sought to stop Iranian mine-layingvessels from blocking the international sea lanes through thePersian Gulf in Operation Prime Chance. The operation lasted until 1989. On April 18, 1988, the U.S. retaliated for the Iranian mining of the USS *Samuel B. Roberts* in Operation Praying Mantis. Simultaneously, the Iranian armed forces had to learn to maintain and keep operational, their large stocks of U.S.-built equipment and weaponry without outside help, due to the American-led sanctions. Reaching back on equipment purchased from the U.S.A. in the 1970s, Iran began establishing its own armaments industry; its efforts in this remained largely unrecognised internationally, until recently. However, Iran was able to obtain limited amounts of American-made armaments, when it was able to buy American spare parts and weaponry for its armed forces, during the Iran-Contra affair. At first, deliveries came via Israel and later, from the USA.

The Iranian government established a five-year rearmament program in 1989 to replace worn-out weaponry from the Iran-Iraq war. Iran spent $10 billion between 1989 and 1992 on arms. Iran ordered weapons designed to prevent other states' naval vessels from accessing the sea, including marines and long-range Soviet planes capable of attacking aircraft carriers.

A former military-associated police force, the Iranian Gendarmerie, was merged with the National Police (Sharbani) and Revolutionary Committees in 1990.

In 1991, the Iranian armed forces received a number of Iraqi military aircraft being evacuated from the Persian Gulf War of that year; most of which were incorporated into the Islamic Republic of Iran Air Force.

From 2003, there have been repeated U.S. and British allegations that Iranian forces have been covertly involved in the Iraq War. In 2004, Iranian armed forces took Royal Navy personnel prisoner, on the Shatt al-Arab (Arvand Rud in Persian) river, between Iran and Iraq. They were released three days later following diplomatic discussions between the UK and Iran.

In 2007, Iranian Revolutionary Guard forces also took prisoner Royal Navy personnel when a boarding party fromHMS *Cornwall* was seized in the waters between Iran and Iraq, in the Persian Gulf. They were released thirteen days later.

According to Juan Cole, Iran has never launched an "aggressive war" in modern history, and its leadership adheres to a doctrine of "no first strike". The country's military budget is the lowest per capita in the Persian Gulf region besides theUAE. Since 1979, there have been no foreign military bases present in Iran. According to Article 146 of the Iranian Constitution, the establishment of any foreign military base in the country is forbidden, even for peaceful purposes.

On 4 December 2011, an American RQ-170 Sentinel unmanned aerial vehicle (UAV) was captured by Iranian forces near the city of Kashmar in northeastern Iran.

In 2012, it was announced that Iran's Quds Force is operating inside Syria providing the government of Bashar al-Assad with intelligence and direction against rebel opposition. There is an emphasis on the monitoring of protesters' use of the internet and mobile phone networks, including text messaging.

In December 2012, Iran stated it had captured an American ScanEagle UAV that violated its airspace over the Persian Gulf. Iran later stated it had also captured two other ScanEagles.

In November 2015, Iranian special forces rescued a Russian pilot that was shot down by Turkey, over Syria. The force involved was made up of men from the Lebanese "Hezbollah" and soldiers from the Syrian special forces, who had undergone special training under the guidance of Iranian instructors.

Apart from this fact, the Syrian soldiers were familiar with the terrain. The general assumed command of the ground operation and Russian aircraft had to carry out air cover and enable satellite surveillance.

Once the location of the Russian pilot was determined via satellite through the built-in GPS device, it became clear that the pilot was located six kilometers behind the front line between the Syrian army forces and the opposition forces. The Special squad that entered the territory controlled by militants was not only able to save the Russian pilot, but also destroy all of the remaining terrorists there who had the most modern weapons in their possession. All of the 24 fighters not only survived, but also returned to their base without injuries.

In April 2016, Iran sent advisors from the 65th Airborne Special Forces Brigade to Syria in support of the government.

In 2016, Revolutionary Guard forces captured U.S. Navy personnel when their boats entered Iranian territorial waters off the coast of Farsi Island in the Persian Gulf. They were released the next day following diplomatic discussions between the U.S. and Iran.

Commanders

- Ayatollah Ali Khamenei (Supreme Leader of the Islamic Revolution and theCommander-in-Chief of the Armed Forces of the Islamic Republic, in Persian: translit. *Fermânande-ye Kol-e Qavâý*)
- Brigadier General Amir Hatami (Minister of Defence)
- Major General Mohammad Bagheri (Commander of the General Staff of the Armed Forces)
- Major General Ataollah Salehi (Deputy commander of General Staff of the Armed Forces, in Persian)
- Major General Yahya Rahim Safavi (Senior Military Advisor to the Leader of the Islamic Revolution)
- Islamic Republic of Iran Army
- Major General Abdolrahim Mousavi (Commander-in-Chief of the Army ýý)
- Brigadier General Ahmad Reza Pourdastan (Deputy Commander in Chief of the Army)
- Brigadier General Mohammad Hossein Dadras (Chief of the Army Joint Headquarters)
- Brigadier General Kioumars Heydari (Commander of the Ground Force)
- Brigadier General Hassan Shahsafi (Commander of the Air Force)
- Brigadier General Farzad Esmaili (Commander of Air Defense Force)
- Rear Admiral Habibollah Sayyari (Commander of the Navy)
- IRGC
- Major General Mohammad Ali Jafari (Commander-in-Chief of the IRGC ýý)
- Brigadier General Hossein Salami (Deputy Commander of the IRGC)
- Brigadier General Mohammad Hejazi (Chief of the IRGC Joint Headquarters)
- Brigadier General Mohammad Pakpour (Commander of IRGC Ground Force)
- Brigadier General Amir Ali Hajizadeh (Commander of the IRGC Aerospace Force)

- Rear Admiral Ali Fadavi (Commander of IRGC Navy)
- Major General Qasem Soleimani (Commander of Quds Force)
- Brigadier General Gholamhossein Gheybparvar (Commander of the BasijResistance Force)
- Law Enforcement Force
- Brigadier General Hossein Ashtari (Commander-in-Chief of the Law Enforcement Force)

Structure

The Iranian regular military, or Islamic Republic of Iran Army, consist of the Islamic Republic of Iran Army Ground Forces,Islamic Republic of Iran Navy, Islamic Republic of Iran Air Force, and the Islamic Republic of Iran Air Defense Force. The regular armed forces have an estimated 398,000 personnel: the Islamic Republic of Iran Army, 350,000 personnel, of which 220,000 are conscripts; the Islamic Republic of Iran Navy, 18,000 personnel, and the Islamic Republic of Iran Air Force, 30,000 airmen. The Islamic Republic of Iran Air Defense Force is a branch split off from the IRIAF.

The Army of the Guardians of the Islamic Revolution, or Revolutionary Guards, has an estimated 125,000 personnel in five branches: Its own Navy, Aerospace Force, and Ground Forces; and the Quds Force (special forces).

The Basij is a paramilitary volunteer force controlled by the Islamic Revolutionary Guards. Its membership is a matter of controversy. Iranian sources claim a membership of 12.6 million, including women, of which perhaps 3 million are combat capable. There are a claimed 2,500 battalions of which some are composed of full-time personnel.GlobalSecurity.org quotes a 2005 study by the Center for Strategic and International Studies estimating 90,000 active-duty full-time uniformed members, 300,000 reservists, and a total of 11 million men that can be mobilised if need be .

Cyberwarfare

It has been reported that Iran is one of the five countries that has a cyber-army capable of conducting cyber-warfare operations. It has also been reported that Iran has immensely increased its cyberwarfare capability since the post presidential election un-rest. Furthermore, China has accused the United States of having initiated a cyber war against Iran, through websites such as Twitter and YouTube and employing a hacker brigade for the purpose of fomenting unrest in

Iran. It has also been reported in early 2010, that two new garrisons for cyberwarfare have been established at Zanjan and Isfahan.

Budget

Iran's 2007 defense budget was estimated to be $11.096 billion by SIPRI (2.5% of GDP). Per capita or percentage of GDP, this was a lower figure than for otherPersian Gulf states.

DEFENSE INDUSTRY

Under the last Shah of Iran, Mohammad Reza Pahlavi, Iran's military industry was limited to assembly of foreign weapons. In the assembly lines that were put up by American firms, such as Bell, Litton and Northrop, Iranian workers put together a variety of helicopters, aircraft, guided missiles, electronic components and tanks.In 1973 the Iran Electronics Industries (IEI) was established. The company was set up in a first attempt to organize the assembly and repair of foreign-delivered weapons. The Iranian Defense Industries Organization was the first to succeed in taking a step into what could be called a military industry by reverse engineeringSoviet RPG-7, BM-21, and SAM-7 missiles in 1979.

Nevertheless, most of Iran's weapons before the Islamic revolution were imported from the United States and Europe. Between 1971 and 1975, the Shah went on a buying spree, ordering $8 billion in weapons from the United States alone. This alarmed the United States Congress, which strengthened a 1968 law on arms exports in 1976 and renamed it the Arms Export Control Act. Still, the United States continued to sell large amounts of weapons to Iran until the 1979 Islamic Revolution.

After the Islamic revolution, Iran found itself severely isolated and lacking technological expertise. Because of economic sanctions and a weapons embargo put on Iran by the United States, it was forced to rely on its domestic arms industry for weapons and spare parts, since there were very few countries willing to do business with Iran.

The Islamic Revolutionary Guards were put in charge of creating what is today known as the Iranian military industry. Under their command, Iran's military industry was enormously expanded, and with the Ministry of Defense pouring investment into the missile industry, Iran soon accumulated a vast arsenal of missiles. Since 1992, it also claiming has produced its own tanks, armored personnel carriers, radar systems, guided missiles, marines, military vessels and fighter planes. Iran is also producing its own submarines.

In recent years, official announcements have highlighted the development of weapons such as the Fajr-3 (MIRV), Hoot, Kowsar, Fateh-110, Shahab-3 missile systems and a variety of unmanned aerial vehicles, at least one of which Israelclaims has been used to spy on its territory.

In 2006, an Iranian UAV acquired and allegedly tracked the American aircraft carrier USS *Ronald Reagan* for 25 minutes without being detected, before returning safely to its base.

On November 2, 2012, Iran's Brigadier General Hassan Seifi reported that the Iranian Army had achieved self-suffiency in producing military equipment, and that the abilities of Iranian scientists have enabled the country to make significant progress in this field. He was quoted saying, Unlike Western countries which hide their new weapons and munitions from all, the Islamic Republic of Iran's Army is not afraid of displaying its latest military achievements and all countries must become aware of Iran's progress in producing weaponry."

UAV program

Iran has produced several domestically developed unmanned aerial vehicle (UAV), which can be used for reconnaissance and combat operations. Iran has also claimed to have downed, captured and later reverse-engineered US and Israeli drones, a claim military experts doubt.

Ballistic missile program

On November 2, 2006, Iran fired unarmed missiles to begin 10 days of military simulations. Iranian state television reported "dozens of missiles were fired includingShahab-2 and Shahab-3 missiles. The missiles had ranges from 300 km to up to 2,000 km. Iranian experts have made some changes to Shahab-3 missiles installing cluster warheads in them with the capacity to carry 1,400 bombs." These launches came after some United States-led military exercises in the Persian Gulf on October 30, 2006, meant to train for blocking the transport of weapons of mass destruction.

Iran is also believed to have started the development of an ICBM/IRBM missile project, known as Ghadr-110 with a range of 3000 km; the program is believed to be a parallel of the advancement of a satellite launcher named IRIS. Iran also dedicatedunderground ballistic missile programs

Weapons of mass destruction

Iran started a major campaign to produce and stockpile chemical weapons after a truce was agreed with Iraq after 1980-88Iran–Iraq War. However, Iran ratified the Chemical Weapons Convention in 1997. Iranian troops and civilians suffered tens of thousands of casualties from Iraqi chemical weapons during the 1980-88 Iran–Iraq War. Even today, more than twenty-four years after the end of the Iran–Iraq War, about 30,000 Iranians are still suffering and dying from the effects of chemical weapons employed by Iraq during the war. The need to manage the treatment of such a large number of casualties has placed Iran's medical specialists in the forefront of the development of effective treatment regimens for chemical weapons victims, and particularly for those suffering from exposure to mustard gas.

Iran ratified the Biological Weapons Convention in 1973. Iran has advanced biological and genetic engineering research programs supporting an industry that produces vaccines for both domestic use and export.

MILITARY AID

In 2013, Iran was reported to supply money, equipment, technological expertise and unmanned aerial vehicles (drones) to Syria's Government and Lebanon's Hezbollah during the Syrian civil war, and to the Iraqi government, Iraqi Shia militia, andPeshmerga during War on ISIL.

Islamic Republic of Iran Army Day

The Iranian Government makes a show of military force on Islamic Republic of Iran Army Day with parades every 18 April, often demonstrating new defense technologies.

The former Supreme leader of Iran, Ruhollah Khomeini named 18 April as Army Day, calling for military parades to exhibit the nation's military preparedness. The Iranian armed forces honor the country's National Army Day by annually parading in many cities of Iran every 18th day of April. The biggest march is held in front of the mausoleum of Ruhollah Khomeini.

DEFENSE INDUSTRY OF IRAN

Iran's military industry manufactures various types of arms and military equipment. According to Iranian officials, the country sold

$100 million worth of military equipment in 2003. and as of 2006 had exported weapons to 57 countries.Iran's military industry, under the command of Iran's Ministry of Defense, is composed of the following main components:

History

Iran's military industry was born under the last Shah of Iran, Mohammad Reza Pahlavi. In 1973, the Iran Electronics Industries (IEI) was founded to organize efforts to assemble and repair foreign-delivered weapons. Most of Iran's weapons before the Islamic revolution were imported from the United States and Europe. Between 1971 and 1975, the Shahwent on a buying spree, ordering $8 billion in weapons from the United States alone. This alarmed the United States Congress, which strengthened a 1968 law on arms exports in 1976 and renamed it the Arms Export Control Act. Still, the United States continued to sell large amounts of weapons to Iran until the 1979 Islamic Revolution.

In 1977, the Iranian Defense Industries Organization began to work on missiles jointly with Israel in Project Flower and requested a joint missile development program with the United States which was rejected. In 1979, the country took the first step into manufacturing by reverse engineering Soviet RPG-7, BM21, and SA-7 missiles.

After the Islamic revolution and the start of the Iran–Iraq War, economic sanctions and an international arms embargo led by the United States coupled with a high demand for military hardware forced Iran to rely on its domestic arms industry for repair and spare parts. The Islamic Revolutionary Guards Corps was put in charge of re-organising the domestic military industry. Under their command Iran's military industry was dramatically expanded, and with the Ministry of Defence pouring capital into the missile industry, Iran soon had an arsenal of missiles.

Since 1992, it also has produced its own tanks, armored personnel carriers, missiles, a submarine, and a fighter plane.

In 2007, following events in Iran's Nuclear Program, the United Nations Security Council placed sanctions on Iran forbidding it from exporting any form of weapons. Despite these sanctions, Iran sold some military equipment to countries such asSudan, Syria, and North Korea. Iran was also unable to import military equipment such as S-300 from Russia and went on to build its own substitute dubbed as Bavar 373.

On November 2, 2012, Iran's Brigadier General Hassan Seifi reported that the Iranian Army had achieved self-suffiency in producing military equipment, and that the abilities of Iranian scientists have enabled the country to make significant progress in this field. He was quoted saying, "Unlike Western countries which hide their new weapons and munitions from all, the Islamic Republic of Iran's Army is not afraid of displaying its latest military achievements and all countries must become aware of Iran's progress in producing weaponry." As of 2016, the Defense Ministry is collaborating with more than 3150 national firms as well as 92 universities.

ISLAMIC REPUBLIC OF IRAN AIR DEFENSE FORCE

The Islamic Republic of Iran Khatam al-Anbia Air Defense Base is a branch split from IRIAF and part of Islamic Republic of Iran Army. It controls all of Iran's military land-based air defense. It is currently commanded by Brigadier General Farzad Esmaili.

History

As of 1996 Iranian Air Defence forces included about 18,000 military personnel. The tradition of aircraft-based air defense, derived from the US-trained Air Force from before the 1978-79 revolution, was giving way to an expanding arsenal of ground-based air defense missile systems. Still, Iran was at the time unable to construct a nationwide, integrated air defense network, and continued to rely on point defense of key locations with surface-to-air missile batteries.

The bulk of Iran's Air Force Air Defence holdings by the mid-1990s revolved around 30 Improved HAWK fire units (12 battalions/ 150+ launchers), 45-60 SA-2 and HQ-2J/23 (CSA-1 Chinese equivalents of the SA-2) launchers. Also available were some 30 Rapier and 15 Tigercat SAM launchers. There are reports of the transfer of SA-6 launchers to Iran from Russia in 1995/1996.In 1997 the Iranian Air Defense forces declared the Almaz S-200 Angara (SA-5 'Gammon') low-to high-altitude surface-to-air missile (SAM) operational.

In December 2005 Iran entered into a contract to purchase 29 TOR-M1 (SA-15 Gauntlet) mobile surface-to-air missile defense systems from Russia worth more than US$700 million (EUR 600 million). Between 1998 and 2002 Iran imported approximately 6 JY-14 surveillance radars from the China National Electronics Import-Export Corporation. The radar can detect targets up to 300 km away and is now part of Iran's air defense system.

On 1 September 2008 it was reported that Russia may proceed with plans to sell advanced S-300 air defence systems to Iran under a secret contract believed to have been signed in 2005. On 22 September 2010 Russian President Dmitry Medvedev signed a decree banning the sale of the S-300 and other military equipment to Iran. The sale was canceled because of United Nations Security Council Resolution 1929 sanctions on Iran. On 10 November 2010 Iran announced that it had developed a version of the S-300 missile.

Iranian land forces have a total of some 1,700 anti-aircraft guns including 14.5mm ZPU-2/-4, 23mm ZSU-23-4, 23mm ZU-23s, 37mm type 55s, 57mm ZSU-57-2 and 100mm KS-19s.Iran also had 100-180 Bofors L/70 40mm guns and modest numbers of Skygaurd 35mm twin anti-aircraft guns.It largest holding consisted of ZU-23s(which it can manufacture).

Recently Iran has built several new anti-aircraft guns including Samavat 35mm Anti-Aircraft Guns, Sa'ir 100mm Anti-Aircraft Guns (Upgraded automatic version of KS-19) and the Mesbah 1 air defense system.

On 21 August 2012 the Iranian military started construction of its largest air defense base in the city of Abadeh in the Southern Fars province. The air defense base is due to be built at the cost of $300 million and will have 6,000 personnel available for a large array of duties, including educational ones. Days later, the defense ministry also announced plans to develop Bavar 373, a new long-range air-defense system, by March 21, 2013.

7

Economy

The economy of Iran is a mixed and transition economy with a large public sector. Some 60 percent of the economy is centrally planned. It is dominated by oil and gas production, although over40 industries are directly involved in the Tehran Stock Exchange, one of the best performing exchanges in the world over the past decade. With 10 percent of the world's proven oil reserves and 15 percent of its gas reserves, Iran is considered an "energy superpower". Iran has fifth highest total estimated value ofnatural resources, valued at US$27.3 trillion in 2016.

It is the world's eighteenth largest by purchasing power parity (PPP) and twenty-seventh by nominal gross domestic product. The country is a member of Next Eleven because of its high development potential. A unique feature of Iran's economy is the presence of large religious foundations called Bonyad, whose combined budgets represent more than 30 percent of central government spending.

Price controls and subsidies, particularly on food and energy,burden the economy. Contraband, administrative controls, widespread corruption, and other restrictive factors undermine private sector-led growth. The legislature in late 2009 passed the subsidy reform plan. This is the most extensive economic reform since the government implemented gasoline rationing in 2007.

Most of the country's exports are oil and gas, accounting for a majority of government revenue in 2010. In 2012, oil exports contributed to about 80% of Iranian public revenue, Oil export revenues enabled Iran to amass well over $135 billion in foreign exchange reserves as of Dec 2016. Iran ranked first in scientific growth in the world in 2011 and has one of the fastest rates of development intelecommunication globally.

Due to its relative isolation from global financial markets, Iran was initially able to avoid recession in the aftermath of the 2008 global financial crisis. However, following expansion of international sanctions related to Iran's nuclear program, the Iranian rial fell to a record low of 23,900 to the US dollar in September 2012.

Exports aided self-sufficiency and domestic investment. Iran'seducated population, high human development, constrained economy and insufficient foreign and domestic investment prompted an increasing number of Iranians to seek overseas employment, resulting in a significant "brain drain". However, in 2015, Iran and the P5+1reached a deal on the nuclear program which will remove sanctions. After removal of most sanctions in 2016 inflation decreased and unemployment was reduced. Many Iranians returned and Iranian tourism industry was significantly improved.

History

In 546 BC, Croesus of Lydia was defeated and captured by the Persians, who then adopted gold as the main metal for their coins. There are accounts in the biblical Book of Esther of dispatches being sent from Susa to provinces as far out as India and the Kingdom of Kush during the reign of Xerxes the Great (485–465 BC). By the time of Herodotus (c. 475 BC), theRoyal Road of the Persian Empire ran some 2,857 km from the city of Susa on the Karun (250 km east of the Tigris) to the port of Smyrna (modernÝzmir in Turkey) on the Aegean Sea.

Modern agriculture in Iran dates back to the 1820s, when Amir Kabirundertook a number of changes to the traditional agricultural system. Such changes included importing modified seeds and signing collaboration contracts with other countries. Polyakov's *Bank Esteqrazi*was bought in 1898 by the Tzarist government of Russia, and later passed into the hands of the Iranian government by a contract in 1920. The bank continued its activities under the name of *Bank Iran*until 1933 when incorporating the newly founded Keshavarzi Bank.

The Imperial Bank of Persia was established in 1885, with offices in all major cities of Persia. Reza Shah Pahlavi (r. 1925–41) improved the country's overall infrastructure, implemented educational reform, campaigned against foreign influence, reformed the legal system, and introduced modern industries. During this time, Iran experienced a period of social change, economic development, and relative political stability.

Reza Shah Pahlavi, who abdicated in 1941, was succeeded by his son, Mohammad Reza Shah Pahlavi (r. 1941–79). No fundamental change occurred in the economy of Iran during World War II (1939–45) and the years immediately following. However, between 1954 and 1960 a rapid increase in oil revenues and sustained foreign aid led to greater investment and fast-paced economic growth, primarily in the government sector. Subsequently, inflation increased, the value of the national currency (the rial) depreciated, and a foreign-trade deficit developed. Economic policies implemented to combat these problems led to declines in the rates of nominal economic growth and per capita income by 1961.

Prior to 1979, Iran developed rapidly. Traditionally agricultural, by the 1970s the country had undergone significant industrialization and modernization. The pace slowed by 1978 as capital flight reached $30 to $40 billion 1980-US dollars just before the revolution.

Following the nationalizations in 1979 and the outbreak of the Iran–Iraq War, over 80% of the economy came under government control. The eight-year war with Iraq claimed at least 300,000 Iranian lives and injured more than 500,000. The cost of the war to the country's economy was some $500 billion. After hostilities ceased in 1988, the government tried to develop the country's communication, transportation, manufacturing, health care, education and energy sectors (including its prospective nuclear power facilities), and began integrating its communication and transportation systems with those of neighboring states.

The government's long-term objectives since the revolution were stated as economic independence, full employment, and a comfortable standard of living but Iran's population more than doubled between 1980 and 2000 and its median age declined. Although many Iranians are farmers, agricultural production has consistently fallen since the 1960s. By the late 1990s, Iran imported much of its food. At that time, economic hardship in the countryside resulted in many people moving to cities.

MACROECONOMIC TRENDS

More than two-thirds of the population (74 million people) are under the age of 30. Net primary school enrollment is almost 100%, suggesting a secondary "demographic boom". Iran's national science budget in 2005 was about $900 million, roughly equivalent to the 1990 figure.

By early 2000, Iran allocated around 0.4% of its GDP to research and development, ranking the country behind the world average of 1.4%. In 2009 the ratio of research to GDP was 0.87% against the government's medium-term target of 2.5%. Iran ranked first in scientific growth in the world in 2011 and 17th in science production in 2012.

Iran has a broad and diversified industrial base. According to The Economist, Iran ranked 39th in a list of industrialized nations, producing $23 billion of industrial products in 2008. Between 2008 and 2009 Iran moved to 28th from 69th place in annual industrial production growth because of its relative isolation from the 2008 international financial crisis.

In the early 21st century the service sector was the country's largest, followed by industry (mining and manufacturing) and agriculture. In 2008 GDP was estimated at $382.3 billion ($842 billion PPP), or $5,470 per capita ($12,800 PPP).

Nominal GDP is projected to double in the next five years. However, real GDP growth is expected to average 2.2% a year in 2012–16, insufficient to reduce the unemployment rate. Furthermore, international sanctions have damaged the economy by reducing oil exports by half before recovering in 2016. The Iranian rial lost more than half of its value in 2012, directing Iran at an import substitution industrialization and a resistive economy. According to the International Monetary Fund, Iran is a "transition economy", i.e., changing from a planned to a market economy.

The United Nations classifies Iran's economy as semi-developed. In 2014, Iran ranked 83rd in the World Economic Forum's analysis of the global competitiveness of 144 countries. Political, policy and currency stability are regarded as the most problematic factors in doing business in Iran. Difficulty in accessing financing is also a major concern, specially for small and medium enterprises. Most of Iran's financial resources are directed at trading, smuggling and speculation instead of production and manufacturing. According to Goldman Sachs, Iran has the potential to become one of the world's largest economies in the 21st century. Iranian President Hassan Rouhani stated in 2014 that the country has the potential to become one of the ten largest economies within the next 30 years.

Economic reform plan

Expansion of public healthcare and international relations are the other main objectives of the fifth plan, an ambitious series of measures that include subsidy reform, banking recapitalization, currency, taxation, customs, construction, employment, nationwide goods and services distribution, social justice and productivity. The intent is to make the country self-sufficient by 2015 and replace the payment of $100 billion in subsidies annually with targeted social assistance. These reforms target the country's major sources of inefficiency and price distortion and are likely to lead to major restructuring of almost all economic sectors. As such, by removing energy subsidies, Iran intends to make its industries more efficient and competitive. By 2016, one third of Iran's economic growth is expected to originate from productivity improvement. Energy subsidies left the country one of the world's least energy-efficient, with energy intensity three times the global average and 2.5 times higher than the Middle Eastern average. The banking sector is seen as a potential hedge against the removal of subsidies, as the plan is not expected to directly impact banks.

NATIONAL ECONOMIC PLANNING

Following annual approval of the government's budget by Majlis, the central bank presents a detailed monetary and credit policy to the Money and Credit Council (MCC) for approval. Thereafter, major elements of these policies are incorporated into the five-year economic development plan. The fifth development plan, for 2010–15, is designed to delegate power to the people and develop a knowledge economy. The plan is part of "Vision 2025", a strategy for long-term sustainable growth.

The sixth five-year development plan for the 2016–2021 period only defined three priorities:

- the development of a resilient economy,
- progress in science and technology,
- and the promotion of cultural excellence.

FISCAL AND MONETARY POLICY

Since the 1979 revolution, government spending has averaged 59% on social policies, 17% on economic matters, 15% onnational defense, and 13% on general affairs. Payments averaged 39% on education, health and social security, 20% on other social programs, 3% on agriculture, 16% on water, power and gas, 5% on manufacturing and mining, 12% on roads and transportation and 5% on other economic affairs. Iran's investment reached 27.7% of GDP in 2009. Between 2002 and 2006, inflation fluctuated around 14%. In 2008, around 55% of government revenue came from oil and natural gas revenue, with 31% from taxes and fees. There are virtually millions of people who do not pay taxes in Iran and hence operate outside the formal economy. The budget for year 2012 was $462 billion, 9% less than 2011. The budget is based on an oil price of $85 per barrel. The value of the US dollar is estimated at IRR 12,260 for the same period.According to the head of the Department of Statistics of Iran, if the rules of budgeting were observed the government could save at least 30 to 35% on its expenses. The central bank's interest rate is 21%, and the inflation rate has climbed to 22% in 2012, 10% higher than in 2011. There is little alignment between fiscal and monetary policy. According to theCentral Bank of Iran the gap between the rich and the poor narrowed because of monthly subsidies but the trend could reverse if high inflation persists.

Iran had an estimated $110 billion in foreign reserves in 2011 and balances its external payments by pricing oil at approximately $75 per barrel. As of 2013, only $30 to $50 billion of those reserves are accessible because of current sanctions. Iranian media has questioned the reason behind Iran's government non-repatriation of its foreign reservesbefore the imposition of the latest round of sanctions and its failure to convert into gold. As a consequence, the Iranian riallost more than 40% of its value between December 2011 and April 2012. Iran's external and fiscal accounts reflect falling oil prices in 2012–13, but remain in surplus. The current account was expected to reach a surplus of 2.1% of GDP in 2012–13, and the net fiscal balance (after payments to Iran's National Development Fund) will register a surplus of 0.3% of GDP. In 2013 the external debts stood at $7.2 billion down from $17.3 billion in 2012. Overall fiscal deficit is expected to deteriorate to 2.7% of GDP in FY 2016 from 1.7% in 2015.

Ownership

Following the hostilities with Iraq the Government declared its intention to privatize most industries and to liberalize and decentralize the economy. Sale of state-owned companies proceeded slowly, mainly due to opposition by a nationalist majority in the parliament. In 2006 most industries, some 70% of the economy, remained state-owned. The majority of heavy industries including steel, petrochemicals, copper, automobiles, and machine tools remained in the public sector, with most light industry privately owned.

Article 44 of the Iranian Constitution declares that the country's economy should consist of state, cooperative and private sectors based. The state sector includes all large-scale industries, foreign trade, major minerals, banking, insurance, power generation, dams and large-scale irrigation networks, radio and television, post, telegraph and telephone services, aviation, shipping, roads, railroads and the like. These are publicly owned and administered by the State. Cooperative companies and enterprises concerned with production and distribution in urban and rural areas form the basis of the cooperative sector and operated in accordance with Shariah law. As of 2012, 5,923 consumer cooperatives, employed 128,396. Consumer cooperatives have over six million members. Private sector operate in construction, agriculture, animal husbandry, industry, trade, and services that supplement the economic activities of the state and cooperative sectors.

Since Article 44 has never been strictly enforced, the private sector has played a much larger role than that outlined in the constitution. In recent years the role of this sector has increased. A 2004 constitutional amendment allows 80% of state assets to be privatized. Forty percent of such sales are to be conducted through the "Justice Shares" scheme and the rest through the Tehran Stock Exchange. The government would retain the remaining 20%. In 2005, government assets were estimated at around $120 billion. Some $63 billion of such assets were privatized from 2005 to 2010, reducing the government's direct share of GDP from 80% to 40%. Many companies in Iran remain uncompetitive because of mismanagement over the years, thus making privatization less attractive for potential investors. According to then-President Mahmoud Ahmadinejad, 60% of Iran's wealth is controlled by just 300 people.

Islamic Revolutionary Guard Corps

The Islamic Revolutionary Guard Corps (IRGC) are thought to control about one third of Iran's economy through subsidiaries and trusts. Estimates by the Los Angeles Times suggest IRGC has ties to over one hundred companies and annual revenue in excess of $12 billion, particularly in construction. The Ministry of Petroleum awarded IRGC billions of dollars in no-bid contracts as well as major infrastructure projects. Tasked with border control, IRGC maintains a monopoly on smuggling, costing Iranian companies billions of dollars each year. Smuggling is encouraged in part by the generous subsidization of domestic goods (including fuel). IRGC also runs the telecommunication company, laser eye-surgery clinics, makes cars, builds bridges and roads and develops oil and gas fields.

Religious foundations

Welfare programs for the needy are managed by more than 30 public agencies alongside semi-state organizations known as *bonyads*, together with several private non-governmental organizations. *Bonyads* are a consortium of over 120 tax-exempt organizations that receive subsidies and religious donations. They answer directly to the Supreme Leader of Iranand control over 20% of GDP. Operating everything from vast soybean and cotton farms to hotels, soft drink, auto-manufacturing and shipping lines, they are seen as overstaffed, corrupt and generally unprofitable. *Bonyad* companies also compete with Iran's unprotected private sector, whose firms complain of the difficulty of competing with the subsidized*bonyads*. *Bonyads* are not subject to audit or Iran's accounting laws. *Setad* is a multi-sector business organization, with holdings of 37 companies, and an estimated value of $95 billion. It is under the control of the Supreme Leader, Ali Khamenei, and created from thousands of properties confiscated from Iranians.

Labor force

After the revolution, the government established a nationaleducation system that improved adult literacy rates: as of 2008 85% of the adult population was literate, well ahead of the regional average of 62%. The Human Development Index was 0.749 in 2013, placing Iran in the "high human development" bracket.

Annual economic growth of above 5% is necessary to absorb the 750,000 new labor force entrants each year. Agriculture contributes just over 11% to GDP and employs one third of the labor force. As of 2004 the industrial sector, which includes mining, manufacturing, and construction, contributed 42% of GDP and employed 31% of the labor force. Mineral products, notably petroleum, account for 80% of Iran's export revenues, even though mining employs less than 1% of the labor force. In 2004 the service sector ranked as the largest contributor to GDP (48%) and employed 44% of workers.Women made up 33% of the labor force in 2005. Youth unemployment (aged 15-24) was 29.1% in 2012, resulting in significant brain drain. According to the government, some 40% of the workforce in the public sector are either in excess or incompetent.

Personal income and poverty

Iran is classed as a middle income country and has made significant progress in provision of health and education services in the period covered by the Millennium Development Goals (MDGs). In 2010, Iran's average monthly income was about $500 (GNI per capita in 2012: $13,000 by PPP). A minimum national wage applies to each sector of activity as defined by the Supreme Labor Council. In 2009 this was about $263 per month ($3,156 per year). The World Bankreported that in 2001, approximately 20% of household consumption was spent on food, 32% on fuel, 12% on health care and 8% on education. Iranians have little debt. Seventy percent of Iranians own their homes.

After the Revolution, the composition of the middle class in Iran did not change significantly, but its size doubled from about 15% of the population in 1979 to more than 32% in 2000. The official poverty line in Tehran for the year ending March 20, 2008, was $9,612, while the national average poverty line was $4,932. In 2010, Iran's Department of Statistics announced that 10 million Iranians live under the absolute poverty line and 30 million live under the relative poverty line.

Social security

Although Iran does not offer universal social protection, in 1996, the Iranian Center for Statistics estimated that more than 73% of the Iranian population was covered by social security. Membership of the social security system for all employees is compulsory.

Social security ensures employee protection against unemployment, disease, old age and occupational accidents. In 2003, the government began to consolidate its welfare organizations to eliminate redundancy and inefficiency. In 2003 the minimum standard pension was 50% of the worker's earnings but no less than the minimum wage. Iran spent 22.5% of its 2003 national budget on social welfare programs of which more than 50% covered pension costs. Out of the 15,000 homeless in Iran in 2015, 5,000 were women.

Employees between the age of 18 and 65 years are covered by the social security system with financing shared between the employee

(7% of salary), the employer (20–23%) and the state, which in turn supplements the employer contribution up to 3%. Social security applies to self-employed workers, who voluntarily contribute between 12% and 18% of income depending on the protection sought. Civil servants, the regular military, law enforcement agencies, and IRGC have their own pension systems.

Trade unions

Although Iranian workers have a theoretical right to form labor unions, there is no union system in the country. Ostensible worker representation is provided by the Workers' House, a state-sponsored institution that attempts to challenge some state policies. Guild unions operate locally in most areas, but are limited largely to issuing credentials and licenses. The right to strike is generally not respected by the state. Since 1979 strikes have often been met by police action.

A comprehensive law covers labor relations, including hiring of foreign workers. This provides a broad and inclusive definition of the individuals it covers, recognizing written, oral, temporary and indefinite employment contracts. Considered employee-friendly, the labor law makes it difficult to lay off staff. Employing personnel on consecutive six-month contracts (to avoid paying benefits) is illegal, as is dismissing staff without proof of a serious offense. Labor disputes are settled by a special labor council, which usually rules in favor of the employee.

Agriculture and foodstuffs

Agriculture contributes just over 11% to the gross national product and employs a third of the labor force. About 11% of Iran's land is arable, with the main food-producing areas located in the Caspian region and in northwestern valleys. Some northern and western areas support rain-fed agriculture, while others requireirrigation.

Primitive farming methods, overworked and under-fertilized soil, poor seed and water scarcity are the principal obstacles to increased production.

About one third of total cultivated land is irrigated. Construction of multipurpose dams and reservoirs along rivers in the Zagros and Alborz mountains have increased the amount of water available for irrigation. Agricultural production is increasing as a result of modernization, mechanization, improvements to crops and livestock as well as land redistribution programs.

Wheat, the most important crop, is grown mainly in the west and northwest. Rice is the major crop in the Caspian region. Other crops include barley, corn, cotton, sugar beets, tea, hemp, tobacco, fruits, potatoes, legumes (beans and lentils), vegetables, fodder plants (alfalfa and clover), almonds, walnuts and spices including cumin andsumac. Iran is the world's largest producer of saffron, pistachios, honey, berberisand berries and the second largest date producer. Meat and dairy products include lamb, goat meat, beef, poultry, milk, eggs, butter and cheese.

Non-food products include wool, leather and silk. Forestry products from the northern slopes of the Alborz Mountains are economically important. Tree-cutting is strictly controlled by the government, which also runs a reforestation program. Rivers drain into the Caspian Sea and are fished for salmon, carp, trout, pike and sturgeon that produce caviar, of which Iran is the largest producer.

Since the 1979 revolution commercial farming has replaced subsistence farming as the dominant mode of agricultural production. By 1997, the gross value reached $25 billion. Iran is 90% self-sufficient in essential agricultural products, although limited rice production leads to substantial imports. In 2007 Iran reached self-sufficiency in wheat production and for the first time became a net wheat exporter. By 2003, a quarter of Iran's non-oil exports were of agricultural products, including fresh and dried fruits, nuts, animal hides, processed foods, and spices. Iran exported $736 million worth of foodstuffs in 2007 and $1 billion (~600,000 tonnes) in 2010. A total of 12,198 entities are engaged in theIranian food industry, or 12% of all entities in the industry sector. The sector also employs approximately 328,000 people or 16.1% of the entire industry sector's workforce.

Manufacturing

Large-scale factory manufacturing began in the 1920s. During the Iran–Iraq War, Iraq bombed many of Iran's petrochemical plants, damaging the large oil refinery at Abadan bringing production to a halt. Reconstruction began in 1988 and production resumed in 1993. In spite of the war, many small factories sprang up to produce import-substitution goods and materials needed by the military.

Iran's major manufactured products are petrochemicals, steel and copper products. Other important manufactures include automobiles, home and electric appliances, telecommunications equipment, cement and industrial machinery. Iran operates the largest operational population of industrial robots in West Asia. Other products include paper, rubber products, processed foods, leather products andpharmaceuticals. In 2000, textile mills, using domestic cotton and wool such as*Tehran Patou* and *Iran Termeh* employed around 400,000 people around Tehran,Isfahan and along the Caspian coast.

A 2003 report by the United Nations Industrial Development Organization regardingsmall and medium-sized enterprises (SMEs) identified the following impediments to industrial development:

- Lack of monitoring institutions;
- Inefficient banking system;
- Insufficient research & development;
- Shortage of managerial skills;
- Corruption;
- Inefficient taxation;
- Socio-cultural apprehensions;
- Absence of social learning loops;
- Shortcomings in international market awareness necessary for global competition,
- Cumbersome bureaucratic procedures;
- Shortage of skilled labor;
- Lack of intellectual property protection;
- Inadequate social capital, social responsibility and socio-cultural values.

Handicrafts

Iran has a long tradition of producing artisanal goods including Persian carpets,ceramics, copperware, brassware, glass, leather goods, textiles and wooden artifacts. The country's carpet-weaving tradition dates from pre-Islamic times and remains an important industry contributing substantial amounts to rural incomes. An estimated 1.2 million weavers in Iran produce carpets for domestic and international export markets. More than $500 million worth of hand-woven carpets are exported each year, accounting for 30% of the 2008 world market. Around 5.2 million people work in some 250 handicraft fields and contribute 3% of GDP.

Automobile manufacturing

As of 2001, 13 public and privately owned automakers within

Iran, led by Iran Khodroand Saipa that accounted for 94% of domestic production. Iran Khodro's Paykan, replaced by the Samand in 2005, is the predominant brand. With 61% of the 2001 market, Khodro was the largest player, whilst Saipa contributed 33% that year. Other car manufacturers, such as the Bahman Group, Kerman Motors, Kish Khodro, Raniran, Traktorsazi, Shahab Khodro and others accounted for the remaining 6%. These automakers produce a wide range of vehicles including motorbikes, passenger cars such as Saipa's Tiba, vans, mini trucks, medium-sized trucks, heavy trucks, minibuses, large buses and other heavy automobiles used for commercial and private activities in the country. In 2009 Iran ranked fifth in car production growth after China, Taiwan, Romania and India. Iran was the world's 12th biggest automaker in 2010 and operates a fleet of 11.5 million cars. Iran produced 1,395,421 cars in 2010, including 35,901 commercial vehicles.

Defense industry

In 2007 the International Institute for Strategic Studies estimated Iran's defense budget at $7.31 billion, equivalent to 2.6% of GDP or $102 per capita, ranking it 25th internationally. The country's defense industry manufactures many types of arms and equipment. Since 1992, Iran's Defense Industries Organization (DIO) has produced its own tanks, armored personnel carriers, guided missiles, radar systems, a guided missile destroyer, military vessels, submarines and a fighter plane. In 2006 Iran exported weapons to 57 countries, including NATO members, and exports reached $100 million. It is also developing a sophisticated mobile air defense system dubbed as Bavar 373.

Construction and real estate

Until the early 1950s construction remained in the hands of small domestic companies. Increased income from oil and gas and easy credit triggered a building boom that attracted international construction firms to the country. This growth continued until the mid-1970s when a sharp rise in inflation and a credit squeeze collapsed the boom. The construction industry had revived somewhat by the mid-1980s, although housing shortages and speculation remained serious problems, especially in large urban centers. As of January 2011, the banking sector, particularly Bank Maskan, had loaned up to 102 trillion rials ($10.2 billion) to applicants of Mehr housing scheme. Construction is one of the most important sectors accounting for 20–50% of total private investment in urban areas and was one of the prime investment targets of well-off Iranians.

Annual turnover amounted to $38.4 billion in 2005 and $32.8 billion in 2011. Because of poor construction quality, many buildings need seismic reinforcement or renovation. Iran has a large dam building industry.

Mines and metals

Mineral production contributed 0.6% of the country's GDP in 2011, a figure that increases to 4% when mining-related industries are included. Gating factors include poor infrastructure, legal barriers, exploration difficulties and government control over all resources. Iran is ranked among the world's 15 major mineral-rich countries.

Although the petroleum industry provides the majority of revenue, about 75% of all mining sector employees work in mines producing minerals other than oil and natural gas. These include coal, iron ore, copper, lead, zinc, chromium, barite, salt,gypsum, molybdenum, strontium, silica, uranium, and gold, the latter of which is mainly a by-product of the Sar Cheshmeh copper complex operation. The mine at Sar Cheshmeh in Kerman Province is home to the world's second largest store of copper. Large iron ore deposits exist in central Iran, near Bafq, Yazdand Kerman. The government owns 90% of all mines and related industries and is seeking foreign investment. The sector accounts for 3% of exports.

Iran has recoverable coal reserves of nearly 1.9 billion short tonnes. By mid-2008, the country produced about 1.3 million short tonnes of coal annually and consumed about 1.5 million short tonnes, making it a net importer. The country plans to increase hard-coal production to 5 million tons in 2012 from 2 million tons in November 2008.

The main steel mills are located in Isfahan and Khuzestan. Iran became self-sufficient in steel in 2009. Aluminum and copper production are projected to hit 245,000 and 383,000 tons respectively by March 2009. Cement production reached 65 million tons in 2009, exporting to 40 countries.

Petrochemicals

Iran manufactures 60–70% of its equipment domestically, including refineries, oil tankers, drilling rigs, offshore platforms and exploration instruments.

Thanks to a fertilizer plant in Shiraz, the world's largest ethylene unit, in Asalouyeh, and the completion of other special economic zone projects, Iran's exports in petrochemicals reached $5.5 billion in 2007, $9 billion in 2008 and $7.6 billion during the first ten months of the Iranian calendar year 2010. National Petrochemical Company's output capacity will increase to over 100 million tpa by 2015 from an estimated 50 million tpa in 2010 thus becoming the world' second largest chemical producer globally after Dow Chemical with Iran housing some of the world's largest chemical complexes.

Major refineries located at Abadan (site of its first refinery), Kermanshah and Tehran failed to meet domestic demand for gasoline in 2009. Iran's refining industry requires $15 billion in investment over the period 2007–2012 to become self-sufficient and end gasoline imports. Iran has the fifth cheapest gasoline prices in the world leading to fuel smuggling with neighboring countries.

Services

Despite 1990s efforts towards economic liberalization, government spending, including expenditure by quasi-governmental foundations, remains high. Estimates of service sector spending in Iran are regularly more than two-fifths of GDP, much government-related, including military expenditures, government salaries and social security disbursements. Urbanization contributed to service sector growth. Important service industries include public services (including education), commerce, personal services, professional services and tourism.

The total value of transport and communications is expected to rise to $46 billion in nominal terms by 2013, representing 6.8% of Iran's GDP. Projections based on 1996 employment figures compiled for the International Labour Organizationsuggest that Iran's transport and communications sector employed 3.4 million people, or 20.5% of the labor force in 2008.

Energy, gas and petroleum

Energy

Electricity:
- *production:* 258 billion kWh (2014)
- *consumption:* 218 billion kWh (2014)
- *exports:* 9.7 billion kWh (2014)

- *imports:* 3.8 billion kWh (2014)

Electricity – production by source:

Iran plans to generate 23,000 MW of electricity through nuclear technology by 2025 to meet its increasing demand for energy.

- *fossil fuels:* 85.6% (2012)
- *hydro:* 12.4% (2012)
- *other:* 0.8% (2012)
- *nuclear:* 1.2% (2012)

Oil:

- *production:* 3,300,000 bbl/d (520,000 m^3/d) (2015)
- *exports:* 1,042,000 bbl/d (165,700 m^3/d) (2013)
- *imports:* 87,440 bbl/d (13,902 m^3/d) (2013)
- *proved reserves:* 157.8 Gbbl (25.09×10^9 m^3) (2016)

Natural gas:

- *production:* 174.5 km^3 (2014)
- *consumption:* 170.2 km^3 (2014)
- *exports:* 9.86 km^3 (2014)
- *imports:* 6.886 km^3 (2014)
- *proved reserves:* 34,020 km^3 (2016)

Iran possesses 10% of the world's proven oil reserves and 15% of its gas reserves. Domestic oil and gas along with hydroelectric power facilities provide power. Energy wastage in Iran amounts to six or seven billion dollars per year, much higher than the international norm. Iran recycles 28% of its used oil and gas, whereas some other countries reprocess up to 60%. In 2008 Iran paid $84 billion in subsidies for oil, gas and electricity. It is the world's third largest consumer of natural gas after United States and Russia. In 2010 Iran completed its first nuclear power plant at Bushehr with Russian assistance.

Iran has been a major oil exporter since 1913. The country's major oil fields lie in the central and southwestern parts of the western Zagros mountains. Oil is also found in northern Iran and in the Persian Gulf. In 1978, Iran was the fourth largest oil producer, OPEC's second largest oil producer and second largest exporter.Following the 1979 revolution the new government reduced production. A further decline in production occurred as result of damage to oil facilities during the Iraq-Iran war. Oil production rose in the late 1980s as pipelines were repaired and newGulf fields exploited. By 2004, annual oil production reached 1.4 billion barrels producing a net profit of $50 billion. Iranian Central Bank data show a declining trend in the share of Iranian exports from oil-products (2006/2007: 84.9%, 2007/2008: 86.5%, 2008/2009: 85.5%, 2009/2010: 79.8%, 2010/2011 (first three quarters): 78.9%). Iranian officials estimate that Iran's annual oil and gas revenues could reach $250 billion by 2015 once current projects come on stream.

Pipelines move oil from the fields to the refineries and to such exporting ports as Abadan, Bandar-e Mashur and Kharg Island. Since 1997, Iran's state-owned oil and gas industry has entered into major exploration and production agreements with foreign consortia. In 2008 the Iranian Oil Bourse (IOB) was inaugurated in Kish Island. The IOB trades petroleum, petrochemicals and gas in various currencies. Trading is primarily in the euro and rial along with other major currencies, not including the US dollar. According to the Petroleum Ministry, Iran plans to invest $500 billion in its oil sector by 2025.

Retail and distribution

Iran's retail industry consists largely of cooperatives (many of them government-sponsored), and independent retailers operating in bazaars. The bulk of food sales occur at street markets with prices set by the Chief Statistics Bureau. Iran has 438,478 small grocery retailers.These are especially popular in cities other than Tehran where the number of hypermarkets and supermarkets is still very limited. More mini-markets and supermarkets are emerging, mostly independent operations. The biggest chainstores are state-owned Etka, Refah, Shahrvand and Hyperstar Market. Electronic commerce in Iran passed the $1 billion mark in 2009.

In 2012, Iranians spent $77 billion on food, $22 billion on clothes and $18.5 billion on outward tourism. In 2015, overallconsumer expenditures and disposable income are projected at $176.4 billion and $287 billion respectively.

Healthcare and pharma

The constitution entitles Iranians to basic health care. By 2008, 73% of Iranians were covered by the voluntary national health insurance system. Although over 85% of the population use an insurance system to cover their drug expenses, the government heavily subsidizes pharmaceutical production/importation. The total market value of Iran's health and medical sector was $24 billion in 2002 and was forecast to rise to $50 billion by 2013. In 2006, 55 pharmaceutical companies in Iran produced 96% (quantitatively) of the medicines for a market worth $1.2 billion. This figure is projected to increase to $3.65 billion by 2013.

Tourism and travel

Although tourism declined significantly during the war with Iraq, it has subsequently recovered. About 1,659,000 foreign tourists visited Iran in 2004 and 2.3 million in 2009 mostly from Asian countries, including the republics of Central Asia, while about 10% came from the European Union and North America.

The most popular tourist destinations are Isfahan, Mashhad and Shiraz. In the early 2000s the industry faced serious limitations in infrastructure, communications, industry standards and personnel training. The majority of the 300,000 tourist visas granted in 2003 were obtained by Asian Muslims, who presumably intended to visit importantpilgrimage sites in Mashhad and Qom. Several organized tours from Germany, France and other European countries come to Iran annually to visit archaeological sites and monuments. In 2003 Iran ranked 68th in tourism revenues worldwide. According to UNESCO and the deputy head of research for Iran Travel and Tourism Organization (ITTO), Iran is rated among the "10 most touristic countries in the world". Domestic tourism in Iran is one of the largest in the world.

Banking, finance and insurance

Government loans and credits are available to industrial and agricultural projects, primarily through banks. Iran's unit of currency is the rial which had an average official exchange rate of 9,326 rials to the U.S. dollar in 2007. Rials are exchanged on the unofficial market at a higher rate. In 1979, the government nationalized private banks. The restructured banking system replaced interest on loans with handling fees, in accordance with Islamic law. This system took effect in the mid-1980s.

The banking system consists of a central bank, the Bank Markazi, which issues currency and oversees all state and private banks. Several commercial banks have branches throughout the country. Two development banks exist and a housing bank specializes in home mortgages. The government began to privatize the banking sector in 2001 when licenses were issued to two new privately owned banks.

State-owned commercial banks predominantly make loans to the state, *bonyad*enterprises, large-scale private firms and four thousand wealthy/connected individuals. While most Iranians have difficulty obtaining small home loans, 90 individuals secured facilities totaling $8 billion. In 2009, Iran's General Inspection Office announced that Iranian banks held some $38 billion of delinquent loans, with capital of only $20 billion.

Foreign transactions with Iran amounted to $150 billion of major contracts between 2000 and 2007, including private and government lines of credit. In 2007, Iran had $62 billion in assets abroad. In 2010, Iran attracted almost $11.9 billion from abroad, of which $3.6 billion was FDI, $7.4 billion was from international commercial bank loans, and around $900 million consisted of loans and projects from international development banks.

As of 2010, the Tehran Stock Exchange traded the shares of more than 330 registered companies. Listed companies were valued at $100 billion in 2011.

Insurance premiums accounted for just under 1% of GDP in 2008, a figure partly attributable to low average income per head. Five state-owned insurance firms dominate the market, four of which are active in commercial insurance. The leading player is the Iran Insurance Company, followed by Asia, Alborz and Dana insurances. In 2001/02 third-party liability insurance accounted for 46% of premiums, followed by health insurance (13%), fire insurance (10%) and life insurance (9.9%).

Communications, electronics and IT

Broadcast media, including five national radio stations and five national television networks as well as dozens of local radio and television stations are run by the government. In 2008 there were 345 telephone lines and 106 personal computers for every 1,000 residents. Personal computers for home use became more affordable in the mid-1990s, since when demand for Internet access has increased rapidly. As of 2010, Iran also had the world's third largest number of bloggers(2010). In 1998 the Ministry of Post, Telegraph & Telephone (later renamed theMinistry of Information & Communication Technology) began selling Internet accounts to the general public. In 2006, revenues from the Iranian telecom industry were estimated at $1.2 billion. In 2006, Iran had 1,223 Internet Service Providers (ISPs), all private sector operated. As of 2014, Iran has the largest mobile market in the Middle East, with 83.2 million mobile subscriptions and 8 million smart-phones in 2012.

According to the World Bank, Iran's information and communications technology sector had a 1.4% share of GDP in 2008. Around 150,000 people work in this sector, including 20,000 in the software industry. 1,200 IT companies were registered in 2002, 200 in software development. In 2014 software exports stood at $400 million. By the end of 2009, Iran's telecom market was the fourth-largest in the Middle East at $9.2 billion and was expected to reach $12.9 billion by 2014 at a compound annual growth rate of 6.9%.

Transport

Iran has an extensive paved road system linking most towns and all cities. In 2011 the country had 173,000 kilometres (107,000 mi) of roads, of which 73% were paved. In 2007 there were approximately 100 passenger cars for every 1,000 inhabitants. Trains operated on 11,106 kilometres (6,901 mi) of track.

The country's major port of entry is Bandar-Abbas on the Strait of Hormuz. After arriving in Iran, imported goods are distributed by trucks and freight trains. The Tehran–Bandar-Abbas railroad, opened in 1995, connects Bandar-Abbas to Central Asia via Tehran and Mashhad. Other major ports include Bandar Anzali and Bandar Torkaman on the Caspian Sea and Khoramshahr and Bandar Imam Khomeini on thePersian Gulf. Dozens of cities have passenger and cargo airports. Iran Air, the national airline, was founded in 1962 and operates domestic and international flights. All large cities have bus transit systems and private companies provide intercity bus services. Tehran, Mashhad,Shiraz, Tabriz, Ahvaz and Isfahan are constructing underground railways. More than one million people work in the transportation sector, accounting for 9% of 2008 GDP.

International trade

Iran is a founding member of OPEC and the Organization of Gas Exporting Countries. Petroleum constitutes 80% of Iran's exports with a value of $46.9 billion in 2006. For the first time, the value of Iran's non-oil exports is expected to reach the value of imports at $43 billion in 2011. Pistachios, liquefied propane, methanol (methyl alcohol), hand-woven carpets and automobiles are the major non-oil exports. Copper, cement, leather, textiles, fruits, saffron and caviar are also export items of Iran.

Technical and engineering service exports in 2007–08 were $2.7 billion of which 40% of technical services went to Central Asia and the Caucasus, 30% ($350 million) to Iraq, and close to 20% ($205 million) to Africa. Iranian firms have developed energy, pipelines, irrigation, dams and power generation in different countries. The country has made non-oil exports a priority by expanding its broad industrial base, educated and motivated workforce and favorable location, which gives it proximity to an estimated market of some 300 million people in Caspian, Persian Gulf and some ECO countriesfurther east.

Total import volume rose by 189% from $13.7 billion in 2000 to $39.7 billion in 2005 and $55.189 billion in 2009. Iran's major commercial partners are China, India,Germany, South Korea, Japan, France, Russia and Italy. From 1950 until 1978, theUnited States was Iran's foremost economic and military partner, playing a major role in infrastructure and industry modernization. It is reported that around 80% of machinery and equipment in Iran is of German origin.

Since the mid-1990s, Iran has increased its economic cooperation with otherdeveloping countries in "south-south integration" including Syria, India, China, South Africa, Cuba and Venezuela. Iran's trade with India passed $13 billion in 2007, an 80% increase within a year. Iran is expanding its trade ties with Turkeyand Pakistan and shares with its partners the common objective to create a common market in West and Central Asia through ECO.

Since 2003, Iran has increased investment in neighboring countries such as Iraq and Afghanistan. In Dubai, UAE, it is estimated that Iranian expatriates handle over 20% of its domestic economy and account for an equal proportion of its population. Migrant Iranian workers abroad remitted less than $2 billion home in 2006. Between 2005 and 2009, trade between Dubai and Iran tripled to $12 billion; money invested in the local real estate market and import-export businesses, collectively known as the *Bazaar*, and geared towards providing Iran and other countries with required consumer goods. It is estimated that one third of Iran's imported goods and exports are delivered through the black market, underground economy, and illegal jetties, thus damaging the economy.

Foreign direct investment

In the 1990s and early 2000s, indirect oilfield development agreements were made with foreign firms, including buyback contracts in the oil sector whereby the contractor provided project finance in return for an allocated production share. Operation transferred to National Iranian Oil Company (NIOC) after a set number of years, completing the contract.

Unfavorable or complex operating requirements and international sanctions have hindered foreign investment in the country, despite liberalization of relevant regulations in the early 2000s. Iran absorbed $24.3 billion of foreign investment between the Iranian calendar years 1993 and 2007. The EIU estimates that Iran's net FDI will rise by 100% between 2010 and 2014.

Foreign investors concentrated their activities in the energy, vehicle manufacture, copper mining, construction, utilities, petrochemicals, clothing, food and beverages, telecom and pharmaceuticals sectors. Iran is a member of the World Bank'sMultilateral Investment Guarantee Agency. In 2006, the combined net worth of Iranian citizens abroad was about 1.3 trillion dollars.

The economic impact of a partial lifting of sanctions extends beyond the energy sector; the New York Times reported that "consumer-oriented companies, in particular, could find opportunity in this country with 81 million consumers, many of whom are young and prefer Western products". The consumer-goods market is expected to grow by $100 billion by 2020.Iran is considered "a strong emerging market play" by investment and trading firms. Opening Iran's market place toforeign investment could also be a boon to competitive multinational firms operating in a variety of manufacturing and service sectors, worth $600 billion to $800 billion in new investment opportunities over the next decade.

Iran and the World Trade Organization

Iran has held observer status at the World Trade Organization (WTO) since 2005. Although the United States has consistently blocked its bid to join the organization, observer status came in a goodwill gesture to ease nuclear negotiations between Iran and the international community. With exports of 60 products with revealedcomparative advantage, Iran is the 65th "most complex country".

Should Iran eventually gain membership status in the WTO, among other prerequisites, copyrights will have to be enforced in the country. This will require a major overhaul.

The country is hoping to attract billions of dollars' worth of foreign investment by creating a more favorable investment climate through freer trade. Free trade zones such as Qeshm,Chabahar and Kish Island are expected to assist in this process. Iran allocated $20 billion in 2010 to loans for the launch of twenty trade centers in other countries.

International sanctions

After the Iranian Revolution in 1979, the United States ended its economic and diplomatic ties with Iran, banned Iranian oil imports and froze approximately $11 billion of its assets. In 1996, the U.S. Government passed the Iran and Libya Sanctions Act (ILSA) which prohibits U.S. (and non-U.S.) companies from investing and trading with Iran in amounts of more than $20 million annually. Since 2000 exceptions to this restriction have been made for items including pharmaceuticalsand medical equipment.

Iran's nuclear program has been the subject of contention with the West since 2006 over suspicions of its intentions. The UN Security Council imposed sanctions against select companies linked to the nuclear program, thus furthering the country'seconomic isolation. Sanctions notably bar nuclear, missile and many military exports to Iran and target investments in oil, gas and petrochemicals, exports of refined petroleum products, as well as the Iranian Revolutionary Guard Corps, banks, insurance, financial transactions and shipping. In 2012 the European Union tightened its own sanctions by joining thethree decade-old US oil embargo against Iran. In 2015, Iran and the P5+1 reached a deal on the nuclear programthat will remove the main sanctions by early 2016. Even though Iran can trade in its own currency some problems subsist mainly due to the fact that it cannot transact in US dollars freely. Given its large reserves of oil and gas, the Iranian rial could become a world reserve currency if parity is established with oil and gas.

Effects

According to Undersecretary of State William Burns, Iran may be losing as much as $60 billion annually in energy investment. Sanctions are making imports 24% more costly on average. In addition, the latest round of sanctions could cost Iran annually $50 billion in lost oil revenues. Iran is increasingly using barter tradebecause its access to the international dollar payment system has been denied. According to Iranian officials, large-scale withdrawal by international companies represents an "opportunity" for domestic companies to replace them.

The IEA estimated that Iranian exports fell to a record of 860,000 bpd in September 2012 from 2.2 million bpd at the end of 2011. This fall led to a drop in revenues and clashes on the streets of Tehran when the local currency, the rial, collapsed. September 2012 output was Iran's lowest since 1988.

The U.S. Energy Department has warned that imposing oil embargoes on Iran would increase world oil prices by widening the gap between supply and demand. According to the U.S. Iran could reduce the world price of crude petroleum by 10%, saving the United States annually $76 billion (at the proximate 2008 world oil price of $100/bbl).

According to NIAC, sanctions cost the United States over $175 billion in lost trade and 279,000 lost job opportunities.Between 2010 and 2012, sanctions cost the E.U. states more than twice as much as the United States in terms of lost trade revenue. Germany was hit the hardest, losing between $23.1 and $73.0 billion between 2010–2012, with Italy and France following at $13.6-$42.8 billion and $10.9-$34.2 billion respectively.

GDP growth turned negative in 2013 (-5%). The unofficial unemployment rate was 20% by mid-2012. Oil exports dropped to 1.4 million bpd in 2014 from 2.5 million bpd in 2011. By 2013, Iran had $80 billion in foreign exchange reserves frozen overseas. Automobile production declined 40% between 2011 and 2013. According to the U.S. government in 2015, Iran's economy has reached a point where it is "fundamentally incapable of recovery" without a nuclear accommodation with the West.

The tentative rapprochement between Iran and the US, which began in the second half of 2013, has the potential to become a world-changing development, and unleash tremendous geopolitical and economic opportunities, if it is sustained if Iran and the US were to achieve a diplomatic breakthrough, geopolitical tensions in the Middle East could decline sharply, and Iran could come to be perceived as a promisingemerging market in its own right.

8

Demographics

Iran's population increased dramatically during the later half of the 20th century, reaching about 80 million by 2016. In recent years, however, Iran's birth rate has dropped significantly. Studies project that Iran's rate of population growth will continue to slow until it stabilizes above 100 million by 2050. More than half of Iran's population is under 35 years old (2012).

In 2009, the number of households stood at 15.3 million (4.8 persons per household). Families earn some 11.8 million rials (about $960) per month on average (2012).

According to the OECD/World Bank statistics population growth in Iran from 1990 to 2008 was 17.6 million and 32%. The literacy rate was 80% in 2007, and 85% in 2008.

Languages and ethnic groups

The largest linguistic group comprises speakers of Iranian languages, like modern Persian, Kurdish, Gilaki, Mazandarani, Luri, Talysh, andBalochi. Speakers of Turkic languages, most notably Azerbaijanis, which is by far the second-most spoken language in the country, but also the Turkmen, and the Qashqai peoples, comprise a substantial minority. The remainder are primarily speakers of Semitic languagessuch as Arabic and Assyrian. There are small groups using other Indo-European languages such as Armenian, Russian, Pashto; Georgian (a member of the Kartvelian language family), spoken in a large pocket only by those Iranian Georgians that live in Fereydan, Fereydunshahr. Most of those Georgians who live in the north Iranian provinces ofGilan, Mazandaran, Isfahan, Tehran Province and the rest of Iran no longer speak the language but keep a Georgian conscience. TheCircassians in Iran, a very large minority in the past and speakers of the Circassian language, have been strongly assimilated and absorbed within the population in the past few centuries. However, significant pockets do exist spread over the country, and they are the second-largest Caucasus-derived group in the nation after the Georgians.

Jews have had a continuous presence in Iran since the time of Cyrus the Great of the Achaemenid Empire. In 1948, there were approximately 140,000–150,000 Jews living in Iran. According to the Tehran Jewish Committee, the Jewish population of Iran was (more recently) estimated at about 25,000 to 35,000, of which approximately 15,000 are in Tehran with the rest residing in Hamadan, Shiraz, Isfahan, Kermanshah, Yazd, Kerman, Rafsanjan, Borujerd, Sanandaj, Tabriz and Urmia. However, the official 2011 state census recorded only 8,756 Jews in Iran.

The CIA World Factbook (which is based on 2013 statistics) gives the following numbers for the languages spoken in Iran today: Persian, Luri, Gilaki and Mazandarani 66%; Azerbaijani and other Turkic languages 18%; Kurdish 10%; Arabic 2%;Baloch 2%; others 1% (Armenian, Georgian, Circassian, Assyrian, etc.).

Other sources, such as the Library of Congress, and the Encyclopedia of Islam (Leiden) give Iran's ethnic groups as following: Persians 65%, Azerbaijanis 16%, Kurds 7%, Lurs 6%, Arabs 2%, Baloch 2%, Turkmens 1%, Turkic tribal groups (e.g. Qashqai) 1%, and non-Persian, non-Turkic groups (e.g. Armenians, Georgians, Assyrians, Circassians, Basseri) less than 1%.

URBAN POPULATION

In addition to its international migration pattern, Iran also exhibits one of the steepest urban growth rates in the world according to the UN humanitarian information unit. According to 2015 population estimates, approximately 73.4 percent of Iran's population lives in urban areas, up from 27 percent in 1950.Changes in urbanization law and regulations eased the urbanization process of rural areas, which created more than 400 cities only in the period of 1996-2005.

RELIGIOUS AFFILIATIONS

About 99% of the Iranians are Muslims; 90% belong to the Shi'a branch of Islam, the official state religion, and about 9% belong to the

Sunni branch, which predominates in neighboring Muslim countries. Less than 1% non-Muslim minorities include Christians, Zoroastrians, Jews, Bahá'ís, Mandeans, and Yarsan. By far the largest group of Christians in Iran are Armenians under the Armenian Apostolic Church which has between 110,000, 250,000, and 300,000, adherents. There are hundreds of Christian churches in Iran.

The Bahá'í Faith, Iran's largest non-Muslim religious minority with a population around 300,000, is not officially recognized (and therefore not included in the census results), and has been persecuted during its existence in Iran. Since the 1979 revolution the persecution of Bahá'ís has increased with executions, the denial of civil rights and liberties, and the denial of access to higher education and employment. Unofficial estimates for the Assyrian Christian population range between 20,000, and 70,000. The number of IranianMandaeans is a matter of dispute. In 2009, there were an estimated 5,000 and 10,000 Mandaeans in Iran, according to the Associated Press. Whereas Alarabiya has put the number of Iranian Mandaeans as high as 60,000 in 2011.

Iranian citizens abroad

The term "Iranian citizens abroad" or " Iranian/Persian diaspora" refers to the Iranian people born in Iran and their children but living outside of Iran. Migrant Iranian workers abroad remitted less than two billion dollars home in 2006.

As of 2010, there are about four to five million Iranians living abroad, mostly in the United States, Canada, Europe, Persian Gulf States, Turkey, Australia and the broader Middle East. According to the 2000 Census and other independent surveys, there are an estimated 1 million Iranian-Americans living in the U.S., in particular, the Los Angeles area is estimated to be host to approximately 72,000 Iranians, earning the Westwood area of LA the nickname Tehrangeles. Other metropolises that have large Iranian populations include Dubai with 300,000 Iranians, Vancouver, London, Toronto, San Francisco Bay Area, Washington D.C., Buenos Aires, Mexico City, Stockholm, Berlin, Hamburg and Frankfurt. Their combined net worth is estimated to be $1.3 trillion.

Note that this differs from the other Iranian peoples living in other areas of Greater Iran, who are of related ethnolinguistical family, speaking languages belonging to the Iranian languages which is a branch of Indo-European languages.

Refugee population

Iran hosts one of the largest refugee population in the world, with more than one million refugees, mostly from Afghanistan(80%) and Iraq (10%). Since 2006, Iranian officials have been working with the UNHCR and Afghan officials for theirrepatriation. Between 1979 and 1997, UNHCR spent more than US$1 billion on Afghan refugees in Pakistan but only $150 million on those in Iran. In 1999, the Iranian government estimated the cost of maintaining its refugee population at US$10 million per day, compared with the US$18 million UNHCR allocated for all of its operations in Iran in 1999. As of 2016, some 300,000 work permits have been issued for foreign nationals in Iran.

CIA World Factbook demographic statistics

The following demographic statistics are from the CIA World Factbook, unless otherwise indicated.

Age structure

0-14 years: 23.69% (male 9,937,715/female 9,449,716)

15-24 years: 17.58% (male 7,386,826/female 6,998,188)

25-54 years: 46.87% (male 19,534,794/female 18,817,480)

55-64 years: 6.58% (male 2,650,049/female 2,731,997)

65 years and over: 5.28% (male 1,990,961/female 2,326,544) (2015 est.)

Median age

total: 28.8 years

male: 28.6 years

female: 29.1 years (2015 est.)

Population growth rate

1.2% (2015 est.)

Birth rate

17.99 births/1,000 population (2015 est.)

Death rate

5.94 deaths/1,000 population (2015 est.)

Urbanization

urban population: 73.4% of total population (2015)

rate of urbanization: 2.07% annual rate of change (2010-15 est.)

Sex ratio

at birth: 1.05 male(s)/female

0-14 years: 1.05 male(s)/female

15-24 years: 1.06 male(s)/female

25-54 years: 1.04 male(s)/female

55-64 years: 0.97 male(s)/female

65 years and over: 0.86 male(s)/female

total population: 1.03 male(s)/female (2015 est.)

Life expectancy at birth

total population: 71.15 years

male: 69.56 years

female: 72.82 years (2015 est.)

Total fertility rate

1.83 children born/woman (2015 est.)

Youth literacy

definition: age 15-24 can read and write

total population: above 90%

male youth: 98%

female youth: 98.0% (2008 est.)

Genetics

Y-chromosome DNA

Y-Chromosome DNA Y-DNA represents the male lineage, the Iranian Y-chromosome pool is as follows where haplogroups,R1 (25%), J2 (23%) G (14%), J1 (8%) E1b1b (5%), L (4%), Q (4%), comprise more than 85% of the total chromosomes.

Mitochondrial DNA

Mitochondrial DNA mtDNA represents the female lineage. The Iranian mitochondrial DNA shows more Western Eurasian lineages than the Y-DNA lineages. Nonetheless, a West Eurasian MtDNA makes up over 90% of the Iranian population on average. (2013).

Among them, U3b3 lineages appear to be restricted to populations of Iran and the Caucasus, while the sub-cluster U3b1a is common in the whole Near East region.

In Iran outliers in the Y-chromosomes and Mitochondrial DNA gene pool are consisted by the north Iranian ethnicities, such as the Gilaki's and Mazandarani's, who's genetic build up including chromosomal DNA are nearly identical to the major South Caucasian ethnicites, namely the Georgians, Armenians and Azerbaijani's. Other outliers are made by the Baloch people, representing a mere 1-2% of the total Iranian population, who have more patrilinial and mitochondrial DNA lines leaning towards northwest South Asian ethnic groups.

Levels of genetic variation in Iranian populations are comparable to the other groups from the Caucasus, Anatolia andEurope.

PEOPLE OF IRANIAN ANCESTRY

Tats (Caucasus)

The "Tats" are an Iranian people, presently living within Azerbaijan and Russia (mainly Southern Dagestan). The Tats are part of the indigenous peoples of Iranian origin in the Caucasus.

Tats use the Tat language, a southwestern Iranian language and a variety of Persian Azerbaijani and Russianare also spoken. Tats are mainly Shia Muslims, with a significant Sunni Muslim minority. Likely the ancestors of modern Tats settled in South Caucasus when the Sassanid Empire from the 3rd to 7th centuries built cities and founded military garrisons to strengthen their positions in this region.

Parsis

The Parsis are the close-knit Zoroastrian community based primarily in India but also found in Pakistan. Parsis are descended from Persian Zoroastrians who emigrated to the Indian subcontinent over 1,000 years ago. Indian census data (2001) records 69,601 Parsis in India, with a concentration in and around the city of Mumbai (previously known as Bombay). There are approximately 8,000 Parsis elsewhere on the subcontinent, with an estimated 2,500 Parsis in the city of Karachiand approximately 50 Parsi families in Sri Lanka. The number of Parsis worldwide is estimated to be fewer than 100,000 (Eliade, 1991:254).

Iranis

In Pakistan and India, the term "Irani" has come to denote Iranian Zoroastrians who have migrated to Pakistan and India within the last two centuries, as opposed to most Parsis who arrived in India over 1000 years ago. Many of them moved during the Qajar era, when persecution of Iranian Zoroastrians was rampant. They are culturally and linguistically closer to the Zoroastrians of Iran. Unlike the Parsis, they speak a Dari dialect, the language spoken by the Iranian Zoroastrians inYazd and Kerman. Their last names often resemble modern Iranian names, however Irani is a common surname among them. In India they are mostly located in modern-day Mumbai while in Pakistan they are mostly located in modern-dayKarachi. In both Pakistan and India, they are famous for their restaurants and tea-houses. Some, such as Ardeshir Irani, have also become very famous in cinema.

Ajam (Bahrain)

The "Ajam" are an ethnic community of Bahrain, of Iranian origin. They have traditionally been merchants living in specific quarters of Manama and Muharraq. The Iranians who adhere to Shiite sect of Islam are Ajam, and they are different from theHuwala, who are Sunnis and some of them have Arab origin.

In addition to this, many names of ancient villages in Bahrain are of Persian origin. It is believed that these names were given during the Safavid rule of Bahrain (1501–1722). i.e. Karbabad, Salmabad, Karzakan, Duraz, Barbar, which indicates that the history of Ajams is much older.

Huwala

Huwala are the descendants of Persians and Persian Arabs who belong to the Sunni sect of Islam. Huwala migrated fromAhwaz in Iran to the Persian Gulf in the seventeenth and eighteenth century.

ETHNICITIES IN IRAN

A majority of the population of Iran (approximately 67–80%) consists of Iranic peoples. The largest groups in this category include Persians (who form the majority of the Iranian population) and Kurds, with smaller communities including Gilakis, Mazandaranis,Lurs, Tats, Talysh, and Baloch.

Turkic groups constitute a substantial minority of about 15–24%, the largest group being the Azerbaijani, who are the second largest ethnicity in Iran as well as the largest minority group. Other Turkic groups include the Turkmen and Qashqai peoples.

Arabs account for about 2–3% of the Iranian population. The remainder, amounting to about 1% of Iranian population, consists of a variety of minor groups, mainly comprising Assyrians, Armenians,Georgians, Circassians, and Mandaeans.

At the beginning of the 20th century, Iran had a total population of just below 10 million, with an approximate ethnic composition of: 6 million Persians (60%), 2.5 million Azeris (25%), 0.2 million Mazandaranis and Gilakis each (2% each).

IRANIAN-SPEAKING PEOPLES

Persians

Iran used to be called Persia until 1935, by that definition all Iranians were considered Persian regardless of their ethnicity. The term "Persians" refers to an ethnic group who speak the Western dialect of Persian and live in the modern country of Iran as well as the descendants of the people who emigrated from the territory of modern-day Iran to other countries.

Ethnic Persians inhabit traditionally the Tehran province, Isfahan province, Fars province, Alborz province, Razavi Khorasan, South Khorasan, Yazd province, Kerman province, Bushehr province, Hormozgan province, Markazi province(Arak), Qom province, Semnan province, Qazvin province, the majority of Hamadan province including the city of Hamadan, majority of the North Khorasan, majority of Khuzestan province, northern half of Sistan and Baluchistan (Zabol), southern and western half of Golestan province including the provincial capital of Gorgan. The majority of the Iranian immigrants in the West and other parts of the world also hail from Persian speaking cities especially fromTehran.

According to the CIA World Factbook, Persians in Iran constitute up to 61% of the country's population. Another source, Library of Congress states Iran's Persians compose 65% of the country's population. However, other sources mention that Persians only comprise 50.5%, or 55.3%. All these numbers include the Mazandaranis and Gilakis as Persian people, though the CIA World Factbook makes a distinction between the Persian language and the Mazandaraniand Gilaki language, respectively.

Kurds

Iranian Kurds make up the majority of the population of Kordestan province, and, together with the Azeris, they are one of the two main ethnic groups in West Azerbaijan province. In West Azerbaijan province, Kurds are concentrated in parts of the southern and western parts of the province. The Feyli tribe of Kurds also make up a significant proportion of the populations of Kermanshah and Ilam provinces, although Kermanshahi and Ilamian Kurds are Shia Muslims, in contrast to the mainstream Kurds, who are adherents of Sunni Islam. Kurmanji-speaking Kurds also form a plurality in North Khorasan province.

Mazandaranis

The Mazanderani people or Tabari people are an Iranian people whose homeland is the North of Iran (Tabaristan). Like the closely related Gilaks, the Mazanderanis are a Caspian people who inhabit the south coast of the Caspian Sea, part of the historical region that used to be called Tabaristan and are currently one of the main ethnic groups residing in the northern parts of Iran. They speak the Mazandarani language, a language native to around 4 million people, but all of them can speak Persian. The Alborz mountains mark the southern boundary of Mazanderani settlement. The Mazanderani peoples number differs between three million and four million (2006 estimate) and many of them are farmers and fishermen.

Gilaks

The Gilaki people or Gilaks are an Iranian people native to the northern Iran province of Gilan and are one of the main ethnic groups residing in the northern part of Iran. Gilaks, along with the closely related Mazandarani people, comprise part of the Caspian people, who inhabit the southern and southwestern coastal regions of the Caspian Sea. They speak theGilaki language and their population is estimated to be between 3 to 4 million (4% of the population). Gilaki people live both alongside the Alborz mountains, and in the surrounding plains. Consequentially, those living along the northern side of the Alborz mountains tend to raise livestock, while those living in the plains farm. Gilaks play an important role in provincial and national economy, supplying a large portion of the region's agricultural staples, such as rice, grains,tobacco and tea. Other major industries include fishing and caviar exports, and the production of silk.

Lurs

Lur people speak the Luri language and inhabit parts of west – south western Iran. Most Lur are Shi'a. They are the fourth largest ethnic group in Iran after the Persians, Azeri, and Kurds. They occupy Lorestan, Chaharmahal and Bakhtiari, Khuzestan, Isfahan, Fars, Bushehr and Kuh-Gilu-Boir Ahmed provinces.

The authority of tribal elders remains a strong influence among the nomadic population. It is not as dominant among the settled urban population.

As is true inBakhtiari and Kurdish societies, Lur women have much greater freedom than women in other groups within the region.The Luri language is Indo-European. The Lur people may be related to the Kurds from whom they "apparently began to be distinguished from... 1,000 years ago." The Sharafnama of Sharaf Khan Bidlisi "mentioned two Lur dynasties among the five Kurdish dynasties that had in the past enjoyed royalty or the highest form of sovereignty or independence." In the Mu'jam Al-Buldan of Yaqut al-Hamawi mention is made of the Lurs as a Kurdish tribe living in the mountains between Khuzestan andIsfahan. The term Kurd according to Richard Frye was used for all Iranian nomads (including the population of Luristan as well as tribes in Kuhistan and Baluchis in Kerman) for all nomads, whether they were linguistically connected to the Kurds or not.

Talysh

The Talysh of Iran are about 430,000 and live mostly in the province of Gilan in north of Iran. They are indigenous to a region shared between Azerbaijan and Iran which spans the South Caucasus and the southwestern shore of the Caspian Sea. Another significant amount of Talysh live therefore also in the Republic of Azerbaijan.

Tats

The Tats of Iran are centralised near the Alborz Mountains, especially in the south of Qazvin province. They speak the Tati language, consisting of a group of northwestern Iranian dialects closely related to the Talysh language. Persian and Azeriare also spoken. Tats of Iran are mainly Shia Muslims and about 300,000 population.

Baloch

The Baloch people of Iran live in southern and central parts of Sistan and Baluchestan province, one of the most remote and isolated areas of Iran, especially from the majority of the people. The northern part of the province is called Sistan and 63% of the population are ethnic Baloch while the rest are Persian Sistani. The Baloch are Sunni Muslims, in contrast to the Sistani Persians who are adherents of Shia Islam. The capital of Sistan and Baluchestan is Zahedan and is inhabited by Baloch people, the next largest city of the province is Zabol in Sistan and is inhabited predominantly by Persians. The town of Jask in neighbouring Hormozgan Province is also inhabited by Baloch people. They form one of the smallest ethnicities in Iran.

TURKIC

The largest Turkic group in Iran are the Iranian Azerbaijanis, forming the second largest ethnicity in the nation after the majority Persian population.

Smaller Turkic groups account for about 2% of Iranian population between them, about half of this number is accounted for by the Iranian Turkmen, the other half comprises various tribal confederacies such as theQashqai or the Khorasani Turks.

Azerbaijanis

Iranian Azerbaijanis (also known as Iranian Turks) are a Turkic-speaking people of mixed Caucasian, Iranian and Turkic origin, who live mainly in Iranian Azerbaijan. Their number or percentage in the country are estimated differently as they are often mentioned to be politically motivated. They are the second largest ethnicity in Iran and the largest ethnic minority. The main estimations are stated below :

- 15%
- 15.5%
- 16%
- 17%
- 21.6
- 24-25 percent
- Minahan, James (2002). Encyclopedia of the Stateless Nations: S-Z. Greenwood Publishing Group. p. 1765. ISBN 978-0-313-32384-3 "Approximately (2002e) 18,500,000 Southern Azeris in

Iran, concentrated in the northwestern provinces of East and West Azerbaijan. It is difficult to determine the exact number of Southern Azeris in Iran, as official statistics are not published detailing Iran's ethnic structure. Estimates of the Southern Azeri population range from as low as 12 million up to 40% of the population of Iran – that is, nearly 27 million..."

In the Azerbaijan region, the population consists mainly of Azerbaijanis. Azeris form the largest ethnic group in Iranian Azerbaijan, while Kurds are the second largest group and a majority in many cities of West Azerbaijan Province. Iranian Azerbaijan is one of the richest and most densely populated regions of Iran. Many of these various linguistic, religious, and tribal minority groups, and Azeris themselves have settled widely outside the region. The majority of Azeris are followers of Shi'a Islam. Iranian Azerbaijanis mainly reside in the northwest provinces, including the Iranian Azerbaijan provinces (East Azerbaijan, West Azerbaijan, Ardabil, and Zanjan), as well as regions of the North to Hamadan Countyand Shara District in the East Hamadan Province, and some regions of Qazvin Province. Some Azerbaijani minorities also live in Markazi, Kordestan, Gilan and Kermanshah provinces. Azerbaijanis also make up significant minorities in various parts of central Iran, especially Tehran, where they constitute around 25% to one-third of the population.

Turkmen

Iranian Turkmen are primarily concentrated in the provinces of Golestân and North Khorasan. The largest Turkmen city in Iran is Gonbad-e Kavoos, followed by Bandar Torkaman.

Turkic tribal groups

The Qashqai people mainly live in the provinces of Fars, Khuzestan and southern Isfahan, especially around the city ofShiraz in Fars. They speak the Qashqai language which is a member of the Turkic family of languages. The Qashqai were originally nomadic pastoralists and some remain so today. The traditional nomadic Qashqai travelled with their flocks each year from the summer highland pastures north of Shiraz roughly 480 km or 300 mi south to the winter pastures on lower (and warmer) lands near the Persian Gulf, to the southwest of Shiraz. The majority, however, have now become partially or wholly sedentary. The trend towards settlement has been increasing markedly since the 1960s.

The Khorasani Turks are Turkic-speaking people inhabiting parts of north-eastern Iran, and in the neighbouring regions ofTurkmenistan up to beyond the Amu Darya River. They speak the Khorasani Turkic and live in North Khorasan, Razavi Khorasan, and Golestan provinces alongside Turkmens.

SEMITIC

Arabs

2% of Iran's citizens are Arabs. A 1998 report by UNCHR reported 1 million of them live in border cities of Khuzestan Province, they are believed to constitute 20% to 25% of the population in the province, most of whom being Shi'a. InKhuzestan, Arabs are a minority in the province. They are the dominant ethnic group only in Shadegan, Hoveyzeh andSusangerd, a minority in the rural areas of Abadan (The city of Abadan is inhabited by ethnic Persians who speak the Abadani dialect), together with Persians, Arabs are one of the two main ethnic groups in Ahvaz. All other cities in Khuzestan province, are either inhabited by the Lur, Bakhtiari or Persian ethnic groups. The historically large and oil rich cities like Mahshahr, Behbahan, Masjed Soleyman, Izeh, Dezful, Shushtar, Andimeshk, Shush, Ramhormoz, Baghemalak, Gotvand, Lali, Omidieh, Aghajari, Hendijan, Ramshir, Haftkel, Bavi are inhabited by people who speak either Luri, Bakhtiari and Persian languages. There are smaller communities in Qom where there are a significant number of Arabs being of Lebanese descent, as well as Razavi Khorasan and Fars provinces. Iranian Arab communities are also found in Bahrain, Iraq, Lebanon, Kuwait, United Arab Emirates, and Qatar.

Assyrians

The Assyrian people of Iran are a Semitic people who speak modern Assyrian, a neo-Aramaic language descended fromClassical Syriac, and are Eastern Rite Christians belonging mostly to the Assyrian Church of the East and, to a lesser extent, to the Chaldean Catholic Church, Syriac Orthodox Church and Ancient Church of the East. They share a common identity, rooted in shared linguistic and religious traditions, with Assyrians in Iraq and elsewhere in the Middle East such asSyria and Turkey, as well as with the Assyrian diaspora.

The Assyrian community in Iran numbered approximately 200,000 prior to the Islamic Revolution of 1979. However, after the revolution many Assyrians left the country, primarily for the United States, and the 1996 census counted only 32,000 Assyrians. Current estimates of the Assyrian population in Iran range from 32,000 (as of 2005) to 50,000 (as of 2007). The Iranian capital, Tehran, is home to the majority of Iranian Assyrians; however, approximately 15,000 Assyrians reside in northern Iran, in Urmia and various Assyrian villages in the surrounding area.

Jews

Judaism is one of the oldest religions practiced in Iran and dates back to late biblical times. The biblical books of Isaiah, Daniel, Ezra, Nehemiah, Chronicles, and Esther contain references to the life and experiences of Jews in Iran.

By various estimates, 10,800 Jews remain in Iran, mostly in Tehran, Isfahan, and Shiraz. BBC reported Yazd is home to ten Jewish families, six of them related by marriage, however some estimate the number is much higher. Historically, Jews maintained a presence in many more Iranian cities. Iran contains the largest Jewish population of any Muslim country.

A number of groups of Jews of Iran have split off since ancient times. They are now recognized as separate communities, such as the Bukharan Jews and Mountain Jews. In addition, there are several thousand in Iran who are, or who are the direct descendants of, Jews who have converted to Islam and the Bahá'í Faith.

Mandaeans

Iranian Mandaeans live mainly in the Khuzestan Province in southern Iran. Mandeans are a Mandaic speaking Semitic people who follow their own distinctive Gnostic religion Mandaeism, venerating John the Baptist as the true Messiah. Like theAssyrians of Iran, their origins lie in ancient Mesopotamia. They number some 10,000 people in Iran, though Alarabiya has put their number as high as 60,000 in 2011.

CAUCASUS-DERIVED GROUPS

Armenians

The current Iranian-Armenian population is somewhere around 500,000. They mostly live in Tehran and Jolfa district. After the Iranian Revolution, many Armenians immigrated to Armenian diasporic communities in North America and western Europe. Today the Armenians are Iran's largest Christian religious minority, followed by Assyrians.

Georgians

Iranian Georgians are Twelver Shia Muslims, whereas the vast majority of Georgians elsewhere in the world are Christian.

The Georgian language is the only Caucasian language fully functioning in Iran and it's spoken only by those that live inFereydan and Fereydunshahr, and in smaller pockets all over Iran. Almost all other communities of Iranian Georgians in Iran have already lost their language, but retain a clear Georgian identity. Once a very large minority in Iran mainly due to mass deportations by the various early modern age and modern age Iranian empires (Safavids, Afsharids, and Qajars), of their Georgian subjects, nowadays, due to intermarrying and assimilating the number of Georgians in Iran is estimated to be over 100,000. However, the amount of Iranians with partial or assimilated Georgian ancestry is estimated to exceed millions.

The Georgian language is still used by many of the Georgians in Iran. The centre of Georgians in Iran is Fereydunshahr, a small city 150 km to the west of Isfahan. The western part of Isfahan province is historically called Fereydan. In this area there are 10 Georgian towns and villages around Fereydunshahr. In this region the old Georgian identity is retained the best compared to other places in Iran. In many major Iranian cities, such as Tehran, Isfahan, Karaj and Shiraz, and Rashtlive Georgians too.

In many other places such as Najafabad, Rahmatabad, Yazdanshahr and Amir Abad (near Isfahan) there are also Georgian pockets and villages. In Mazandaran Province in northern Iran, there are ethnic Georgians too. They live in the town ofBehshahr, and also in Behshahr county, in Farah Abad, and many other places, which are usually called "Gorji Mahalle" (Georgian Neighbourhood). Most of these Georgians no longer speak the Georgian language, but retain aspects ofGeorgian culture and a Georgian identity. Some argue that Iranian Georgians retain remnants of Christian traditions, but there is no evidence for this.

Circassians

Like with the Georgians, once a very large minority in Iran all the way from the Safavid to the Qajar era, the vast majority of the

Circassians have been assimilated into the population nowadays. However, significant numbers remain present, and they are the second-largest Caucasian ethnic group in the nation after the Georgians.

From Sir John Chardin's "Travels in Persia, 1673–1677":

There is scarce a Gentleman in Persia, whose Mother is not a Georgian, or a Circassian Woman; to begin with the King, who commonly is a Georgian, or a Circassian by the Mother's side.

Circassians alongside the Georgians were deported en masse by the Shah's to fulfil roles in the civil administration, the military, and the royal Harem, but also as craftsmen, farmers, amongst other professions. Circassian women were both in Ottoman Turkey and Persia desired for their beauty, while the men were known as fearsome warriors. Notable Iranians of Circassian descent of the past include Teresia Sampsonia, Shah Abbas II, Shah Suleiman I, Pari Khan Khanum (daughter ofShah Tahmasp, involved in many court intrigues), Shamkhal Sultan, Jamshid Beg (the assassinator of Shah Ismail II), andAnna Khanum.

Traces of Circassian settlements have lasted into the 20th century, and small pockets still exist scattered over the country, even after centuries of absorbing and assimilating, such as in Fars, Rasht, Aspas, Gilan,Mazandaran, and the capital Tehran (due to contemporary internal migration). Their total number nowadays is unknown due to heavy assimilation and lack of censuses based on ethnicity, but are known to be significant. Due to the same assimilation however, no sizeable number speaks the Circassian language anymore.

RECENT IMMIGRATION

Most of the large Circassian migrational waves towards mainland Iran stem from the Safavid and Qajar era, however a certain amount also stem from the relatively recent arrivals that migrated as the Circassians were displaced from the Caucasus in the 19th century. A Black African population exists due to historical slavery. A substantial number of Russiansarrived in the early 20th century as refugees from the Russian revolution, but their number has dwindled following the Iran crisis of 1946 and the Iranian Revolution. In the 20th to 21st centuries, there has been limited immigration to Iran fromTurkey, Iraqis (especially huge numbers during the 1970s known as Moaveds), Afghanistan (mostly arriving as refugees in 1978), Lebanese (especially in Qom, though a Lebanese community has been present in the nation for centuries), Indians(mostly arriving temporarily during the 1950s to 1970s, typically working as doctors, engineers, and teachers), Koreans(mostly in the 1970s as labour migrants) and China (mostly since the 2000s working in engineering or business projects). Limited immigration from Pakistan is partly due to labour migrants and partly to Balochi ties across the Iranian-Pakistani border. About 200,000 Iraqis arrived as refugees in 2003, mostly living in refugee camps near the border; an unknown number of these has since returned to Iraq.

Over the same period, there has also been substantial emigration from Iran, especially since the Iranian revolution (seeIranian diaspora, Human capital flight from Iran, Jewish exodus from Iran), especially to the United States, Canada, Germany,Israel, and Sweden.

9

Culture and Society

CULTURE OF IRAN

The culture of Iran or culture of Persia is one of the oldest in the world. Owing to its dominant geo-political position and culture in the world, Iran has directly influenced cultures and peoples as far away as Italy, Macedonia, and Greece to the West, Russia to the North, the Arabian Peninsula to the South, and South and East Asia to the East. Thus an eclectic cultural elasticity has been said to be one of the key defining characteristics of the Persian spirit and a clue to its historical longevity. Furthermore, Iran's culture has manifested itself in several facets throughout the history of Iran as well as theCaucasus, Central Asia, Anatolia, and Mesopotamia.

The article uses the words *Persian* and *Iranian* interchangeably, sometimes referring to the language and its speakers, and other times referring to the name of pre-20th century Iran, a nomenclature which survives from western explorers and orientalists. They are not the same and the cultures of the peoples of Greater Persia are the focus of this chapter.

Art

Iran has one of the richest art heritages in world history and encompasses many disciplines including architecture, painting, weaving, pottery, calligraphy,metalworking and stonemasonry. There is also a very vibrant Iranian modern and contemporary art scene.

Iranian art has gone through numerous phases. The unique aesthetics of Iran is evident from the Achaemenid reliefs in Persepolis to the mosaic paintings ofBishapur. The Islamic era brought drastic changes to the styles and practice of the arts, each dynasty with its own particular foci. The Qajarid era was the last stage of classical Persian art, before modernism was imported and suffused into elements of traditionalist schools of aesthetics.

Language and literature

Several languages are spoken in different regions of Iran. The predominant language and national language is Persian, which is spoken across the country.Azerbaijani is spoken primarily and widely in the northwest, Kurdish primarily in the west as well as Luri, Mazandarani and Gilaki at the Caspian Sea coastal regions,Arabic primarily in the Persian Gulf coastal regions, Balochi primarily in the desolate and remote far southeast, and Turkmen primarily in northern border regions. Smaller languages spread in other regions notably include Talysh, Georgian,Armenian, Assyrian, and Circassian, amongst others.

Persian literature inspired Goethe, Ralph Waldo Emerson, and many others, and it has been often dubbed as a most worthy language to serve as a conduit for poetry. Dialects of Persian are sporadically spoken throughout the region from China to Syria to Russia, though mainly in the Iranian Plateau.

Contemporary Iranian literature is influenced by classical Persian poetry, but also reflects the particularities of modern-day Iran, through writers such as Houshang Moradi-Kermani, the most translated modern Iranian author, and poet Ahmad Shamlou.

RELIGION IN IRAN

Zoroastrianism was the national faith of Iran for more than a millennium before theArab conquest. It has had an immense influence on Iranian philosophy, culture andart after the people of Iran converted to Islam.

Today of the 98% of Muslims living in Iran, around 89% are Shi'a and only around 9% are Sunni.This is quite the opposite trend of the percentage distribution of Shi'a to Sunni Islam followers in the rest of the Muslim population from state to state (primarily in the Middle East) and throughout the rest of the world.

Followers of the Baha'i faith comprise the largest non-Muslim minority in Iran. Followers of the Baha'i faith are scattered throughout small communities in Iran, although there seems to be a large population of people who follow the Baha'i faith in Tehran. Most of the Baha'i are of Persian descent, although there seem to be many among the Azerbaijani and Kurdish people. The Baha'i are severelypersecuted.

Followers of the Christian faith comprise around 250,000 Armenians, around 32,000 Assyrians, and a small number of Roman Catholic, Anglican, and Protestant Iranians that have been converted by missionaries in earlier centuries. Thus, Christians that live in Iran are primarily descendants of indigenous Christians that were converted during the 19th and 20th centuries. Judaism is an officially recognized faith in Iran, and in spite of the hostilities between Iran and Israel over the Palestinian issue, the millennia old Jewish community in Iran enjoys the right to practice their religion freely as well as a dedicated seat in parliament to a representative member of their faith. In addition to Christianity and Judaism, Zoroastrianismis another officially recognized religion in Iran, although followers of this faith do not hold a large population in Iran. In addition, although there have been isolated incidences of prejudice against Zoroastrians, most followers of this faith have not been persecuted for being followers of this faith.

HOLIDAYS IN IRAN

The Persian year begins in the vernal equinox: if the astronomical vernal equinox comes before noon, then the present day is the first day of the Persian year. If the equinox falls after noon, then the next day is the official first day of the Persian year. The Persian Calendar, which is the official calendar of Iran, is a solar calendar with a starting point that is the same as the Islamic calendar. According to the Iran Labor Code, Friday is the weekly day of rest. Government official working hours are from Saturday to Wednesday (from 8 am to 4 pm).

Although the date of certain holidays in Iran are not exact (due to the calendar system they use, most of these holidays are around the same time), some of the major public holidays in Iran include Oil Nationalization Day (20 March), Nowrooz—which is the Iranian equivalent of New Years (20 March), the Prophet's Birthday and Imam Sadeq (4 June), and the Death of Imam Khomeini (5 June). Additional holidays include The Anniversary of the Uprising Against the Shah (30 January), Ashoura (11 February), Victory of the 1979 Islamic Revolution (2 April), Sizdah-Bedar—Public Outing Day to end Nowrooz (1 April), and Islamic Republic Day (20 January).

WEDDING CEREMONIES

There are two stages in a typical wedding ritual in Iran. Usually both phases take place in one day. The first stage is known as "Aghd", which is basically the legal component of marriage in Iran. In this process, the Bride and Groom as well as their respective guardians sign a marriage contract. This phase usually takes place in the bride's home. After this legal process is over, the second phase, "Jashn-e Aroosi" takes place. In this step, which is basically the wedding reception, where actual feasts and celebrations are held, typically lasts from about 3–7 days. The ceremony takes place in a decorated room with flowers and a beautifully decorated spread on the floor. This spread is typically passed down from mother to daughter and is composed of very nice fabric such as "Termeh" (cashmere), "Atlas" (gold embroidered satin), or "Abrisham" (silk).

Items are placed on this spread: a Mirror (of fate), two Candelabras (representing the bride and groom and their bright future), a tray of seven multi-colored herbs and spices (including poppy seeds, wild rice, angelica, salt, nigella seeds, black tea, and frankincense). These herbs and spices play specific roles ranging from breaking spells and witchcraft, to blinding the evil eye, to burning evil spirits.

In addition to these herbs/spices, a special baked and decorated flatbread, a basket of decorated eggs, decorated almonds, walnuts and hazelnuts (in their shell to represent fertility), a basket of pomegranates/ apples (for a joyous future as these fruits are considered divine), a cup of rose water (from special Persian roses)—which helps perfume the air, a bowl made out of sugar (apparently to sweeten life for the newlywed couple), and a brazier holding burning coals and sprinkled with wild rue (as a way to keep the evil eye away and to purify the wedding ritual) are placed on the spread as well.

Finally, there are additional items that must be placed on the spread, including a bowl of gold coins (to represent wealth and prosperity), a scarf/shawl made of silk/fine fabric (to be held over the bride and groom's head at certain points in the ceremony), two sugar cones—which are ground above the bride and groom's head, thus symbolizing sweetness/happiness, a cup of honey (to sweeten life), a needle and seven strands of colored thread (the shawl that is held above the bride and groom's head is sewn together with the string throughout the ceremony), and a copy of the couple's Holy Book (other religions require different texts); but all of these books

symbolize God's blessing for the couple. An early age in marriage—
especially for brides—is a long documented feature of marriage in
Iran. While the people of Iran have been trying to legally change this
practice by implementing a higher minimum in marriage, there have
been countless blocks to such an attempt. Although the average age
of women being married has increased by about five years in the past
couple decades, young girls being married is still common feature of
marriage in Iran—even though there is an article in the Iranian Civil
Code that forbid the marriage of women younger than 15 years of age
and males younger than 18 years of age.

PERSIAN RUGS

In Iran, Persian rugs have always been a vital part of the Persian
culture. Iranians were some of the first people in history to weave
carpets. First deriving from the notion of basic need, the Persian rug
started out as a simple/pure weave of fabric that helped nomadic
people living in ancient Iran stay warm from the cold, damp ground.
As time progressed, the complexity and beauty of rugs increased to
a point where rugs are now bought as decorative pieces. Because of
the long history of fine silk and wool rug weaving in Iran, Persian rugs
are world-renowned as some of the most beautiful, intricately designed
rugs available. Around various places in Iran, rugs seem to be some
of the most prized possessions of the local people. Iran currently
produces more rugs and carpets than all other countries in the world
put together.

MODERN CULTURE

Cinema

With 300 international awards in the past 10 years, Iranian films
continue to be celebrated worldwide. The best known Persian directors
are Abbas Kiarostami, Majid Majidi, Jafar Panahi and Asghar Farhadi.

Contemporary art

There is a resurgence of interest in Iranian contemporary artists
and in artists from the larger Iranian diaspora. Key notables include
Shirin Aliabadi, Mohammed Ehsai, Ramin Haerizadeh, Rokni
Haerizadeh, Golnaz Fathi, Monir Shahroudy Farmanfarmaian, Parastou
Forouhar, Pouran Jinchi, Farhad Moshiri, Shirin Neshat, Parviz
Tanavoli, Y. Z. Kami, and Charles Hossein Zenderoudi.

Music

The music of Persia dates to before the days of Barbod in the royal Sassanid courts. This is where many music cultures trace their distant origins.

Architecture

Traditional tea-houses

There are countless numbers of traditional tea-houses (*chai khooneh*) throughout Iran, and each province features its own unique cultural presentation of this ancient tradition. However, there are certain traits which are common to all tea-houses, especially the most visible aspects, strong *chai* (tea) and the ever-present *ghalyanhookah*. Almost all tea-houses serve *baqleh*, steam boiled fava beans (in the pod), served with salt and vinegar, as well as a variety of desserts and pastries. Many tea-houses also serve full meals, typically a variety of kebabs, as well as regional specialties.

Persian gardens

The Persian garden was designed as a reflection of paradise on earth; the word "garden" itself coming from Persian roots. The special place of the garden in the Iranian heart can be seen in their architecture, in the ruins of Iran, and in their paintings.

Cuisine

Cuisine in Iran is considered to be one of the most ancient forms of cuisine around the world. Bread is arguably the most important food in Iran, with a large variety of different bread, some of the most popular of which include: nan and hamir, which are baked in large clay ovens (also called "tenurs"). In Iranian cuisine, there are many dishes that are made from dairy products. One of the most popular of which includes yoghurt ("mast") — which has a specific fermentation process that is widely put to use amongst most Iranians. In addition, mast is used to make soup and is vital in the production of oil. In addition to these dairy products, Iranian cuisine involves a lot of dishes cooked from rice. Some popular rice dishes include boiled rice with a variety of ingredients such as meats, vegetables, and seasonings ("plov") including dishes like chelo-horesh, shish kebab with rice, chelo-kebab, rice with lamb, meatballs with rice, and kofte (plain boiled rice). In addition, Iranian cuisine is famous for its sweets. One of the most famous of which includes "baklava" with almonds, cardamom, and egg yolks. Iranian sweets typically involve the use of honey, cinnamon, lime juice, and sprouted wheat grain. One very popular dessert drink in Iran, "sherbet sharbat-portagal", is made from a mixture of orange peel and orange juice boiled in thin sugar syrup and diluted with rose water. Just like the people of many Middle Eastern countries the most preferred drink of the people of Iran is tea (without milk) or "kakhve-khana".

SPORTS

- The game of Polo originated with Iranian tribes in ancient times and was regularly seen throughout the country until the revolution of 1979 where it became associated with the monarchy. It continues to be played, but only in rural areas and discreetly. Recently, as of 2005, it has been acquiring an increasingly higher profile. In March 2006, there was a highly publicised tournament and all significant matches are now televised.

- The Iranian Zoor Khaneh

WOMEN IN PERSIAN CULTURE

Since the 1979 Revolution, Iranian women have had more opportunities in some areas and more restrictions in others. One of the striking features of the Revolution was the large scale participation of women from traditional backgrounds in demonstrations leading up to the overthrow of the monarchy. The Iranian women who had gained confidence and higher education during the Pahlavi era participated in demonstrations against the Shah to topple the monarchy. The culture of education for women was established by the time of revolution so that even after the revolution, large numbers of women entered civil service and higher education, and in 1996 fourteen women were elected to the Islamic Consultative Assembly. In 2003, Iran's first woman judge during the Pahlavi era, Shirin Ebadi, won the Nobel Peace Prize for her efforts in promoting human rights.

According to a UNESCO world survey, at the primary level of enrollment Iran has the highest female to male ratio in the world among sovereign nations, with a female to male ratio of 1.22 : 1.00. By 1999, Iran had 140 female publishers, enough to hold an exhibition of books and magazines published by women. As of 2005, 65% of

Iran's university students and 43% of its salaried workers were women. and as of early 2007 nearly 70% of Iran's science and engineering students are women. This has led to many female school and university graduates being under-utilized. This is beginning to have an effect on Iranian society and was a contributing factor to protests by Iranian youth.

During recent decades, Iranian women have had significant presence in Iran's scientific movement, art movement, literary new wave and contemporary Iranian cinema. Women account for 60% of all students in the natural sciences, including one in five PhD students.

TRADITIONAL HOLIDAYS/CELEBRATIONS

Iranians celebrate the following days based on a solar calendar, in addition to important religious days of Islamic and Shiacalendars, which are based on a lunar calendar.

- Nowruz (Iranian New Year) - Starts from 21 March
- Sizdah be dar (Nature Day)
- Jashn-e-Tirgan (Water Festival)
- Jashn-e-Sadeh (Fire Festival)
- Jashn-e-Mehregan (Autumn Festival)
- Shab-e-Yalda (Winter Feast)
- Charshanbeh Suri

Traditional cultural inheritors of the old Persia

Like the Persian carpet that exhibits numerous colors and forms in a dazzling display of warmth and creativity, Persian culture is the glue that bonds the peoples of western and central Asia. The Caucasus and Central Asia "occupy an important place in the historical geography of Persian civilization. Much of the region was included in the Pre-Islamic Persian empires, and many of its ancient peoples either belonged to the Iranian branch of the Indo-European peoples (e.g. Medes andSoghdians), or were in close cultural contact with them (e.g. the Armenians). In the words of Iranologist Richard Nelson Frye:

Many times I have emphasized that the present peoples of central Asia, whether Iranian or Turkic speaking, have one culture, one religion, one set of social values and traditions with only language separating them.

The Culture of Persia has thus developed over several thousand years. But historically, the peoples of what are now Iran, Armenia,

Azerbaijan, Turkey, Georgia, are related to one another as part of the larger group of peoples of the Greater Iranian cultural and historical sphere. The Northern Caucasus is well within the sphere of influence of Persian culture as well, as can be seen from the many remaining relics, ruins, and works of literature from that region.(e.g. 1) (e.g. 2)

Contributions to humanity in ancient history

From the humble brick, to the windmill, Persians have mixed creativity with art and offered the world numerous contributions. What follows is a list of just a few examples of the cultural contributions of Greater Iran.

- (10,000 BC) - Earliest known domestication of the goat.
- (6000 BC) - The modern brick. Some of the oldest bricks found to date are Persian, from c. 6000 BC.
- (5000 BC) - Invention of wine. Discovery made by University of Pennsylvaniaexcavations at Hajji Firuz Tepe in northwestern Iran.
- (5000 BC) - Invention of the Tar (lute), which led to the development of theguitar.
- (3000 BC) - The ziggurat. The Sialk ziggurat, according to the Cultural Heritage Organization of Iran, predates that of Ur or any other of Mesopotamia's 34 ziggurats.
- (3000 BC) - A game resembling backgammon appears in the east of Iran.
- (1400 BC - 600 BC) - Zoroastrianism: where the first prophet of a monotheistic faith arose according to some scholars, claiming Zoroastrianism as being "the oldest of the revealed credal religions, which has probably had more influence on mankind directly or indirectly, more than any other faith".
- (576 BC - 529 BC) - The Cyrus Cylinder: The world's first charter of human rights.
- (576 BC - 529 BC) - Under the rule of Cyrus the Great, Cyrus frees the Jews from Babylonian captivity.
- (521 BC) - The game of Polo.
- (500 BC) - First Banking System of the World, at the time of the Achaemenid, establishment of Governmental Banks to help farmers at the time of drought, floods, and other natural disasters in form of loans and forgiveness loans to restart their

farms and husbandries. These Governmental Banks were effective in different forms until the end of Sassanian Empire before invasion of Arabs to Persia.

- (500 BC) - The word Check has a Persian root in old Persian language. The use of this document as a check was in use from Achaemenid time to the end of Sassanian Empire. The word of [Bonchaq, or Bonchagh] in modern Persian language is new version of old Avestan and Pahlavi language "Check". In Persian it means a document which resembles money value for gold, silver and property. By law people were able to buy and sell these documents or exchange them.

- (500 BC) - World's oldest staple.

- (500 BC) - The first taxation system (under the Achaemenid Empire).

- (500 BC) - "Royal Road" - the first courier post.

- (500 BC) - Source for introduction of the domesticated chicken into Europe.

- (500 BC) - First cultivation of spinach.

- (400 BC) - Yakhchals, ancient refrigerators.

- (400 BC) - Ice cream.

- (250 BC) - Original excavation of a Suez Canal, begun under Darius, completed under the Ptolemies.

- (50 AD) - Peaches, a fruit of Chinese origin, were introduced to the west through Persia, as indicated by their Latinscientific name, *Prunus persica*, from which (by way of the French) we have the English word "peach."

- (271 AD) - Academy of Gundishapur - The first hospital.

- (700 AD) - The cookie.

- (700 AD) - The windmill.

- (864 AD - 930 AD) - First systematic use of alcohol in Medicine: Rhazes.

- (1000 AD) - Tulips were first cultivated in medieval Persia.

- (1000 AD) - Introduction of paper to the west.

- (935 AD - 1020 AD) - Ferdowsi writes the Shahnama (Book of Kings) that resulted in the revival of Iranian culture and the expansion of the Iranian cultural sphere.

- (980 AD - 1037 AD) - Avicenna, a physician, writes The Canon of Medicine one of the foundational manuals in the history of modern medicine.

- (1048 AD - 1131 AD) - Khayyam, one of the greatest polymaths of all time, presents a theory of heliocentricity to his peers. His contributions to laying the foundations of algebra are also noteworthy.

- (1207 AD - 1273 AD) - Rumi writes poetry and in 1997, the translations were best-sellers in the United States.

- Algebra and Trigonometry: Numerous Iranians were directly responsible for the establishment of Algebra, the advancement of Medicine and Chemistry, and the discovery of Trigonometry.

- Qanat, subterranean aqueducts.

- Wind catchers, ancient air residential conditioning.

10

Tourism

Tourism in Iran is diverse, providing a range of activities from hiking and skiing in theAlborz and Zagros mountains, to beach holidays by the Persian Gulf and the Caspian Sea. The Iranian government has been making concerted efforts to attract tourists to the various destinations in the country and arrivals have increased during the past years. Kish Islandalone attracts around 1 million visitors per year, the majority of whom are Iranian but also this its attractive for non-Iranian Muslim who like to have beach holiday with Islamic style that let men and women use separate beaches .

Before the Iranian revolution, tourism was characterized by significant numbers of visitors traveling to Iran for its diverse attractions, boasting cultural splendours and a diverse and beautiful landscape suitable for a range of activities. Tourism declined dramatically during the Iran–Iraq War in the 1980s.

Since the Iranian revolution in 1979, the majority of foreign visitors to Iran have been religious pilgrims and business people, In Iran there are many Shi'ite Shrines, the two main ones being Imam Reza Shrine in Mashhad and Fatimah al-Ma'sûmah Shrine in Qom Each year millions of pilgrims from Iran and other Shi'ite countries visit these holy places.Official figures do not distinguish between those traveling to Iran for business and those coming for pleasure, and they also include a large number of diaspora Iranians returning to visit their families in Iran or making pilgrimages to holy Shia sites near Mashhad, Qom and else where . Domestic tourism in Iran is one of the largest in the world. the government continues to project strong rises in visitor numbers and tourism revenue for the foreseeable future, and to talk of projects to build an additional 100 hotels, for example, to expand its currently limited stock. In 2013, the number of foreign tourists in Iran reached 4.76 million, contributing more than $2 billion to the national economy. The strong devaluation of the Iranian Rial since early 2012 is also a positive element for tourism in Iran. Over five million tourists visited Iran in the fiscal year of 2014-2015, ending March 21, four percent more year-on-year.

According to a report published by World Travel and Tourism Council in 2015 the size of its tourism industry – including cultural and ecotourism as major components of it – is estimated as having the potential to create jobs for 1,285,500 and rise by 4.1% pa to 1,913,000 jobs in 2025. based on the report in the year of 2014 Travel & Tourism directly supported 413,000 jobs (1.8% of total employment). This is expected to rise by 4.4% in 2015 and rise by 4.3% pa to 656,000 jobs (2.2% of total employment) by 2025.

FOREIGN VISITORS

The most up-to-date figures from the World Tourism Organisation for the origin of visitors to Iran show that building up visitors from the Islamic and wider Asian world will have to start from a low base. Around three-quarters of those entering Iran in 1999 came from Europe. According to the New York Times, unlike most Americans who stopped visiting Iran after the Revolution, European tourists continued to visit the country in similar numbers after the revolution. This was mainly because the Revolution was far more Anti-American and not so muchAnti-European. it doesn't means American can't travel to Iran, Just Americanmust have tour guide as long as they are in Iranian territory, this low is also applicable for UK citizen and Canadians.

The majority of the 300,000 tourist visas granted in 2003 were obtained by Asian Muslims, who presumably intended to visit important pilgrimage sites inMashhad and Qom. Several organized tours from Germany, France, UK and other European countries come to Iran annually to visit archaeological sites andmonuments. Iran have 21 places in world cultural heritages list, because of this lots of cultural tourist each year comes to visit Iran

According to Iranian officials, about 1,659,000 foreign tourists visited Iran in 2004 - although government statistics don't distinguish between tourism, business and religious pilgrims; most came from Asian countries, including the republics of Central Asia, while a small share (about 10%) came from North Americaand the European Union including Germany, Italy, Bulgaria, France, Belgium. The most popular tourist destinations are Northern Iran, Isfahan, Mashhad, Yazd andShiraz. There is undoubtedly great scope for increased visitors from the Islamic world, and possibly also from non-Muslim countries with which Iran is developing business and political links, such as China and India.

From 2004, the country experienced a 100-percent growth in foreign tourist arrivals until mid-2008 when the number of foreign arrivals surged up to 2.5 million. Specially, there has been an enormous increase in the number of German tourists traveling to Iran in 2008.

The World Travel and Tourism Council claims that business and personal tourism rose by 11.3% and 4.6%, respectively, in real terms in 2007, with the growth in personal tourism only modestly below that of the preceding year.

In 2011, most of Iran's international visitors arrived in Iran solely for the purpose of leisure travel. Leisure tourists arriving from abroad are also often relatives of Iranian citizens or expatriates residing outside of Iran returning to visit. Another key segment of international arrival traffic are pilgrims come to pay a visit to one of the many holy sites scattered throughout the country.

The number of international arrivals has been steadily increasing, up from 2.2 million people in 2009 to 3.6 million in 2011, with per capita spending of $1,850 per visit on average.

Over five million tourists visited Iran in the fiscal year of 2014-2015, ending March 21, four percent more year-on-year.

Visa requirement

In general, Iran has tried to improve its complex and time-consuming visa application process and has begun to issue week-long visas for the nationals of 68 countries at airports. An online hotel reservation system has been developed. Iran will equip all airports with electronic visa facilities by February 2009 to issue online entry permits to foreign nationals. Visas can now be secured electronically and be collected from Iranian consulates or international airports. Iran has 15 road border crossings connecting it with Iraq, Turkey, Afghanistan, Pakistan, Turkmenistan, Armenia and Azerbaijan. Rail lines from Turkey and Turkmenistan can also be used to enter Iran.About 70% of visitors arrived by land in 2002, about 29% by air and less than 1% by sea. The price of internal flights is heavily subsidised, deterring competition and hampering profitability. In April 2005 the Imam Khomeini International Airportwas reopened under the management of a consortium of four local airlines — Mahan Air, Aseman, Caspian Air and Kish Air — although no formal contract appeared to have been awarded.

INFRASTRUCTURE AND THE ECONOMY

In the early 2000s the industry still faced serious limitations in infrastructure,communications, regulatory norms, and personnel training. In late 2003 there were about 640 hotels in Iran and around 63,000 beds.

In FY 2003 Iran had about 69,000 restaurants and 6,000 hotels and other lodging places; about 80 percent of these establishments were in urban areas. Some 875 restaurants and hotels were publicly managed by cooperatives and government organizations. More than 95 percent of restaurants and hotels had fewer than five employees, and only 38 had more than 100 employees. In FY 2002 this sector employed more than 166,000 people, 42,000 of whom worked in places of lodging. Of the 56,618 beds in all hotels, about half were located in three- to five-star hotels.

In recent years, 235 hotels, hotel apartments, motels and guesthouses have become operational nationwide. As at 2010, 400 hotels and 200 hotel apartments are under construction nationwide. Some 66 percent of these projects are underway in the provinces of Tehran, Gilan, Mazandaran, Razavi Khorasan and Isfahan.

Cultural Heritage, Handicrafts and Tourism Organization of Iran

Iran's Cultural Heritage, Tourism and Handicrafts Organization is responsible for the establishment, development and operation of tourism facilities in Iran, planning for the repair or extension of tourism facilities through direct investment or providing loans to the private sector or entering into partnership with the private sector, issuing licenses and supervising the establishment and administration of hotels and restaurants and travel agencies and qualification and rating of these units.

Area considered for further expansion in the tourism sector in Iran are eco tourism,coastlines, restoration of historical relics, handicraft townships, and health tourism (e.g.water therapy). 30,000 people come to Iran each year to receive medical treatment (2012). As a matter of fact, Iran might become the leading country in the Islamic World when it comes to the medical tourism field due to a number of reasons that include the country's unique geographical position, the fluctuation of Iranian currency that leads to lower prices in healthcare services, as well as the development in medical research and technology. The rapid growth rate of the healthcare system which, according to the World Tourism Organization, has increased of 5% in last decade, seems to indicate that in the future Iran will be one of the most visited countries bymedical tourists, above all coming from the neighbouring countries, such as Arzebaijan, Iraq and the Gulf States.

Officials state that Iran has in recent years earned about US$1bn a year from tourism.Close to 1.8% of national employment is generated in the tourism sector. Weak advertising, unstable regional conditions, a poor public image in some parts of the world, and absence of efficient planning schemes in the tourism sector have all hindered the growth of tourism.

Iran's '20-Year Vision' document projects investment of over $32 billion in the country's tourism sector and tragets 20 million tourists by 2025. In order to encourage domestic and foreign direct investment in this sector, the 50 percent tax exemption previously granted to tourism enterprises has been extended to include five-star hotels. In 2016 Iran announced that it will grant 100 percent tax holidays between five to 13 years depending on the region for hoteliers investing in Iran. Tariffs for utilities comply with industrial ones.Investment in Iran's free trade zones are exempt from taxes for up to 20 years. As of 2016, international hotel operators investing in Iran are Rotana (Abu Dhabi), Accor (France), Meliá (Spain) and Steigenberger (Germany) among others.

Outward tourism

Traditionally, only a small number of wealthy Iranian tourists traveled abroad, and the majority of the trips were business departures, mostly to neighboring states in the Persian Gulf and the wider Middle East (1 million each year), Central Asia andTurkey (~1 million). Although this is likely to continue to characterize much Iranian travel abroad, since the change of regime in Iraq in 2003, Iranians from all walks of life have visited their western neighbor. In addition, a large proportion of Iranians traveling abroad are likely to be visiting family, especially in Europe, the US and Australia (~1 million). Up until early

2012, because the Iranian rial was overvalued, the Iranian government was subsidizing its travelers abroad (2010). In 2011, some 27 million travelers and businessmen passed the Iranian custom departments. Following the Iranian subsidy reform plan, airfares in Iran went up by 65% in 2012. In 2012, Iranians spent $18.5 billion on outward tourism. They spent $12 billion to purchase airplane tickets from foreign airliners between the years 2012-2015.

TRANSPORT IN IRAN

Iran has a long paved road system linking most of its towns and all of its cities. In 2011 the country had 173,000 kilometres (107,000 mi) of roads, of which 73% were paved. In 2008 there were nearly 100 passenger cars for every 1,000 inhabitants.

Trains operate on 11,106 km (6,942 mi) of railroad track. The country's major port of entry is Bandar-Abbas on the Strait of Hormuz. After arriving in Iran, imported goods are distributed throughout the country by trucks and freight trains. The Tehran-Bandar-Abbas railroad, opened in 1995, connects Bandar-Abbas to the railroad system of Central Asia via Tehran and Mashhad. Other major ports include Bandar e-Anzali and Bandar e-Torkeman on the Caspian Sea and Khorramshahr and Bandar-e Emam Khomeyni on the Persian Gulf.

Dozens of cities have airports that serve passenger and cargo planes. Iran Air, the national airline, was founded in 1962 and operates domestic and international flights. All large cities have mass transit systems using buses, and several private companies provide bus service between cities. Tehran,Mashhad, Shiraz, Tabriz, Ahwaz and Esfahan have underground mass transit rail lines, in different stages of operation and construction.

Transport in Iran is inexpensive because of the government's subsidization of the price of gasoline. The downside is a huge draw on government coffers, economic inefficiency because of highly wasteful consumption patterns, contraband with neighboring countries and air pollution. In 2008, more than one million people worked in the transportation sector, accounting for 9% of GDP.

Ministry of Road and Transportation

The Ministry of Roads and Transportation is in charge of studying and deciding pricing policy of the transportation; as well as issuing licenses for the establishment of transportation firms. In addition, the

Ministry is in charge of implementing comprehensive and integrated transportation policies in Iran. As of 2016, plans for foreign direct investment in the transport sector include over 5,600 km of highways, 745 km of freeways, and close to 3,000 km of main roads. These projects and others are worth $25 billion (not including airplanes purchases worth another $50 billion). Iran says it needs more than $40 billion to complete 258 major unfinished transportation projects (2016).

Railways

- Total: 11,106 km Plan to increase total railways length from 13,500 km in 2016 to 20,000 km by 2025.
    - o Standard gauge: 8,273 km of 1,435 mm (4 ft 8 $\frac{1}{2}$ in) gauge (146 km electrified) (2006)
    - o Broad gauge: 94 km of 1,676 mm (5 ft 6 in) gauge (connected to Pakistan Railways)

Electrified railway is 146 km from Tabriz to Jolfa and the tender for electrification ofTehran- Mashhad has been finished according to Railway electrification in Iran. Note: Broad-gauge track is employed at the borders with Azerbaijan Republic andTurkmenistan which have 1,520 mm (4 ft 11 $\frac{27}{32}$ in) broad gauge rail systems; 41 km of the standard gauge, electrified track is in suburban service at Tehran (2007).

The majority of transportation in Iran is road-based. The government plans to transport 3.5% of the passenger volume and 8.5% of the freight volume by rail. Extensive electrification is planned. The railway network expands by about 500 km per year according to the Ministry of R&T.

Railway links with adjacent countries

In December 2014, a rail line from Iran opened to Turkmenistan and Kazakhstan. The opening of the line marks the first direct rail link between Iran, Kazakhstan and China and upon completion of the Marmaray rail project direct rail transport between China and Europe (while avoiding Russia) will be possible.

- Afghanistan - planned
- Azerbaijan - break-of-gauge 1,435 mm (4 ft 8 $\frac{1}{2}$ in)/1,520 mm (4 ft 11 $\frac{27}{32}$ in) (Only to Nakhichevan, planned link to Azerbaijan proper for building Russia-Iran corridor)
- Armenia - planned - break of gauge 1,435 mm (4 ft 8 $\frac{1}{2}$ in)/ 1,520 mm (4 ft 11 $\frac{27}{32}$ in)

- Iraq - part under construction, part planned.
    - o one long link from Arak via Kermanshah to Baghdad
    - o one short link of about 50 km links Khorramshahr to Basra and is due for completion in 2006.
- Pakistan - break-of-gauge 1,435 mm (4 ft 8 $\frac{1}{2}$ in)/1,676 mm (5 ft 6 in) - missing link from Bam to Zahedan completed 2009.
- Turkey - via Lake Van - train ferry - 1,435 mm (4 ft 8 $\frac{1}{2}$ in)
- Turkmenistan - break-of-gauge 1,435 mm (4 ft 8 $\frac{1}{2}$ in)/1,520 mm (4 ft 11 $\frac{27}{32}$ in)

Couplings, brakes and electrification

- Couplers - SA3 and buffers
- Brakes - air
- Electrification - 25 kV AC

Rapid transit

Tehran Metro

The Tehran Metro is a rapid transit system in Tehran carrying 5 million passengers a day and consisting of seven lines that run a total of 200 kilometres (~120 mi) with two further lines under construction. The metro will have a final length of 430 kilometres (270 mi) once all nine lines are constructed by 2028. Metro services run from 5:30 to 23:00 throughout the city and the ticket price is 3,000-8,000 IRR($0.10-$0.30 USD) and is based on distance of the trip.

Tehran Bus Rapid Transit

The Tehran Bus Rapid Transit (BRT) is a rapid transit system serving Tehran which was officially inaugurated in 2008. The BRT has a network of over 150 kilometres, transporting 1.8 million passengers on a daily basis. The BRT has a total of ten lines with a further expansion planned to bring the total length to 300 kilometres. The price of Tehran's BRT is somewhere between 4,000IRR to 9,500IRR (0.15$ to 0.35$ USD).

Mashhad Urban Railway

The Mashhad Urban Railway is urban rail line in Mashhad, construction on line one began in 1999 and was opened on 24 April 2011. Line two has also been opened recently and finished construction. Furthermore, four other lines are either being constructed or are planned to be. Mashhad Urban Railway operates its single line from 6:30 to 21:30 daily. It has a daily ridership of 130 000 passengers and has a total length of 24 kilometres (14.9 mi).

Isfahan Metro

The Isfahan Metro construction of line one commenced in 2001 and was finally opened to the public on 15 October 2015. Line one has a total length of 11 kilometres. The city is planning a second East to West line to serve the city.

Shiraz Metro

The Shiraz Metro is a rapid transit system in Shiraz. Line one was officially inaugurated on 11 October 2014 after being in construction since 2011; the single line has a length of 10.5 kilometres (6.5 mi) and stops at six stations. Line 2 is currently under construction and has a length of 15 kilometres (9.3 mi). The metro currently has a daily ridership of 500 000 passengers with 27 trains in operation.

Tabriz Metro

The Tabriz Metro is a metro system serving the city of Tabriz. The first line was opened on 28 August 2015 with a 7-kilometre length and six stations. There is also a regional commuter line planned to the city of Sahand. Line one runs Northwest from El Goli Station to Ostad Shahriar Station.

Roadways and automobiles

Note: There were more than 11 million vehicles in Iran by 2010 mostly manufactured or assembled locally. As of 2015, 34,000 km of roads provided essential corridors of transportation, while 45,000 km of major roads and 100,000 km of roads connecting villages and rural areas have seen no maintenance and upkeep practices (worth a total of $57 billion).

Road accidents

Iran ranks 23d worldwide in traffic deaths per 100,000 population per year, with a rate of 24.3, half the rate of the worst country, Eritrea. Iran ranks first worldwide in terms of having the largest number of road accidents with 38,000 deaths and injuries per year. Other sources place the total number of fatalities at 100,000 over the past 6 years or 20,000 per year on average (2008).

Transport officials say 46.8 percent of car accidents take place in cities, 21.5 percent outside, 19.5 percent on rural routes, 4.2 percent on urban highways and 4.2 percent on suburban highways.

The high death tolls in car accidents are blamed on high speed, unsafe vehicles, widespread disregard of traffic laws and inadequate emergency services.

Motorcycles account for 50 percent of sound pollution in Tehran and 40-45 percent of accidents.

WATERWAYS

850 km (on Karun River; additional service on Lake Urmia) (2006)

Note: the Shatt al-Arab is usually navigable by maritime traffic for about 130 km; channel has been dredged to 3 m and is in use.

Pipelines

- Condensate 7 km; condensate/gas 12 km; gas 19,246 km; liquid petroleum gas 570 km; oil 7,018 km; refined products 7,936 km

- Iran is currently undergoing negotiations with neighboring Pakistan for the construction of an oil and gas pipeline to that country to help integrate their respective economies and solve the energy shortage being faced by Pakistan.

Ports and harbors

The capacity of container loading and unloading in the country's ports is currently at 4.4 million which will increase to 7 million by the end of 2015. Port capacity will increase to 200 million tons in 2015 from 150 million tons in 2010.

- *All ports:* Abadan (largely destroyed in fighting during 1980-88 war), Ahvaz, Bandar Abbas, Bandar-e Anzali (Caspian sea), Bushehr, Bandar-e Emam Khomeyni, Bandar-e Lengeh, Bandar-e Mahshahr, Bandar-e Torkaman(Caspian sea), Chabahar (Bandar-e Beheshti), Kharg island, Lavan island, Sirriisland, Khorramshahr (limited operation since November 1992), Noshahr(Caspian sea), Arvand Kenar.
    - o *Main:* Assaluyeh, Bandar Abbas, Bandar-e Eman Khomeyni. Bandar Abbas, with capacity of 2.5 million TEU in 2010 and 3.3 million TEU in 2016, is in southern Iran and handles 90% of the country's container throughput. Bandar Abbas is run by the *Shaheed Rajaee* Port Authority.

    o *Major Export Terminals (loading capacity):* Kharg Island 5,000,000 bbl/d (790,000 m^3/d), Lavan Island 200,000 bbl/d (32,000 m^3/d), Neka (Caspian sea) 50,000 bbl/d (7,900 m^3/d), Assaluyeh 250,000 bbl/d (40,000 m^3/d) gas liquids, Kish Island, Abadan (aka Bandar-e Eman Khomeyni) and Bandar Mahshahr (latter 2 are used mostly by NPC for petrochemicals export).

- *Major Oil/Gas Ports:*
- Kharg Island: is the largest and main export terminal in Iran. Roughly 90% of Iran's exports are sent via Kharg. Kharg's loading system has a capacity of 5.0 million bbl/d. The terminal processes all onshore production (the Iranian Heavy and Iranian Light Blends) and offshore production from the Froozan field (the Froozan Blend). The Kharg terminal includes the main T-jetty, the Sea Island that is located on the west side of Kharg, and the Dariush terminal to the south. Kharg Island relies on storage to ensure even operations, and its current storage capacity is expected to increase to 28 million barrels of oil in 2014.
- Lavan Island, mostly handles exports of the Lavan Blend sourced from offshore fields. Lavan is Iran's highest-quality export grade and one of Iran's smallest streams. Lavan's production averaged less than 100,000 bbl/d in 2013, but the Lavan facilities have the capacity to process 200,000 bbl/d of crude oil. Lavan has a two-berth jetty, which can accommodate vessels up to 250,000 deadweight tons. Lavan's storage capacity is 5.5 million barrels.
- Sirri Island: serves as a loading port for the Sirri Blend that is produced in the offshore fields of the same name. The Sirri terminal includes a loading platform equipped with four loading arms that can load tankers from 80,000 to 330,000 deadweight tons. Its storage capacity is 4.5 million barrels.
- Ras Bahregan.

MERCHANT MARINE

Total: 76 (2013)

- By type: bulk carrier 8, cargo 51, chemical tanker 3, container 4, liquefied gas 1, passenger/cargo 3, petroleum tanker 2, refrigerated cargo 2, roll on/roll off 2

- Foreign-owned: 2 (UAE 2)
- Registered in other countries: 71 (Barbados 5, Cyprus 10, Hong Kong 3, Malta 48, Panama 5) (2010)
- Shipping freight (important for liquid natural gas (LNG) exports) will grow by an average of 5.3 percent a year in the 2009-2013.

Over the next two decades, Iran would need 500 new ships, including 120 oil tankers, 40 liquefied natural gas (LNG) carriers and over 300 commercial vessels.

AIRPORTS AND AIRLINES

Iran handles about 50 million passengers annually (2016). Iran's airports are improving their international connections, and Arak Airport in Markazi province has recently begun to operate international flights, making a total of five such airports in the country, in addition to ten local airports. In May 2007 international flights into the capital, Tehran, were moved to the Imam Khomeini International Airport (IKIA), just outside the city because of capacity constraints at the existing central Mehrabad Airport.

- Airports: 319 (2013)
- There are 54 "major" airports in Iran (2008): 8 international, 21 air border, and 25 domestic.
- Number of flights from airports nationwide reached 31,088 in a month (October 20-November 20, 2008): 10,510 domestic, 4,229 international and 15,404 transit.
- Airport capacity for departures and arrivals: 73 million persons (2011)
- Number of passengers departing and arriving at airports: 40.1 million persons (2011)
- Share of non-public sector in domestic flights: 60% (2011)
- Share of non-public sector in international flights: 58.7% (2011)

National airline:

- Iran Air handles 6 million passengers annually (2016)

Airports - with paved runways

Total: 140 (2013)

over 3,047 m: 42

2,438 to 3,047 m: 29

1,524 to 2,437 m: 26

914 to 1,523 m: 36

under 914 m: 7 (2013)

Airports - with unpaved runways

Total: 179 (2013)

over 3,047 m: 1

1,524 to 2,437 m: 2

914 to 1,523 m: 135

under 914 m: 32 (2013)

Heliports

Total: 26 (2013)

Transit statistics

People

- In 2011, some 27 million travelers and businessmen passed custom departments.
- Over five million passengers have been transported via border points mainlyMehran and Bazargan.
- In 2002, about 70% of visitors arrived by land, about 29% by air and less than 1% by sea

Commodities

- In 2011, cargos and commodities from 100 countries have been transited across Iran. Over 10.5 million tons of oil products and non-oil commodities were transited via land (91% via road and 9% via railroad) and marine borders.
- In 2010, 10 million tons of commodities from 110 countries, worth $31.5 billion, transited through Iran for 82 destinations.
- In 2009, the value of goods transited was about $25 billion. This figure constitutes seven percent of the GDP.
- From March 22, 2009 until September 22, 2009 over 3 million tons of goods worth some $11.3 billion were transited through Iran. Regarding the countries of origin, China was first in terms of volume, Turkmenistan ranked second,Uzbekistan came third, Turkey fourth and UAE fifth. Among the destinations, Afghanistan was first, Iraq second,Azerbaijan third, UAE fourth

and Turkmenistan ranked fifth.

- Some 33 million tons of goods and 29 million passengers are transported annually by the rail transportation network, accounting for 9 percent and 11 percent of the whole transportations in the country (2011).

- Per capita parcel post for each Iranian stands at 15 per annum (2008).

- One million tons of commodities, fuel and barter have been transited abroad per month (2008).

- Fuel is transported in Iran by road tankers, tank wagons, tanker ships as well as through pipelines. Nearly 10,000 tankers from 400 private sector companies transport fuel by road. In 2013, nearly 87 billion liters of fuel were transported by Iranian tankers. Iran's tank wagons and ships transported 3 billion liters and 8 billion liters of fuel, respectively.

- 3.498 million tons of non-oil commodities were transited abroad via Iran during March 20-November 20, 2008 (79% of the commodities were transited by road).

Mode of transport

- More than 90 percent of the country's imports and exports, particularly in the fisheries and oil sectors, are undertaken through the sea (2009).

- In 2008, 84% of the transited goods through Iran were transported through roads while the rest was transported via railroad.

Port of entry

- In 2011, Bandar Abbas was the country's most active border in terms of transit (37 percent), followed by Parvizkhan (17 percent), Bazargan (9 percent) and Bashmaq (7 percent).

- In 2008, some 24 border crossings except Kileh in Sardasht (West Azarbaijan) and Yazdan in Southern Khorasan were active nationwide. Bandar Abbas, contributing 40.8% of transit operations, was considered the most dynamic in terms of transiting cargo. It was followed by Bazargan (16.6 percent), Sarakhs (14.1 percent), Bandar Anzali (9.2 percent) and Pileh-Savar (3.9 percent).

Economics

- Every ton of transit cargo earns $150 for the country and creates 40 jobs. Iran will earn a revenue of USD 12 billion when the volume of goods transported through the country reaches 40 million tons annually.

TRACECA

In September 2009, Iran formally joined the Transport Corridor Europe – Caucasus – Asia (TRACECA) programme, also known as the "new Silk Road." TRACECA was founded in 1998 with the aim of promoting economic relations, trade and transport communications between Europe, the Caucasus and Asia. This programme consists of the EU and 14 member states (including Iran) from Eastern Europe and the Caucasus. Iran's strategic location means that it is a key transport corridor between Europe and Central Asia.

In August 2010, Iran declared that it "did not sign on to TRACECA project" and said it has been fostering improved transport links through a series of bilateral agreements with neighboring states instead. According to Iran's first Vice-PresidentMohammad-Reza Rahimi "If all the potential of the country's transit sector is tapped, it can bring in as much revenues as[the] oil [industry]". He also announced that Iran will join China and Europe by rail in the near future.

11

Education

Education in Iran is centralized and divided into K-12 education plushigher education. K-12 education is supervised by the Ministry of Education and higher education is under supervision of Ministry of Science and Technology and Ministry of Health and Medical Education (Iran). As of September 2015, 93% of the Iranian adult population are literate. In 2008, 85% of the Iranian adult population were literate, well ahead of the regional average of 62%. This rate increases to 97% among young adults (aged between 15 and 24) without any gender discrepancy. By 2007, Iran had a student to workforce populationratio of 10.2%, standing among the countries with highest ratio in the world.

Primary school starts at the age of 6 for a duration of 6 years. Middle school, also known as First 3 years of Dabirestân (*Dabirestân ÏÑæå Çæá ÏÈÌÑÓÊÇ*), goes from the seventh to the ninth grade. High school (*Dabirestân ÏæÑå Ïæã ÏÈÌÑÓÊÇ*), for which the last three years is not mandatory, is divided between theoretical, vocational/technical and manual, each program with its own specialties. The requirement to enter into higher education is to have a High school diploma, and finally pass the national university entrance examination, Iranian University Entrance Exam (*Konkur ˜ä˜æÑ*), which is the equivalent of the Frenchbaccalauréat exam.

Universities, institutes of technology, medical schools and community colleges, provide the higher education. Higher education is sanctioned by different levels of diplomas: *Fogh-e-Diplom* or *Kârdâni* after 2 years of higher education,*Kârshenâsi* (also known under the name "licence") is delivered after 4 years of higher education (Bachelor's degree).*Kârshenâsi-ye Arshad* is delivered after 2 more years of study (Master's degree). After which, another exam allows the candidate to pursue a doctoral program (PhD).

HISTORY OF EDUCATION IN IRAN

Modern education

The first Western-style public schools were established by Haji-Mirza Hassan Roshdieh. Amir Kabir (the Grand Minister) helped the first modern Iranian college establish in the mid-nineteenth century, and the first Iranian University modelled after European Universities established during the first Pahlavi period.

There are both free public schools and private schools in Iran at all levels, from elementary school through university. Education in Iran is highly centralized. The Ministry of Education is in charge of educational planning, financing, administration, curriculum, and textbook development. Teacher training, grading, and examinations are also the responsibility of the Ministry. At the university level, however, every student attending public schools is required to commit to serve the government for a number of years typically equivalent to those spent at the university, or pay it off for a very low price (typically a few hundred dollars). During the early 1970s, efforts were made to improve the educational system by updating school curriculation, introducing modern textbooks, and training more efficient teachers.

The 1979 revolution continued the country's emphasis on education with the new government putting its own stamp on the process. The most important change was the Islamization of the education system. All students were segregated by sex. In 1980, the Cultural Revolution Committee was formed to oversee the institution of Islamic values in education. An arm of the committee, the Center for Textbooks (composed mainly of clerics), produced 3,000 new college-level textbooks reflecting Islamic views by 1983. Teaching materials based on Islam were introduced into the primary grades within six months of the revolution.

Budget

Each year, 20% of government spending and 5% of GDP goes to education, a higher rate than most other developing countries. 50% of education spending is devoted to secondary education and 21% of the annual state education budget is devoted to the provision of tertiary education.

EDUCATION REFORM

The *Fourth Five-Year Development Plan (2005-2010)* has envisaged upgrading the quality of the educational system at all levels, as well as reforming education curricula, and developing appropriate programs of vocational training, a continuation of the trend towards labor market oriented education and training.

With the new education reform plan in 2012, the Pre-university year will be replaced with an additional year in elementary school. Students will have the same teacher for the first 3 years of primary school. Emphasis will be made on research, knowledge production and questioning instead of math and memorizing alone. In the new system the teacher will no longer be the only instructor but a facilitator and guide.

Other more general goals of the education reform are:
- Making the education more global in terms of knowledge.
- Nurturing children who believe in the one God.
- Providing a socially just education system.
- Increasing the role of the family in the education system.
- Increasing the efficiency of the education system.
- Achieving the highest standard of education in the region.

TEACHER EDUCATION

Farhangian University is the university of teacher education and human resource development in Ministry of Education. Teacher Training Centers in Iran are responsible for training teachers for primary, orientation cycle, and gifted children's schools. These centers offer two-year programs leading to a Fogh-Diploma (associate degree). Students that enter Teacher Training Centers, have at minimum, completed the orientation cycle of education; most have a High school diploma. A national entrance examination is required for admission.

In order to teach 9-12 grades, in theory, a bachelor's degree is required; however due to a shortage of teachers in Iran, schools have been compelled to use teaching staff with other educational backgrounds. Teachers are trained in universities and higher institutes. There are seven teacher-training colleges in Iran.

FOREIGN LANGUAGES

Persian is officially the national language of Iran. Arabic language, as the language of Koran is taught grades 6-11. In addition to Arabic, students are required to take one foreign language class in grades 7-12. Although other foreign languages such as German, French, Spanish and Chinese are offered in most urban schools, English continues to be the most desired language.

Kanoun-e-Zabaan-e-Iran or Iran's Language Institute affiliated to Center for Intellectual Development of Children and Young Adults was founded in 1979. Persian, English, French, Spanish, German and Arabic are taught to over 175,000 students during each term.

English language is studied in rahnamaei (literally meaning, guidance or orientation), an equivalent for middle school in other countries. Middle school is a period of three years and it covers grades 6-8 for students aged 11 to 13 years old. The government is now considering teaching English language from primary school level. However, the quality of English education in schools is not satisfactory and most of students in order to obtain a better English fluency and proficiency have to take English courses in private institutes.

Presently, there are over 5000 foreign language schools in the country, 200 of which are situated in Tehran. A few television channels air weekly English and Arabic language sessions, particularly for university candidates who are preparing for the annual entrance test.

INTERNET AND DISTANCE EDUCATION

Full Internet service is available in all major cities and it is very rapidly increasing. Many small towns and even some villages now have full Internet access. The government aims to provide 10% of government and commercial services via the Internetby end-2008 and to equip every school with computers and connections by the same date.

Payame Noor University (established 1987) as a provider exclusively of distance education courses is a state university under the supervision of the Ministry of Science, Research and Technology.

HIGHER EDUCATION

As of 2013, 4.5 million students are enrolled in universities, out of a total population of 75 million. Iranian universities churn out almost 750,000 skilled graduates annually. The tradition of university education in Iran goes back to the early centuries of Islam. By the 20th century, however, the system had become antiquated and was remodeled along French lines. The country's 16 universities were closed after the 1979 revolution and were then reopened gradually between 1982 and 1983 under Islamic supervision.

While the universities were closed, the Cultural Revolution Committee investigated professors and teachers and dismissed those who were believers in Marxism, liberalism, and other "imperialistic" ideologies. The universities reopened with Islamic curricula. In 1997, all higher-level institutions had 40,477 teachers and enrolled 579,070 students.

The syllabus of all the universities in Iran is decided by a national council as a result the difference of the quality of education among the universities is only based on the location and the quality of the students and the faculty members. Among all top universities in the country there are three universities each notable for some reasons:

The University of Tehran (founded in 1934) has 10 faculties, including a department of Islamic theology. It is the oldest (in the modern system) and biggest university in Iran. It has been the birthplace of several social and political movements.

Tarbiat Modares University (means: professor training university) also located in Tehran is the only exclusively post-graduate institute in Iran. It only offers Master's, PhD, and Postdoc programs. It is also the most comprehensive Iranian university in the sense that it is the only university under the Iranian Ministry of Science System that has a Medical School. All other Medical Schools in Iran are a separate university and governed under the Ministry of Health; for example Tehran University of Medical Sciences (commonly known as Medical School of Tehran University) is in fact separate from Tehran University.

Sharif University of Technology also located in Tehran is nationally well known for taking in the top undergraduate Engineering and Science students; and internationally recognized for training competent under graduate students. It has probably the highest percentage of graduates who seek higher education abroad.

K.N.Toosi University of Technology and Amirkabir University of Technology are among most prestigious universities in Tehran. Other major universities are at Shiraz, Tabriz, Esfahan, Mashhad, Ahvaz, Kerman, Kermanshah, Babolsar, Rasht, and Orumiyeh. There are about 50 colleges and 40 technological institutes.

In 2009, 33.7% of all those in the 18-25 age group were enrolled in one of the 92 universities, 512 Payame Noor Universitybranches, and 56 research and technology institutes around the country. There are currently some 3.7 million university students in Iran and 1.5 million study at the 500 branches of Islamic Azad University. Iran had 1 million medical students in 2011.

Entrepreneurship

In recent decades Iran has shown an increasing interest in various entrepreneurship fields, in higher educational settings, policy making and business. Although primary and secondary school textbooks do not address entrepreneurship, severaluniversities including Tehran University and Sharif University, offer courses on entrepreneurship to undergraduate and graduate students.

In accordance with the third five-year development plan, the "entrepreneurship development plan in Iranian universities", (known as KARAD Plan) was developed, and launched in twelve universities across the country, under the supervision ofManagement and Planning Organization and the Ministry of Science, Research and Technology.

WOMEN IN EDUCATION

In September 2012, women made up more than 60% of all universities' student body in Iran. However, the numbers were not always this promising; this high level of achievement and involvement in high education is a recent development of the past decades. The right to a respectable education has been a major demand of the Iranian women's movement starting in the early twentieth century. Before the 1979 revolution a limited number of women went to male-dominated schools and most traditional families did not send their girls to school because the teachers were men or the school was not Islamic. During the 1990s, women's enrolment in educational institutions began to increase. The establishment and the expansion of private universities "daneshgah-e-azad-e islami" also contributed to the increasing enrollment for both women and men. Under the presidency of Rafsanjani and the High council of cultural Revolution, the Women's social and cultural council was set up and charged with studying the legal, social, and economic problems of women. The council, with the support of Islamic feminists worked to lift all restrictions on women entering any fields of study in 1993. After the Islamic Revolution, Ayatollah Ruhollah Khomeini and his new regime prioritized the Islamization of the Iranian education system for both women and men. When Khomeini died in 1989, under president Akbar Hashemi Rafsanjani, many but not all restrictions on women's education were lifted, albeit with controversy. The right to education for everyone without discrimination is explicitly guaranteed under Iran's constitution and international documents, which Iran has accepted or to which it is a party. Some scholars believe that women have poor access to higher education because of certain policies and the oppression of women's right in Iran's strictly Islamic society. However, Iranian women do have fair access to higher education as seen by a significant increase in female enrollment and graduation rates as women university students now outnumber males, Iranian women emerge to more prominent positions in the labor force, and the presence and confidence of professional women in the public sphere. The opportunities for women education and their involvement in higher education has grown exponentially after the Iranian Revolution. According to UNESCO world survey, Iran has the highest female to male ratio at primary level of enrollment in the world among sovereign nations, with a girl to boy ratio of 1.22 : 1.00.

Schools for Gifted Children

The National Organization for Development of Exceptional Talents (NODET), also known as SAMPAD, maintains middle and high schools in Iran. These schools were shut down for a few years after the revolution, but later re-opened. Admittance is based on an entrance examination, and is very competitive, especially in Tehran. Their tuition is similar to private schools, but may be partially or fully waived depending on the students financial condition. Some NODET alumni are world leading scientists. Another schools are Selective Schools which are called "Nemoone Dolati".These schools are controlled by government and have no fees.Students take this entrance exam alongside with NODET exams.

Organization for Educational Research and Planning (OERP)

OERP is a government affiliated, scientific, learning organization. It has qualitative and knowledge-based curricula consistent with the scientific and research findings, technological, national identity, Islamic and cultural values.

OERP's Responsibilities:

1. To research on the content of the educational,

2. To study and develop simple methods for examinations and educational assessments,

3. To write, edit and print text-books,

4. To identify and provide educational tools and the list of standards for educational tools and equipments,

5. To run pure research on improving the quality and quantity of education,

6. To perform other responsibilities issued by the OERP Council.

PROMINENT HIGH SCHOOLS IN IRAN: HISTORICAL AND CURRENT

In alphabetical order:

- Aboureihan High School
- Alborz High School
- Allameh Helli High Schools (NODET)
- Allameh Tabatabaei High School
- Bagherol Oloom High School
- Daneshmand High School
- Danesh High School
- Energy Atomi High School
- Farzanegan High Schools (NODET)
- Firouz Bahram High School
- Hadaf No.3 High School
- Imam Mousa Sadr High School
- Kamal High school
- Mirza Koochak Khan High School (NODET)
- Mofid No.1 and No.2 High School
- Nikan High School
- Rahyar Educational Complex
- Razi High School
- Salam High Schools
- Shahid Beheshti High School, Soheil
- Shahid Dastgheib High School(NODET)
- Shahid Ejei High School (NODET)
- Shahid Soltani School (NODET)
- Imam Ali High School (NODET)

International Baccalaureate schools

Iran has three International Baccalaureate (IB) schools. They are Mehr-e-Taban International School, Shahid Mahdavi International School, and Tehran International School.

Mehr-e-Taban International School is an authorized IB world school in Shiraz offering the Primary Years Programme, Middle Years Programme and Diploma Programme. Shahid Mahdavi School is an IB world school in Tehran offering the Primary Years Programme and Middle Years Programme. Tehran International School is an IB world school in Tehran offering theDiploma Programme.

Statistics

- In 2010, 64% of the country's population was under the age of 30.

- There are approximately 92,500 public educational institutions at all levels, with a total enrollment of approximately 17,488,000 students.

- According to 2008 estimates, 89.3% of males and 80.7% of females over the age of 15 are literate; thus 85% of the population is literate. Virtually all children of the relevant age group enrolled into primary schools in 2008 while enrollment into secondary schools increased from 66% in 1995 to 80% in 2008. As a result, youth literacy rates increased from 86% to 94% over the same period, rising significantly for girls.

- A *literacy corps* was established in 1963 to send educated conscripts to villages. During its first 10 years, the corps helped 2.2 million urban children and 600,000 adults become literate. This corps was replaced with the Literacy Movement Organization after the Islamic Revolution.

- In 1997, there were 9,238,393 pupils enrolled in 63,101 primary schools, with 298,755 teachers. The student-to-teacher ratio stood at 31 to 1. In that same year, secondary schools had 8,776,792 students and 280,309 teachers. The pupil-teacher ratio at the primary level was 26 to 1 in 1999. In the same year, 83% of primary-school-age children were enrolled in school. As of 1999, public expenditure on education was estimated at 4.6% of GDP (not budget).

- In 2007, the majority of students (60%) enrolled in Iranian universities were women.

- According to UNESCO world survey, Iran has the highest female to male ratio at primary level of enrollment in the world among sovereign nations, with a girl to boy ratio of 1.22 : 1.00.
- Each year, 20% of government spending and 5% of GDP goes to education, a higher rate than most other developing countries. 50% of education spending is devoted to secondary education and 21% of the annual state education budget is devoted to the provision of tertiary education.

SCIENCE AND TECHNOLOGY IN IRAN

Iran has made considerable advances in science and technology through education and training, despite international sanctions in almost all aspects of research during the past 30 years. Iran's university population swelled from 100,000 in 1979 to 2 million in 2006. In recent years, the growth in Iran's scientific output is reported to be the fastest in the world. Iran has made great strides in different sectors, including aerospace, nuclear science, medical development, as well as stem cell and cloning research.

Throughout the history Persia was always a cradle of science, contributing to medicine, mathematics, astronomy and philosophy. Trying to revive the golden time of Persian science, Iran's scientists now are cautiously reaching out to the world. Many individual Iranian scientists, along with the Iranian Academy of Medical Sciences and Academy of Sciences of Iran, are involved in this revival.

Science in ancient Iran (Persia)

Science in Persia evolved in two main phases separated by the arrival and widespread adoption of Islam in the region.

References to scientific subjects such as natural science and mathematics occur in books written in the Pahlavi languages.

Ancient technology in Persia

The Qanat (a water management system used for irrigation) originated in pre-Achaemenid Persia. The oldest and largest known qanat is in the Iranian city of Gonabad, which, after 2,700 years, still provides drinking and agricultural water to nearly 40,000 people.

Persian philosophers and inventors may have created the first batteries (sometimes known as the Baghdad Battery) in the Parthian or Sassanid eras. Some have suggested that the batteries may have been used medicinally. Other scientists believe the batteries were used for electroplating — transferring a thin layer of metal to another metal surface — a technique still used today and the focus of a common classroom experiment.

Windwheels were developed by the Babylonians ca. 1700 BC to pump water for irrigation. In the 7th century, Persian engineers in Greater Iran developed a more advanced wind-power machine, the windmill, building upon the basic model developed by the Babylonians.

Mathematics

The 9th century mathematician Muhammad Ibn Musa-al-Kharazmi created theLogarithm table, developed algebra and expanded upon Persian and Indian arithmetic systems. His writings were translated into Latin by Gerard of Cremonaunder the title: *De jebra et almucabola*. Robert of Chester also translated it under the title *Liber algebras et almucabala*. The works of Kharazmi "exercised a profound influence on the development of mathematical thought in the medieval West".

Other Persian scientists included Abu Abbas Fazl Hatam, the Banu Musa brothers, Farahani, Omar Ibn Farakhan, Abu Zeid Ahmad Ibn Soheil Balkhi (9th century AD), Abul Vafa Bouzjani, Abu Jaafar Khan, Bijan Ibn Rostam Kouhi, Ahmad Ibn Abdul Jalil Qomi, Bu Nasr Araghi, Abu Reyhan Birooni, the noted Iranian poet Hakim Omar Khayyam Neishaburi, Qatan Marvazi, Massoudi Ghaznavi (13th century AD), Khajeh Nassireddin Tusi, and Ghiasseddin Jamshidi Kashani.

Medicine

The practice and study of medicine in Iran has a long and prolific history. Situated at the crossroads of the East and West, Persia was often involved in developments in ancient Greek and Indian medicine; pre- and post-Islamic Iran have been involved in medicine as well.

For example, the first teaching hospital where medical students methodically practiced on patients under the supervision of physicians was the Academy of Gundishapur in the Persian Empire. Some experts go so far as to claim that: "to a very large extent, the credit for the whole hospital system must be given to Persia".

The idea of xenotransplantation dates to the days of Achaemenidae (the Achaemenian dynasty), as evidenced by engravings of many mythologic chimeras still present in Persepolis.

Several documents still exist from which the definitions and treatments of the headache in medieval Persia can be ascertained. These documents give detailed and precise clinical information on the different types of headaches. The medieval physicians listed various signs and symptoms, apparent causes, and hygienic and dietary rules for prevention of headaches. The medieval writings are both accurate and vivid, and they provide long lists of substances used in the treatment of headaches. Many of the approaches of physicians in medieval Persia are accepted today; however, still more of them could be of use to modern medicine.

In the 10th century work of Shahnameh, Ferdowsi describes a Caesarean section performed on Rudabeh, during which a special wine agent was prepared by a Zoroastrian priest and used to produce unconsciousness for the operation. Although largely mythical in content, the passage illustrates working knowledge of anesthesia in ancient Persia.

Later in the 10th century, Abu Bakr Muhammad Bin Zakaria Razi is considered the founder of practical physics and the inventor of the special or net weight of matter. His student, Abu Bakr Joveini, wrote the first comprehensive medical book in the Persian language. Razi is also the inventor of alcohol.

After the Islamic conquest of Iran, medicine continued to flourish with the rise of notables such as Rhazes and Haly Abbas, albeit Baghdad was the new cosmopolitan inheritor of Sassanid Jundishapur's medical academy.

An idea of the number of medical works composed in Persian alone may be gathered from Adolf Fonahn's *Zur Quellenkunde der Persischen Medizin*, published in Leipzig in 1910. The author enumerates over 400 works in the Persian language on medicine, excluding authors such as Avicenna, who wrote in Arabic. Author-historians Meyerhof, Casey Wood, and Hirschberg also have recorded the names of at least 80 oculists who contributed treatises on subjects related to ophthalmologyfrom the beginning of 800 AD to the full flowering of Muslim medical literature in 1300 AD.

Aside from the aforementioned, two other medical works attracted great attention in medieval Europe, namely Abu Mansur Muwaffaq's *Materia Medica*, written around 950 AD, and the illustrated *Anatomy* of *Mansur ibn Muhammad*, written in 1396 AD.

Modern academic medicine began in Iran when Joseph Cochran established a medical college in Urmia in 1878. Cochran is often credited for founding Iran's "first contemporary medical college". The website of Urmia University credits Cochran for "lowering the infant mortality rate in the region" and for founding one of Iran's first modern hospitals (Westminster Hospital) in Urmia.

Astronomy

In 1000 AD, Biruni wrote an astronomical encyclopaedia that discussed the possibility that the earth might rotate around the sun. This was before Tycho Brahe drew the first maps of the sky, using stylized animals to depict the constellations.

In the tenth century, the Persian astronomer Abd al-Rahman al-Sufi cast his eyes upwards to the awning of stars overhead and was the first to record a galaxy outside our own. Gazing at the Andromeda galaxy he called it a "little cloud" – an apt description of the slightly wispy appearance of our galactic neighbour.

Chemistry

Tusi believed that a body of matter is able to change but is not able to disappear entirely. He wrote "a body of matter cannot disappear completely. It only changes its form, condition, composition, color, and other properties, and turns into a different complex or elementary matter". Five hundred years later, Mikhail Lomonosov (1711–1765) and Antoine-Laurent Lavoisier(1743–1794) created the law of conservation of mass, setting down this same idea.

However, it should be noted that Tusi argued for evolution within a firmly Islamic context—he did not, like Darwin, draw materialist conclusions from his theories. Moreover, unlike Darwin, he was arguing hypothetically: he did not attempt to provide empirical data for his theories. Nonetheless his arguments, which in some ways prefigure natural selection, are still considered remarkably 'advanced' for their time.

Jaber Ibn Hayyan, the famous Iranian chemist who died in 804 at Tous in Khorasan, was the father of a number of discoveries recorded in an encyclopaedia and of many treatises covering two thousand topics, and these became the bible of European chemists of the 18th century, particularly of Lavoisier. These works had a variety of uses including tinctures and their applications in tanning and textiles; distillations of plants and flowers; the origin of perfumes; therapeutic pharmacy, and gunpowder, a powerful military instrument possessed by Islam long before the West. Jabir ibn Hayyan, is widely regarded as the founder of chemistry, inventing many of the basic processes and equipment still used by chemists today such as distillation.

Physics

Abu Ali al-Hasan ibn al-Haytham is known in the West as Alhazen, born in 965 in Persia and dying in 1039 in Egypt. He is known as the father of optics for his writings on, and experiments with, lenses, mirrors, refraction, and reflection. He correctly stated that vision results from light that is reflected into the eye by an object, not emitted by the eye itself and reflected back, as Aristotle believed. He solved the problem of finding the locus of points on a spherical mirror from which light will be reflected to an observer. From his studies of refraction, he determined that the atmosphere has a definite height and that twilight is caused by refraction of solar radiation from beneath the horizon.

Biruni was the first scientist to formally propose that the speed of light is finite, before Galileo tried to experimentally prove this.

Kamal al-Din Al-Farisi (1267–1318) born in Tabriz, Iran, is known for giving the first mathematically satisfactory explanation of the rainbow, and an explication of the nature of colours that reformed the theory of Ibn al-Haytham. Al-Farisi also "proposed a model where the ray of light from the sun was refracted twice by a water droplet, one or more reflections occurring between the two refractions." He verified this through extensive experimentation using a transparent sphere filled with water and a camera obscura.

SCIENCE POLICY

The Iranian Research Organization for Science and Technology and the National Research Institute for Science Policy come under the Ministry of Science, Research and Technology. They are in charge of establishing national research policies.

The government first set its sights on moving from a resource-based economy to one based on knowledge in its 20-year development plan, *Vision 2025*, adopted in 2005. This transition became a priority after international sanctions were progressively hardened from 2006 onwards and the oil embargo tightened its grip. In February 2014, the Supreme Leader Ayatollah Ali Khamenei introduced what he called the 'economy of resistance', an economic plan advocating innovation and a lesser dependence on imports that reasserted key provisions of *Vision 2025*.

Vision 2025 challenged policy-makers to look beyond extractive industries to the country's human capital for wealth creation. This led to the adoption of incentive measures to raise the number of university students and academics, on the one hand, and to stimulate problem-solving and industrial research, on the other.

Iran's successive five-year plans aim to realize collectively the goals of *Vision 2025*. For instance, in order to ensure that 50% of academic research was oriented towards socio-economic needs and problem-solving, the *Fifth Five-Year Economic Development Plan* (2010–2015) tied promotion to the orientation of research projects.

It also made provision for research and technology centres to be set up on campus and for universities to develop linkages with industry. The *Fifth Five-Year Economic Development Plan* had two main thrusts relative to science policy.

The first was the "islamization of universities', a notion that is open to broad interpretation. According to Article 15 of the *Fifth Five-Year Economic Development Plan*, university programmes in the humanities were to teach the virtues of critical thinking, theorization and multidisciplinary studies. A number of research centres were also to be developed in the humanities. The plan's second thrust was to make Iran the second-biggest player in science and technology by 2015, behind Turkey. To this end, the government pledged to raise domestic research spending to 3% of GDP by 2015.

Vision 2025 fixed a number of targets, including that of raising domestic expenditure on research and development to 4% of GDP by 2025. In 2012, spending stood at 0.33% of GDP.

In 2009, the government adopted a *National Master Plan for Science and Education* to 2025 which reiterates the goals of Vision 2025. It lays particular stress on developing university research and fostering university–industry ties to promote the commercialization of research results.

Human resources

line with the goals of *Vision 2025*, policy-makers have made a concerted effort to increase the number of students and academic researchers. To this end, the government raised its commitment to higher education to 1% of GDP in 2006. After peaking at this level, higher education spending stood at 0.86% of GDP in 2015. Higher education spending has resisted better than public expenditure on education overall. The latter peaked at 4.7% of GDP in 2007 before slipping to 2.9% of GDP in 2015. *Vision 2025* fixed a target of raising public expenditure on education to 7% of GDP by 2025.

Student enrollment trends

The result of greater spending on higher education has been a steep rise in tertiary enrollment. Between 2007 and 2013, student rolls swelled from 2.8 million to 4.4 million in the country's public and private universities. Some 45% of students were enrolled in private universities in 2011. There were more women studying than men in 2007, a proportion that has since dropped back slightly to 48%.

Enrollment has progressed in most fields. The most popular in 2013 were social sciences (1.9 million students, of which 1.1 million women) and engineering (1.5 million, of which 373 415 women). Women also made up two-thirds of medical students. One in eight bachelor's students go on to enroll in a master's/PhD programme. This is comparable to the ratio in the Republic of Korea and Thailand (one in seven) and Japan (one in ten).

The number of PhD graduates has progressed at a similar pace as university enrollment overall. Natural sciences and engineering have proved increasingly popular among both sexes, even if engineering remains a male-dominated field. In 2012, women made up one-third of PhD graduates, being drawn primarily to health (40% of PhD students), natural sciences (39%), agriculture (33%) and humanities and arts (31%). According to the UNESCO Institute for Statistics, 38% of master's and PhD students were studying science and engineering fields in 2011.

There has been an interesting evolution in the gender balance among PhD students. Whereas the share of female PhD graduates in health remained stable at 38–39% between 2007 and 2012, it rose in all three other broad fields. Most spectacular was the leap in female PhD graduates in agricultural sciences from 4% to 33% but there was also a marked progression in science (from 28% to 39%) and engineering (from 8% to 16% of PhD students). Although data are not readily available on the number of PhD graduates choosing to stay on as faculty, the relatively modest level of domestic research spending would suggest that academic research suffers from inadequate funding.

The *Fifth Five-Year Economic Development Plan* (2010–2015) fixed the target of attracting 25 000 foreign students to Iran by 2015. By 2013, there were about 14 000 foreign students attending Iranian universities, most of whom came from Afghanistan, Iraq, Pakistan, Syria and Turkey. In a speech delivered at the University of Tehran in October 2014, President Rouhani recommended greater interaction with the outside world. He said that 'scientific evolution will be achieved by criticism and the expression of different ideas. Scientific progress is achieved, if we are related to the world. We have to have a relationship with the world, not only in foreign policy but also with regard to the economy, science and technology. I think it is necessary to invite foreign professors to come to Iran and our professors to go abroad and even to create an English university to be able to attract foreign students.'

One in four Iranian PhD students were studying abroad in 2012 (25.7%). The top destinations were Malaysia, the USA, Canada, Australia, UK, France, Sweden and Italy. In 2012, one in seven international students in Malaysia was of Iranian origin. There is a lot of scope for the development of twinning between universities for teaching and research, as well as for student exchanges.

Trends in researchers

According to the UNESCO Institute for Statistics, the number of (full-time equivalent) researchers rose from 711 to 736 per million inhabitants between 2009 and 2010. This corresponds to an increase of more than 2 000 researchers, from 52 256 to 54 813. The world average is 1 083 per million inhabitants. One in four (26%) Iranian researchers is a woman, which is close to the world average (28%). In 2008, half of researchers were employed in academia (51.5%), one-third in the government sector (33.6%) and just under one in seven in the business sector (15.0%). Within the business sector, 22% of researchers were women in 2013, the same proportion as in Ireland, Israel, Italy and Norway. The number of firms declaring research activities more than doubled between 2006 and 2011, from 30 935 to 64 642. The increasingly tough sanctions regime oriented the Iranian economy towards the domestic market and, by erecting barriers to foreign imports, encouraged knowledge-based enterprises to localize production.

Research expenditure

Iran's national science budget was about $900 million in 2005 and it had not been subject to any significant increase for the previous 15 years. In 2001, Iran devoted 0.50% of GDP to research and development.

Expenditure peaked at 0.67% of GDP in 2008 before receding to 0.33% of GDP in 2012, according to the UNESCO Institute for Statistics. The world average in 2013 was 1.7% of GDP. Iran's government has devoted much of its budget to research on high technologies such as nanotechnology, biotechnology, stem cell research and information technology (2008). In 2006, the Iranian government wiped out the financial debts of all universities in a bid to relieve their budget constraints. According to theUNESCO science report 2010, most research in Iran is government-funded with the Iranian government providing almost 75% of all research funding. Domestic expenditure on research stood at 0.7% of GDP in 2008 and 0.3% of GDP in 2012. Iranian businesses contributed about 11% of the total in 2008. The government's limited budget is being directed towards supporting small innovative businesses, business incubators and science and technology parks, the type of enterprises which employ university graduates.

The share of private businesses in total national R&D funding according to the same report is very low, being just 14%, as compared with Turkey's 48%. The rest of approximately 11% of funding comes from higher education sector and non-profit organizations. A limited number of large enterprises (such as IDRO, NIOC, NIPC, DIO, Iran Aviation Industries Organization, Iranian Space Agency, Iran Electronics Industries or Iran Khodro) have their own in-house R&D capabilities.

Funding the transition to a knowledge economy

Vision 2025 foresaw an investment of US$3.7 trillion by 2025 to finance the transition to a knowledge economy. It was intended for one-third of this amount to come from abroad but, so far, FDI has remained elusive. It has contributed less than 1% of GDP since 2006 and just 0.5% of GDP in 2014. Within the country's *Fifth Five-Year Economic Development Plan* (2010–2015), a National Development Fund has been established to finance efforts to diversify the economy. By 2013, the fund was receiving 26% of oil and gas revenue.

Much of the US$3.7 trillion earmarked in *Vision 2025* is to go towards supporting investment in research and development by knowledge-based firms and the commercialization of research results. A law passed in 2010 provides an appropriate mechanism, the Innovation and Prosperity Fund. According to the fund's president, Behzad Soltani, 4600 billion Iranian rials (circa US$171.4 million) had been allocated to 100 knowledge-based companies by late 2014. Public and private universities wishing to set up private firms may also apply to the fund.

Some 37 industries trade shares on the Tehran Stock Market. These industries include the petrochemical, automotive, mining, steel, iron, copper, agriculture and telecommunications industries, 'a unique situation in the Middle East'. Most of the companies developing high technologies remain state-owned, including in the automotive and pharmaceutical industries, despite plans to privatize 80% of state-owned companies by 2014. It was estimated in 2014 that the private sector accounted for about 30% of the Iranian pharmaceutical market.

The Industrial Development and Renovation Organization (IDRO) controls about 290 state-owned companies. IDRO has set up special purpose companies in each high-tech sector to co-ordinate investment and business development. These entities are the Life Science Development Company, Information Technology Development Centre, Iran InfoTech Development Company and the Emad Semiconductor Company. In 2010, IDRO set up a capital fund to finance the intermediary stages of product- and technology-based business development within these companies.

TECHNOLOGY PARKS

As of 2012, Iran had officially 31 science and technology parks nationwide. Furthermore, as of 2014, 36 science and technology parks hosting more than 3,650 companies were operating in Iran. These firms have directly employed more than 24,000 people. According to the *Iran Entrepreneurship Association*, there are totally 99 parks of science and technology, which operate without official permits. Twenty-one of those parks are located in Tehran and affiliated withUniversity Jihad, Tarbiat Modares University, Tehran University, Ministry of Energy (Iran), Ministry of Health and Medical Education, and Amir Kabir University among others. Fars Province, with 8 parks and Razavi Khorasan Province, with 7 parks, are ranked second and third after Tehran respectively. Iran has nearly 3,000 knowledge-based companies in 2016.

Innovation

As of 2004, Iran's national innovation system (NIS) had not experienced a serious entrance to the technology creation phase and mainly exploited the technologies developed by other countries (e.g.

in the petrochemicals industry). In 2016, Iran ranked second in the percentage of graduates in science and engineering in the Global Innovation Index. Iran also ranked fourth in tertiary education, 26 in knowledge creation, 31 in gross percentage of tertiary enrollment, 41 in general infrastructure, 48 in human capital as well as research and 51 in innovation efficiency ratio.

In recent years several drugmakers in Iran are gradually developing the ability to innovate, away from generic drugsproduction itself.

According to the *State Registration Organization of Deeds and Properties*, a total of 9,570 national inventions was registered in Iran during 2008. Compared with the previous year, there was a 38-percent increase in the number of inventions registered by the organization.

Iran has several funds to support entrepreneurship and innovation:

- Innovation and Flourishing/Prosperity Fund of the Directorate of Science and Technology of the Presidential Office,
- National Researchers and Industrialists Support Fund,
- Nokhbegan Technology Development Institute,
- Biotechnology Fund,
- Nanotechnology Fund,
- Novin Technology Development Fund,
- Sharif Export Development Research and Technology Fund,
- Support Fund of Researchers and Technologists,
- Payambar Azam (the great prophet) Scientific and Technological Award,
- Student Entrepreneurs Support Fund,
- +6,000 private interest-free funds & 3 venture capital funds (Shenasa, Simorgh and Sarava Pars).

Private sector

Because of its weakness or absence, the support industry makes little contribution to the innovation/technology development activities. Supporting the development ofsmall and medium enterprises in Iran will strengthen greatly the supplier network.

As of 2014, Iran had 930 industrial parks and zones, of which 731 are ready to beceded to the private sector. The government of Iran has plans for the establishment of 50–60 new industrial parks by the end of the fifth Five-Year Socioeconomic Development Plan (2015).

A 2003-report by the United Nations Industrial Development Organization regarding small and medium-sized enterprises (SMEs) identified the following impediments to industrial development:

- Lack of monitoring institutions;
- Inefficient banking system;
- Insufficient research & development;
- Shortage of managerial skills;
- Corruption;
- Inefficient taxation;
- Socio-cultural apprehensions;
- Absence of social learning loops;
- Shortcomings in international market awareness necessary for global competition,
- Cumbersome bureaucratic procedures;
- Shortage of skilled labor;
- Lack of intellectual property protection;
- Inadequate social capital, social responsibility and socio-cultural values.

The economic complexity ranking of Iran has increased by 1 places over the past 50 years from 66th in 1964 to 65th in 2014. According to UNCTAD in 2016, private companies in Iran need better marketing strategies with emphasis oninnovation.

Despite these problems, Iran has progressed in various scientific and technological fields, including petrochemical,pharmaceutical, aerospace, defense, and heavy industry. Even in the face of economic sanctions, Iran is emerging as anindustrialized country.

Parallel to academic research, several companies have been founded in Iran during last few decades. For example,CinnaGen, established in 1992, is one of the pioneering biotechnology companies in the region. CinnaGen won*Biotechnology Asia 2005 Innovation Awards* due to its achievements and innovation in biotechnology research. In 2006,Parsé Semiconductor Co. announced it had designed and produced a 32-bit computer microprocessor inside the country for the first time. Software companies are growing rapidly. In CeBIT 2006, ten Iranian software companies introduced their products. Iran's National Foundation for Computer Games unveiled the country's first online video game in 2010, capable of supporting up to 5,000 users at the same time.

Science in modern Iran

Theoretical and computational sciences are highly developed in Iran. Despite the limitations in funds, facilities, and international collaborations, Iranian scientists have been very productive in several experimental fields such as pharmacology,pharmaceutical chemistry, and organic and polymer chemistry. Iranian biophysicists, especially molecular biophysicists, have gained international reputations since the 1990s. High field nuclear magnetic resonance facility, microcalorimetry,circular dichroism, and instruments for single protein channel studies have been provided in Iran during the past two decades. Tissue engineering and research onbiomaterials have just started to emerge in biophysics departments.

Considering the country's brain drain and its poor political relationship with the United States and some other Western countries, Iran's scientific community remains productive, even while economic sanctionsmake it difficult for universities to buy equipment or to send people to the United States to attend scientific meetings.Furthermore, Iran considers scientific backwardness, as one of the root causes of political and military bullying by developed countries over developing states. After the Iranian Revolution, there have been efforts by the religious scholars to assimilate Islam with modern science and this is seen by some as the reason behind the recent successes of Iran to augment its scientific output. Currently Iran aims for a national goal of self-sustainment in all scientific arenas. Many individual Iranian scientists, along with the Iranian Academy of Medical Sciences and Academy of Sciences of Iran, are involved in this revival. The *Comprehensive Scientific Plan* has been devised based on about 51,000 pages of documents and includes 224 scientific projects that must be implemented by the year 2025.

Medical sciences

With over 400 medical research facilities and 76 medical magazine indexes available in the country, Iran is the 19th country in medical research and is set to become the 10th within 10 years (2012). Clinical sciences are invested in highly in Iran. In areas such as rheumatology, hematology, and bone marrow trasplantation, Iranian medical scientists publish regularly. The Hematology, Oncology and Bone Marrow Transplantation Research Center (HORC) of Tehran University of Medical Sciences in Shariati Hospital was established in 1991. Internationally, this center is one of the largest bone marrow transplantation centers and has carried out a large number of successful transplantations. According to a study conducted in 2005, associated specialized pediatric hematology and oncology (PHO) services exist in almost all major cities throughout the country, where 43 board-certified or eligible pediatric hematologist–oncologists are giving care to children suffering from cancer or hematological disorders. Three children's medical centers at universities have approved PHO fellowship programs. Besides hematology, gastroenterology has recently attracted many talented medical students. The gasteroenterology research center based at Tehran University of Medical Sciences has produced increasing numbers of scientific publications since its establishment.

Modern organ transplantation in Iran dates to 1935, when the first cornea transplant in Iran was performed by Professor Mohammad-Qoli Shams at Farabi Eye Hospital in Tehran, Iran. The Shiraz Nemazi transplant center, also one of the pioneering transplant units of Iran, performed the first Iranian kidney transplant in 1967 and the first Iranian liver transplant in 1995.

The first heart transplant in Iran was performed 1993 in Tabriz. The first lung transplant was performed in 2001, and the first heart and lung transplants were performed in 2002, both at Tehran University of Medical Sciences. Iran developed the first artificial lung in 2009 to join five other countries in the world that possess such technology. Currently, renal, liver, and heart transplantations are routinely performed in Iran. Iran ranks fifth in the world in kidney transplants. The Iranian Tissue Bank, commencing in 1994, was the first multi-facility tissue bank in country. In June 2000, the Organ Transplantation Brain Death Act was approved by the Parliament, followed by the establishment of the Iranian Network for Transplantation Organ Procurement. This act helped to expand heart, lung, and liver transplantation programs. By 2003, Iran had performed 131 liver, 77 heart, 7 lung, 211 bone marrow, 20,581 cornea, and 16,859 renal transplantations. 82 percent of these were donated by living and unrelated donors; 10 percent by cadavers; and 8 percent came from living-related donors. The 3-year renal transplant patient survival rate was 92.9%, and the 40-month graft survival rate was 85.9%.

Neuroscience is also emerging in Iran. A few PhD programs in cognitive and computational neuroscience have been established in the country during recent decades. Iran ranks first in Mideast and region in ophthalmology.

Iranian surgeons treating wounded Iranian veterans during Iran–Iraq War invented a new neurosurgical treatment for brain injured patients that laid to rest the previously prevalent technique developed by US Army surgeon Dr Ralph Munslow. This new surgical procedure helped devise new guidelines that have decreased death rates for comatosed patients with penetrating brain injuries from 55% of 1980 to 20% of 2010. It has been said that these new treatment guidelines benefited US congresswoman Gabrielle Giffords who had been shot in the head.

Biotechnology

Iran has a growing biotechnology sector that is one of the most advanced in the developing world. The Razi Institute for Serums and Vaccines and the Pasteur Institute of Iran are leading regional facilities in the development and manufacture of vaccines. In January 1997, the Iranian Biotechnology Society (IBS) was created to oversee biotechnology research in Iran.

Agricultural research has been successful in releasing high yielding varieties with higher stability as well as tolerance to harsh weather conditions. The agriculture researchers are working jointly with international Institutes to find the best procedures and genotypes to overcome produce failure and to increase yield. In 2005, Iran's first genetically modified (GM) rice was approved by national authorities and is being grown commercially for human consumption. In addition to GM rice, Iran has produced several GM plants in the laboratory, such as insect-resistant maize; cotton; potatoes and sugar beets; herbicide-resistant canola; salinity- and drought-tolerant wheat; and blight-resistant maize and wheat. The Royan Instituteengineered Iran's first cloned animal; the sheep was born on 2 August 2006 and has passed the critical first two months of his life.

In the last months of 2006, Iranian biotechnologists announced that they, as the third manufacturer in the world, have sent CinnoVex (a recombinant type ofInterferon b1a) to the market. According to a study by David Morrison and Ali Khademhosseini (Harvard-MIT and Cambridge), stem cell research in Iran is amongst the top 10 in the world. Iran will invest 2.5 billion dollars in the country's stem cell research over the next five years (2008–2013). Iran ranks 2nd in world in transplantation of stem cells.

In 2010, Iran begun mass-producing ocular bio-implants named SAMT. Iran began investing in biotechnological projects in 1992 and this is the tenth facility in Iran. 'Lifepatch' is the fourth bio-implant mass-produced by Iran after bone, heart valve, and tendon bio-implants. 12 countries in the world produce bio-tech drugs, which Iran is one of them. According to Scopus, Iran ranked 21st in biotechnology by producing nearly 4,000 related-scientific articles in 2014.

In 2010, AryoGen Biopharma established the biggest and most modern knowledge-based facility for production of therapeutic monoclonal antibodies in the region. As at 2012, Iran produces 15 types of monoclonal/anti-body drugs. These anti-cancer drugs are now produced by only two to three western companies.

In 2015, Noargen company established as first officially registered CRO & CMO in Iran. Noargen uses concept of CMO and CRO servicing to biopharma sector of Iran as its main activity to fill the gap and promote developing biotech ideas/products toward commercialization.

Physics and materials

Iran had some significant successes in nuclear technology during recent decades, especially in nuclear medicine. However, little connection exists between Iran's scientific society and that of the nuclear program of Iran. Iran is the 7th country in production of uranium hexafluoride (or UF_6). Iran now controls the entire cycle for producing nuclear fuel. Iran is among the 14 countries in possession of nuclear [energy] technology. In 2009, Iran was developing its first domestic Linear particle accelerator (LINAC). It is among the few countries in the world that has the technology to produce zirconium alloys. Iran produces a wide range of lasersin demand within the country in medical and industrial fields. In 2011, Iranian scientists at the Atomic Energy Organization of Iran (AEOI) have designed and built a nuclear fusion device, named IR-IECF. Iran is the 6th country with such technology.

Computer science, electronics and robotics

Center of Excellence in Design, Robotics, and Automation was established in 2001 to promote educational and research activities in the fields of design, robotics, and automation. Besides these professional groups, several robotics groups work in Iranian high schools. "Sorena 2" Robot, which was designed by engineers atUniversity of Tehran, was unveiled in 2010. The robot can be used for handling sensitive tasks without the need for cooperating with human beings. The robot is taking slow steps similar to human beings, harmonious movements of hands and feet and other movements similar to humans. Next the researchers plan to develop speech and visioncapabilities and greater intelligence for this robot. the Institute of Electrical and Electronics Engineers (IEEE) has placed the name of Surena among the five prominent robots of the world after analyzing its performance. In 2010, Iranian researchers have, for the first time in the country, developed ten robots for the nation's automotive industry using domesticknow how.

Ultra Fast Microprocessors Research Center in Tehran's Amirkabir University of Technology successfully built asupercomputer in 2007. Maximum processing capacity of the supercomputer is 860 billion operations per second. Iran's first supercomputer launched in 2001 was also fabricated by Amirkabir University of Technology. In 2009, a SUSE Linux-based HPC system made by the Aerospace Research Institute of Iran (ARI) was launched with 32 cores and now runs 96 cores. Its performance was pegged at 192 GFLOPS. Iran's National Super Computer made by Iran Info-Tech Development Company (a subsidiary of IDRO) was built from 216 AMD processors. The Linux-cluster machine has a reported "theoretical peak performance of 860 gig-flops". The Routerlab team at the University of Tehran successfully designed and implemented an access-router (RAHYAB-300) and a 40Gbit/s high capacity switch fabric (UTS). In 2011Amirkabir University of Technology and Isfahan University of Technology produced 2 new supercomputers with processing capacity of 34,000 billion operations per second. The supercomputer at Amirkabir University of Technology is expected to be among the 500 most powerful computers in the world.

Research in nanotechnology has taken off in Iran since the Nanotechnology Initiative Council (NIC) was founded in 2002. The council determines the general policies for the development of nanotechnology and co-ordinates their implementation. It provides facilities, creates markets and helps the private sector to develop relevant R&D activities. In the past decade, 143 nanotech companies have been established in eight industries. More than one-quarter of these are found in the health care industry, compared to just 3% in the automotive industry.

Today, five research centres specialize in nanotechnology, including the Nanotechnology Research Centre at Sharif University, which established Iran's first doctoral programme in nanoscience and nanotechnology a decade ago. Iran also hosts the International Centre on Nanotechnology for Water Purification, established in collaboration with UNIDO in 2012. In 2008, NIC established an Econano network to promote the scientific and industrial development of nanotechnology among fellow members of the Economic Cooperation Organization, namely Afghanistan, Azerbaijan, Kazakhstan, Kyrgyzstan, Pakistan, Tajikistan, Turkey, Turkmenistan and Uzbekistan.

In 2007, Iranian scientists at the Medical Sciences and Technology Center succeeded in mass-producing an advanced scanning microscope — the Scanning Tunneling Microscope (STM). By 2017, Iran ranked 4th in nanotechnologies. Iran has designed and mass-produced more than 35 kinds of advanced nanotechnology devices. These include laboratory equipment, antibacterial strings, power station filters and construction related equipment and materials.

Aviation and space

On 17 August 2008, The Iranian Space Agency proceeded with the second test launch of a three stages Safir SLV from a site south of Semnan in the northern part of the Dasht-e-Kavir desert. The *Safir* (Ambassador) satellite carrier successfully launched the Omid satellite into orbit in February 2009. Iran is the 9th country to put a domestically-built satellite into orbit since the Soviet Union launched the first in 1957. Iran is among a handful of countries in the world capable of developing satellite-related technologies, including satellite navigation systems.Iran's first astronaut will be sent into space on board an Iranian shuttle by 2019. Iran is also the sixth country to send animals in space. Iran is one of the few countries capable of producing 20-25 ton sea patrol aircraft. In 2013, Iran constructed its first hypersonic wind tunnel for testing missiles and doing aerospace research. Iran is the 8th country capable of manufacturing jet engines.

Astronomy

The Iranian government has committed 150 billion rials (roughly 16 million US dollars) for a telescope, an observatory, and a training program, all part of a plan to build up the country's astronomy base. Iran wants to collaborate internationally and become internationally competitive in astronomy, says the University of Michigan's Carl Akerlof, an adviser to the Iranian project. "For a government that is usually characterized as wary of foreigners, that's an important development". In July 2010, Iran unveiled its largest domestically-manufactured telescope dubbed "Tara". in 2016, Iran unveiled its new optical telescope for observing celestial objects as part of APSCO. It will be used to understand and predict the physical location of natural and man-made objects in orbit around the Earth.

Energy

Iran has achieved the technical expertise to set up hydroelectric, gas and combined cycle power plants. Iran is among the four world countries that are capable of manufacturing advanced V94.2 gas turbines. Iran is able to produce all the parts needed for its gas refineries and is now the third country in the world to have developed Gas to liquids(GTL) technology. Iran produces 70% of its industrial equipment domestically including various turbines, pumps,catalysts, refineries, oil tankers, oil rigs, offshore platforms and exploration instruments. Iran is among the few countries that has reached the technology and "know-how" for drilling in the deep waters. Iran's indigenously designed Darkhovin Nuclear Power Plant is scheduled to come online in 2016.

Armaments

Iran possesses the technology to launch superfast anti-submarine rockets that can travel at the speed of 100 meters per second under water, making the country second only to Russia in possessing the technology. Iran is among the five countries in the world to have developed ammunitions with laser targetingtechnology. Iran is among the few countries that possess the technological know-how of the unmanned aerial vehicles (UAV) fitted with scanning and reconnaissance systems. Iran is among the 12 countries with missile technology and advanced mobile air defense systems. Over the past years, Iran has made important breakthroughs in its defense sector and attained self-sufficiency in producing important military equipment and systems. Since 1992, it also has produced its own tanks, armored personnel carriers, sophisticated radars, guided missiles, a submarine, and fighter planes.

Scientific collaboration

Iran annually hosts international science festivals. The *International Kharazmi Festival in Basic Science* and The *Annual Razi Medical Sciences Research Festival* promote original research in science, technology, and medicine in Iran. There is also an ongoing R&D collaboration between large state-owned companies and the universities in Iran.

Iranians welcome scientists from all over the world to Iran for a visit and participation in seminars or collaborations. Many Nobel laureates and influential scientists such as Bruce Alberts, F. Sherwood Rowland, Kurt Wüthrich, Stephen Hawking, and Pierre-Gilles de Gennes visited Iran after the Iranian revolution. Some universities also hosted American and European scientists as guest lecturers during recent decades.

Although sanctions have caused a shift in Iran's trading partners from West to East, scientific collaboration has remained largely oriented towards the West. Between 2008 and 2014, Iran's top partners for scientific collaboration were the USA, Canada, the UK and Germany, in that order. Iranian scientists co-authored almost twice as many articles with their counterparts in the USA (6 377) as with their next-closest collaborators in Canada (3 433) and the UK (3 318). Iranian and U.S. scientists have collaborated on a number of projects.

Malaysia is Iran's fifth-closest collaborator in science and India ranks tenth, after Australia, France, Italy and Japan. One-quarter of Iranian articles had a foreign co-author in 2014, a stable proportion since 2002. Scientists have been encouraged to publish in international journals in recent years, a policy that is in line with *Vision 2025*.

The volume of scientific articles authored by Iranians in international journals has augmented considerably since 2005, according to Thomson Reuters' Web of Science (Science Citation Index Expanded). Iranian scientists now publish widely in international journals in engineering and chemistry, as well as in life sciences and physics. Women contribute about 13% of articles, with a focus on chemistry, medical sciences and social sciences. Contributing to this trend is the fact that PhD programmes in Iran now require students to have publications in the Web of Science.

Iran has submitted a formal request to participate in a project which is building an International Thermonuclear Experimental Reactor (ITER) in France by 2018. This megaproject is developing nuclear fusion technology to lay the groundwork for tomorrow's nuclear fusion power plants. The project involves the European Union, China, India, Japan, Republic of Korea, Russian Federation and USA. A team from ITER visited Iran in November 2016 to deepen its understanding of Iran's fusion-related programmes.

Iran hosts several international research centres, including the following established between 2010 and 2014 under the auspices of the United Nations: the Regional Centre for Science Park and

Technology Incubator Development (UNESCO, est. 2010), the International Centre on Nanotechnology (UNIDO, est. 2012) and the Regional Educational and Research Centre for Oceanography for Western Asia (UNESCO, est. 2014).

Iran is stepping up its scientific collaboration with developing countries. In 2008, Iran's Nanotechnology Initiative Council established an Econano network to promote the scientific and industrial development of nanotechnology among fellow members of the Economic Cooperation Organization, namely Afghanistan, Azerbaijan, Kazakhstan, Kyrgyzstan, Pakistan, Tajikistan, Turkey, Turkmenistan and Uzbekistan. The Regional Centre for Science Park and Technology Incubator Development is also initially targeting these same countries. It is offering them policy advice on how to develop their own science parks and technology incubators.

Iran is an active member of COMSTECH and collaborates on its international projects. The coordinator general of COMSTECH, Dr. Atta ur Rahman has said that Iran is the leader in science and technology among Muslim countries and hoped for greater cooperation with Iran in different international technological and industrialization projects. Iranian scientists are also helping to construct the Compact Muon Solenoid, a detector for the Large Hadron Collider of the European Organization for Nuclear Research (CERN) that is due to come online in 2008. Iranian engineers are involved in the design and construction of the first regional particle accelerator of the Middle East in Jordan, calledSESAME.

Since the lifting of international sanctions, Iran has been developing scientific and educational links with Kuwait, Switzerland, Italy, Germany, China and Russia.

Contribution of Iranians and people of Iranian origin to modern science

Scientists with an Iranian background have made significant contributions to the international scientific community. In 1960, Ali Javan invented first gas laser. In 1973, the fuzzy set theory was developed by Lotfi Zadeh. Iranian cardiologist Tofy Mussivand invented the first artificial heart and afterwards developed it further. HbA1c was discovered by Samuel Rahbar and introduced to the medical community. The Vafa-Witten theorem was proposed by Cumrun Vafa, an Iranian string theorist, and his co-worker Edward Witten. The Kardar-Parisi-Zhang (KPZ) equation has been named after Mehran Kardar, notable Iranian physicist. Other notable discoveries and innovations by Iranian scientists and engineers (or of Iranian origin) include:

- Karim Nayernia: discovery of spermatagonial stem cells
- Reza Ghadiri: 1998 Feynman prize for invention of a self-organized replicating molecular system
- Mehdi Vaez-Iravani: invention of shear force microscopy
- Siavash Alamouti and Vahid Tarokh: invention of space–time block code
- Shirin Dehghan: 2006 Women in Technology Award
- Nader Engheta, inventor of "invisibility shield" (plasmonic cover) and research leader of the year 2006, *Scientific American* magazine, and winner of a Guggenheim Fellowship (1999) for "Fractional paradigm of classical electrodynamics"
- Ali Safaeinili: coinventor of Mars Advanced Radar for Subsurface and Ionosphere Sounding (MARSIS)
- Pierre Omidyar: economist, founder and chairman of eBay
- Rouzbeh Yassini: inventor of the cable modem
- Homayoun Seraji: most-published author in the 20-year history of the *Journal of Robotic Systems* (declared in 2007).
- Moslem Bahadori: reported the first case of plasma cell granuloma of the lung.
- Mohammad Abdollahi: The Laureate of IAS-COMSTECH 2005 Prize in the field of Pharmacology and Toxicology and an IAS Fellow. MA is ranked as an International Top 1% outstanding Scientists of the World in the field of Pharmacology & Toxicology according to Essential Science Indicator from USA Thompson Reuters ISI. An award named "Mohammad Abdollahi Prize" has been established by Asian Network for Scientific Information and Science Alert Publishing company and The International Journal of Pharmacology in the recognition of MA efforts in the field of Pharmacology & Toxicology. MA is also known as one of outstanding leading scientists of OIC member countries.
- Maysam Ghovanloo: inventor of Tongue-Drive Wheelchair.
- Mansour Ahmadian and Jila Nazari: Developers of PARS (Parallel Application from Rapid Simulation), which won the IET Innovation award 2008 in software design

- Mohammad-Nabi Sarbolouki, invention of dendrosome
- Shekoufeh Nikfar: The awardee of the top women scientists by TWAS-TWOWS-Scopus in the field of Medicine in 2009.
- Afsaneh Rabiei: inventor of an ultra-strong and lightweight material, known as Composite Metal Foam (CMF).
- Maryam Mirzakhani: In August 2014, Mirzakhani became the first-ever woman, as well as the first-ever Iranian, to receive the Fields Medal, the highest prize in mathematics.
- Ramin Golestanian: In August 2014, Ramin Golestanian won the Holweck Prize for his research work in physics.

International rankings

- According to Scopus, Iran ranked 17th in terms of science production in the world in 2012 with the production of 34,155 articles above Switzerland and Turkey.
- According to the Institute for Scientific Information (ISI), Iran increased its academic publishing output nearly tenfold from 1996 to 2004, and has been ranked first globally in terms of output growth rate (followed by China with a 3 fold increase). In comparison, the only G8 countries in top 20 ranking with fastest performance improvement are Italy at tenth and Canada at 13th globally. Iran, China, India and Brazil are the only developing countries among 31 nations with 97.5% of the world's total scientific productivity. The remaining 162 developing countries contribute less than 2.5% of the world's scientific output. Despite the massive improvement from 0.0003% of the global scientific output in 1970 to 0.29% in 2003, still Iran's total share in the world's total output remained small. According toThomson Reuters, Iran has demonstrated a remarkable growth in science and technology over the past one decade, increasing its science and technology output fivefold from 2000 to 2008. Most of this growth has been in engineering and chemistry producing 1.4% of the world's total output in the period 2004–2008. By year 2008, Iranian science and technology output accounted for 1.02% of the world's total output (That is ~340000% growth in 37 years of 1970–2008). 25% of scientific articles published in 2008 by Iran were international coauthorships. The top five countries coauthoring with Iranian scientists are US, UK, Canada, Germany and France.

- A 2010 report by Canadian research firm Science-Metrix has put Iran in the top rank globally in terms of growth in scientific productivity with a 14.4 growth index followed by South Korea with a 9.8 growth index. Iran's growth rate in science and technology is 11 times more than the average growth of the world's output in 2009 and in terms of total output per year, Iran has already surpassed the total scientific output of countries like Sweden, Switzerland, Israel, Belgium, Denmark, Finland, Austria or that of Norway. Iran with a science and technology yearly growth rate of 25% is doubling its total output every three years and at this rate will reach the level of Canadian annual output in 2017. The report further notes that Iran's scientific capability build-up has been the fastest in the past two decades and that this build-up is in part due to the Iraqi invasion of Iran, the subsequent bloody Iran Iraq war and Iran's high casualties due to the international sanctions in effect on Iran as compared to the international support Iraq enjoyed. The then technologically superior Iraq and its use of chemical weapons on Iranians, made Iran to embark on a very ambitious science developing program by mobilizing scientists in order to offset its international isolation, and this is most evident in the country's nuclear sciences advancement, which has in the past two decades grown by 8,400% as compared to the 34% for the rest of the world. This report further predicts that though Iran's scientific advancement as a response to its international isolation may remain a cause of concern for the world, all the while it may lead to a higher quality of life for the Iranian population but simultaneously and paradoxically will also isolate Iran even more because of the world's concern over Iran's technological advancements. Other findings of the report point out that the fastest growing sectors in Iran are Physics, Public health sciences, Engineering, Chemistry and Mathematics. Overall the growth has mostly occurred after 1980 and specially has been becoming faster since 1991 with a significant acceleration in 2002 and an explosive surge since 2005. It has been argued that scientific and technological advancement besides the nuclear program is the main reason for United States worry about Iran, which may become a superpower in the future. Some in Iranian scientific community see sanctions as a western conspiracy to stop Iran's rising rank in modern science and allege that some (western) countries want to monopolize modern technologies.

- As per US government report on science and engineering titled "Science and Engineering Indicators: 2010" prepared byNational Science Foundation, Iran has the world's highest growth rate in Science & Engineering article output with an annual growth rate of 25.7%. The report is introduced as a factual and policy neutral "...volume of record comprising the major high-quality quantitative data on the U.S. and international science and engineering enterprise". This report also notes that the very rapid growth rate of Iran inside a wider region was led by its growth in scientific instruments, pharmaceuticals, communications and semiconductors.

- The subsequent National Science Foundation report published in 2012 by US government under the name "Science and Engineering Indicators: 2012", had put Iran first globally in terms of growth in science and engineering article output in the first decade of this millennium with an annual growth rate of 25.2%.

- The latest updated National Science Foundation report published in 2014 by US government titled "Science and Engineering Indicators 2014", has again ranked Iran first globally in terms of growth in science and engineering article output at an annualized growth rate of 23.0% with 25% of Iran's output having been produced through international collaboration.

- Iran ranked 49th for citations, 42nd for papers, and 135th for citations per paper in 2005. Their publication rate in international journals has quadrupled during the past decade. Although it is still low compared with the developed countries, this puts Iran in the first rank of Islamic countries. According to a British government study (2002), Iran ranked 30th in the world in terms of scientific impact.

- According to a report by SJR (A Spanish sponsored scientific-data data) Iran ranked 25th in the world in scientific publications by volume in 2007 (a huge leap from the rank of 40 few years before). As per the same source Iran ranked 20th and 17th by total output in 2010 and 2011 respectively.

- In 2008 report by Institute for Scientific Information (ISI), Iran ranked 32, 46 and 56 in Chemistry, Physics and

Biologyrespectively among all science producing countries. Iran ranked 15th in 2009 in the field of nanotechnology in terms of presenting articles.

* Science Watch reported in 2008 that Iran has the world's highest growth rate for citations in medical, environmental and ecological sciences. According to the same source, Iran during the period 2005–2009, had produced 1.71% of world's total engineering papers, 1.68% of world's total chemistry papers and 1.19% of world's total material sciences papers.

* According to the sixth report on "international comparative performance of UK research base" prepared in September 2009 by Britain-based research firm *Evidence* and Department for Business, Innovation and Skills, Iran has increased its total output from 0.13% of world's output in 1999 to almost 1% of world's output in 2008. As per the same report Iran had doubled its biological sciences and health research out put in just two years (2006–2008). The report further notes that Iran by 2008 had increased its output in physical sciences by as much as ten times in ten years and its share in world's total output had reached 1.3%, comparing with US share of 20% and Chinese share of 18%. Similarly Iran's engineering output had grown to 1.6% of the world's output being greater than Belgium or Sweden and just smaller than Russia's output at 1.8%. During the period 1999–2008, Iran improved its science impact from 0.66 to 1.07 above the world's average of 0.7 similar to Singapore's. In engineering Iran improved its impact and is already ahead of India, South Korea and Taiwan in engineering research performance. By 2008, Iran's share of most cited top 1% of world's papers was 0.25% of the world's total.

THE NEW BUSINESS OF EDUCATION IN IRAN

Enghelab Square lies at the heart of Tehran's urban and revolutionary landscape, just meters away from the gates of Tehran University. The site of some of the most pitched battles of the 1979 revolution, the square today bustles as an open-air market of goods. There, among the booksellers and fruit vendors, visitors can buy bootleg DVDs, banned books, drugs and alcohol and, if need be, an entire master's thesis — written from scratch and prepared for oral defense, in less than a month.

The illicit buying and selling of advanced degrees is the logical, if unhappy, consequence of the commodification of education in post-revolutionary Iran. Fueled by an insatiable mania for credentials by employers and ordinary Iranians alike, students who pay others to write their research are not unlike their peers who purchase their degrees in installments from private and public universities. They do so in order to survive in the country's cutthroat labor and marriage markets where possession of a credential is the principle criterion of success.

More interested in "getting the paper" than bearing witness to political Islam, ordinary Iranians have appropriated the university system for themselves, transforming an ideological apparatus designed to produce Islamic citizens into a transactional relationship between the pedagogical state and its population.

Although Iran's 4.5 million university students comprise only 5 percent of the country's overall population, gross enrollment rates show that more than half of people ages 18 to 24 are enrolled in some form of higher education, well on pace to reach the official goal of 60 percent by 2025. Of these, around 85 percent will pay out-of-pocket for their education, whether enrolling in night school, participating in Iran's open university system (Payam-e Noor) or attending one of the nearly 400 local campuses of Islamic Azad University, billed as one of world's largest university systems with a reported $200 billion in assets. All told, Iranian parents annually spend more than $3 billion to put their children's through college.

Yet less than 10 years ago, Iran was a country of high school dropouts and junior high graduates. In 2006, less than half of all 14- to 17-year-olds were enrolled in the correct high school level, and no more than 34 percent among those living in Iran's rural provinces. Some 1 million teenagers were either in the wrong grade because of late enrollment or because they had failed the previous grade. More than 2.4 million students eligible for high school had gone missing and were not in the system at all.

These seemingly puzzling figures are evidence of an educational system that, until very recently, had been incapable of meeting the unrelenting demand for college education. Prospective high school students faced the daunting choice of either entering a labor market that punished the poorly educated but in which menial jobs were always available or seeking entry into a public university system that had historically accepted only 10 percent of all applicants. Given this balance of odds, it is not surprising that large numbers of teenagers dropped out of school to seek their fortune in the workforce.

Supply finally met demand during the administration of President Mahmoud Ahmadinejad, which ended in 2013. Growth in the private and fee-based public sectors of higher education has been nothing short of astonishing, fueled by the unprecedented expansion of distance-learning and part-time universities from just over 383,000 available spots in 2005 to 1.1 million in 2011. For the first time in Iran's modern history, anyone who is willing to pay can go to university. Figures released this summer confirm a nearly perfect chance of being accepted to most majors, if not specific degree programs. For math majors, where vacancies outnumber total applicants, that figure is over 100 percent.

The effects of this transformation have already been felt downstream. Iran's vice-minister for high school education announced in late July that net enrollment rates for the first cycle of high school (grades 7 through 9) had reached 94 percent and an impressive 82 percent for the second cycle (grades 10 through 12).

The movement of the invisible hand across Iran's educational market has not been entirely efficient. During the final year of Ahmadinejad's presidency, many university campuses reported that they were operating well under capacity, leading to accusations that the administration was profiting off of the desperation of families by illegally expanding fee-based schooling.

Given the recent revelations of corruption and gross incompetence during Ahmadinejad's tenure, there may be some basis to such claims. However the problem of credentialism is hardly state-manufactured. In Iran, demand drives capacity: even as bachelor's degrees have become ubiquitous, new bottlenecks are emerging at the top of the educational food chain. Of the approximately 900,000 students who applied in 2011 for a master's degree, only 60,000 were accepted, some 6 percent. The figures for PhD candidates were even worse: only 4 percent of those seeking a doctorate made it into a program, a meager 6,000 students out of 127,000 applicants.

The transformation of schooling from a public good into a private resource has come at a cost, as much political as financial. By conceding the ideological character of the school system, state authorities have secured the cooperation of families and the withdrawal of their children from oppositional activities. Going to college has, in effect, demobilized large segments of Iranian society by rendering much of the country's youth quiet, if not entirely quiescent, on campus.

To be clear, careerism does not preclude oppositional politics. Indeed, significant segments of the student population consistently put their own futures at risk in spite of the extraordinary sacrifices that they and their families have made to be accepted into the university system. It is not uncommon to find student activist leaders drawn from the best students (daneshjuyan-e nabegheh) enrolled in the country's most prestigious departments and universities, by definition those who have the most to lose by their protests and the most to gain through their quiescence. Nothing in this essay denies the virtue of their actions or the righteousness of their cause.

EDUCATION IN IRAN: OPPORTUNITIES AND CHALLENGES

Four decades of economic sanctions and political isolation have affected every facet of life in Iran. Yet despite the obstacles, science and research have flourished. According to Towards 2030, a UNESCO science report, 'the sanctions ... have accelerated the shift from a resource-based economy to a knowledge economy by challenging policymakers to look beyond extractive industries to the country's human capital for wealth creation ... between 2006 and 2011 the number of firms declaring R&D activities more than doubled.'

The same report highlighted that in 2017, Iran ranked seventh worldwide for the number of scientific papers related to nanotechnology. However, it would be a mistake to consider sanctions as a positive force for science and research in Iran. Although paralyzing sanctions pushed the education system to be more creative, they have posed numerous challenges for students and scholars. For example, as a result of the sanctions on the Iranian banking system, many universities lost their subscriptions to international academic journals, simply because they could not transfer the money to pay for access to the journals.

Despite these challenges, significant progress has been made in higher education in recent years. For example, between 1996 and 2008, scientific output increased 18-fold, from 736 published papers to 13,238. In 2011, scientific output grew 11 times faster in Iran than the global average and faster than any other country in the world. Iran now has a staggering number of science and engineering students – over two million, an increase of 161 per cent since 2004. Also notable is that 70 per cent of these students are women. In recent months, new bibliometric data have identified Tehran as potentially being as important as Delhi and Beijing, in terms of cities growing their academic international collaboration in certain fields. Energy research, for example, has a field-weighted citation impact approaching 50 per cent above the world average. There are several socio-cultural factors that can partly explain these achievements, but at the same time it is fair to assume that this rapid scientific growth could not happen without a sufficient educational infrastructure. After all, such an educational leap requires both horizontal and vertical development.

According to UNESCO statistics published by the World Bank, Iran spent 2.95 per cent of its GDP on education at all levels in 2014. This figure represents 19.7 per cent of overall government spending, which is higher than the majority of developing countries. Globally, governments spent an average of 14.25 per cent of total expenditure on education. Iran has a high literacy rate by Middle Eastern standards. The country's adult literacy rate was 84.6 per cent in 2013, compared to 78 per cent in the neighbouring Arab states. The literacy rate among 15-24-year-olds is even higher at 98 per cent.

In Iran, basic education is compulsory and lasts nine years. Prior to the education reform act of 2012, basic education lasted eight years and was divided into a five-year elementary education and a three-year lower secondary education. The reforms extended the elementary cycle to six years, extending basic education to a total of nine years.

During elementary school, pupils attend 24 hours of class per week. The curriculum covers subjects such as mathematics, science, Islamic studies, Persian reading, writing and comprehension and social studies.

At lower secondary school, other subjects such as history, vocational studies, Arabic and English are introduced, and students attend more hours of class each week. The curriculum at this level is national and consistent across all schools.

Upper secondary education is not compulsory but is free and lasts three years. At this level, students can choose from one of the available streams such as academic (nazari), technical (fani herfei), and vocational/skills (kar-danesh). The academic stream has traditionally been the most popular.

Over the last four decades, higher education has rapidly expanded. In 1977, Iran had only 16 universities with a reported 154,315 students.

In 2008, it had over 3.5 million students enrolled in universities. The overwhelming majority of students are enrolled in the private sector. More than one third attend the semi-private Islamic Azad University (IAU), Iran's largest university and one of the largest mega universities in the world with 1.7 million students. In 2013, 57.9 per cent of the 921,386 students taking the konkur standardized entrance exam were admitted to public university. Konkur is extremely competitive and takes place only once a year. It is a 4.5-hour multiple-choice test that covers all subjects taught in high school. In recent years, legislation has been passed to eliminate konkur and replace it with a different system.

Medical universities are supervised by the Ministry of Health, Treatment and Medical Education, but all other institutions are under the control of the Ministry of Science, Research and Technology. Despite the rapid expansion of the higher education sector, Iran faces a shortage of educational opportunities at the graduate level, because most of the programmes at private universities are at the undergraduate level. Only six per cent of the approximately 900,000 applicants to master programmes and four per cent of the 127,000 doctoral applicants reportedly secured a spot in 2011.

The other major challenge facing higher education institutions is political, which is connected to the ideological nature of the ruling regime. Even before the revolution in 1979, universities were considered as epicentres of political activism. In fact, university students played a vital role in overthrowing the shah. After the revolution and the establishment of the Islamic Republic, political activism in Iranian universities intensified. This resulted in the temporary closure of all universities and colleges throughout the country in 1980, an event that marked the beginning of the cultural revolution. Thousands of students and scholars were purged and textbooks were rewritten in accordance with the ideological doctrine of the Islamic Republic.

Although the universities were reopened three years later, the state maintained strict control over higher education. During the presidency of Mohammad Khatami (1997-2005), who was a reformist, higher education was significantly reinvigorated both in terms of resources and student freedoms. Yet in 1999, there was a major clash between students and the security forces connected to the hardliners, which resulted in violence and destruction in and around a university campus in Tehran. Under Mahmoud Ahmadinejad (2005-2013), the hardliners took drastic measures to 'Islamize' higher education again and put more pressure on scholars and students. In recent years, the supreme leader, Ayatollah Ali Khamenei, has warned against 'un-Islamic' universities and subjects and has pushed for ideological conformity.

Today, the Iranian education system presents both opportunities and challenges. It is clear that the system, and in particular higher education, is facing challenges both externally and internally. Internally, hardline factions of the regime see higher education as an ideological tool; externally, sanctions imposed by the West make universities' everyday operations significantly harder. Despite the 2015 nuclear deal that saw some of the sanctions lifted, heavy embargoes still overshadow life in the country.

Despite these challenges, Iran's education system seems to be dynamic. Especially in scientific and engineering subjects, Iran is now considered as a leader in West Asia and continues to produce world-class researchers such as Maryam Mirzakhani (the first female winner of the Fields Medal, the most prestigious award in mathematics) who make important contributions to human knowledge. Although the Iranian education system has the potential to do a lot better, its future depends on the ongoing power struggle between the hardliners and reformists in the country.

Bibliography

Abrahamian, Ervand.*Iran Between Two Revolutions*, 1982.

Afshar, Haleh.*Islam and Feminisms: An Iranian Case-Study*, 1998.

Akhavi, Shahrough.*Religion and Politics in Contemporary Iran: Clergy-State Relations in the Pahlavi Period*, 1980.

Amân Allâhî Bahârvand, Sikander.*Tribes of Iran*, 1988.

Amjad, Mohammed.*Iran: From Royal Dictatorship to Theocracy*, 1989.

Ardalan, Nader, and Laleh Bakhtiar.*The Sense of Unity: The Sufi Tradition in Persian Architecture*, 1973.

Atkinson, Rick, *Crusade: The Untold Story of the Persian Gulf War*, NYC, Houghton Mifflin Co, 1994.

Azimi, Fakhreddin.*Iran: The Crisis of Democracy*, 1989.

Bakhash, Shaul.*The Reign of the Ayatollahs: Iran and the Islamic Revolution*, rev. ed., 1990.

Bayat, Mangol.*Mysticism and Dissent: Socioreligious Thought in Qajar Iran*, 1982.

Beeman, William O., *Language, status, and power in Iran*, Bloomington, IND, Indiana University Press, 1986.

Bill, James A.*The Eagle and the Lion: The Tragedy of American-Iranian Relations*, 1988.

Brauer, Erich, *The Jews of Kurdistan*, Detroit, Wayne State University Press, 1993.

Chubin, Shahram, and Charles Tripp.*Iran and Iraq at War*, 1988.

Cole, Juan R.I. and Nikki R. Keddie , *Shiism and Social Protest*, New Haven, Yale University Press, 1986.

Cole, Juan, *Modernity and the Millennium: The Genesis of the Baha'i Faith in the Nineteenth-Century Middle East. Studies in the Babi and Baha'i religions, vol. 9*, NYC, Columbia University Press, 1998.

Cole, Juan, *Sacred Space and Holy War: The Politics, Culture and History of Shi'ite Islam*, IB Tauris, 2002.

Cordesman, Anthony H., *The Iran-Iraq War: 1984-1986*, Rosslyn, Virginia, Eaton Analytical Assessments Center, 1986.

El-Azhary, M.S, *The Iran-Iraq War: An Historical, Economic, and Political Analysis*, NYC, St. Martin's Press, 1984.

Farhat, Hormoz.*The Traditional Art Music of Iran*, 1973.

Fathi, Asghar, ed.*Women and the Family in Iran*, 1985.

Ferrier, R.W., ed.*The Arts of Persia*, 1989.

Fesharaki, Fereidun.*Development of the Iranian Oil Industry: International and Domestic Aspects*, 1976.

Fischer, Michael M. J.*Iran: From Religious Dispute to Revolution*, 1980.

Floor, Willem, *Traditional Crafts in Qajar Iran (1800-1925)*, Costa Mesa, MAZDA, 2003.

Forbis, William, *Fall of the Peacock Throne: the Story of Iran*, NYC, Harper and Row, 1980.

Friedl, Erika.*Women of Deh Koh: Lives in an Iranian Village*, 1989.

Frye, Richard N.*The Golden Age of Persia: The Arabs in the East*, 1975.

Hooglund, Eric J.*Land and Revolution in Iran, 1960–1980*, 1982.

Horne, Lee.*Village Spaces: Settlement and Society in Northeastern Iran*, 1994.

Keddie, Nikki R., and Eric Hooglund, eds.*The Iranian Revolution and the Islamic Republic.*1986.

Keddie, Nikki R.*Roots of Revolution: An Interpretive History of Modern Iran*, 1981.

Khadduri, Majid.*The Gulf War: The Origins and Implications of the Iraq-Iran Conflict*, 1988.

Lamberg-Karlovsky, C. C.*Excavations at Tepe Yahya, Iran, 1967–1975: The Early Periods*, 1986.

Looney, Robert E.*Economic Origins of the Iranian Revolution*, 1982.

Maull, Hanns W., and Otto Pick, eds.*The Gulf War: Regional and International Dimensions*, 1989.

Milani, Farzaneh.*Veils and Words: The Emerging Voices of Iranian Women Writers.*1992.

Milani, Mohsen M.*The Making of Iran's Islamic Revolution: From Monarchy to Islamic Republic*, 1988.

Nettl, Bruno.*Daramad of Chahargah: A Study in the Performance Practice of Persian Music*, 1972.

Parsa, Misagh.*Social Origins of the Iranian Revolution*, 1989.

Salzman, Philip Carl.*Black Tents of Baluchistan*, 2000.

Tabataba'i, 'Allamah Sayyid Muhammad Husayn.*Shi'ite Islam*, 2nd ed., 1977.

Talattof, Kamran.*The Politics of Writing in Iran: A History of Modern Persian Literature*, 1999.

Tapper, Richard.*The Conflict of Tribe and State in Iran and Afghanistan*, 1983.

Wilbur, Donald N.*Iran, Past and Present: From Monarchy to Islamic Republic*, 9th ed., 1981.

Index

❑❑❑